THE
FRENCH
LITERARY
HORIZON

JUSTIN O'BRIEN

THE
FRENCH
LITERARY
HORIZON

RUTGERS UNIVERSITY PRESS
New Brunswick   *New Jersey*

Permission to reprint has been kindly granted by the following:

The Book Find Club, Inc.: review of *Jean Barois*, 1949. / *Columbia University Forum:* "Albert Camus, Militant" (Winter 1961). / Columbia University Press: Introduction to *The Maxims of Marcel Proust*, edited with a translation by Justin O'Brien. Copyright 1948. / *Decision:* "Please Pass the Ill Will" (June 1941). / Farrar, Straus & Giroux, Inc.: Introduction to *From the N.R.F.*, edited by Justin O'Brien. Copyright © 1958 by Justin O'Brien. Reprinted with permission of Farrar, Straus & Giroux, Inc. / *The Kenyon Review:* "French Poetry in the Thirties" (Autumn 1939). / Alfred A. Knopf, Inc.: Introductions to *The Journals of André Gide*, Vols. I and IV, *Madeleine, So Be It, or The Chips Are Down, Resistance, Rebellion and Death, The New French Writers.* Copyright 1947, 1951, 1952, © 1959, © 1960, 1947, by Alfred A. Knopf, Inc. / Helen Macy, The Limited Editions Club: Introduction to *Swann's Way*, 1954. / *The Nation:* "*The Counterfeiters* and *Point Counter Point*," reviews of *Pity for Women, Seven Mysteries of Europe, The World of the Thibaults, Harvest, Death on the Installment Plan, Paris France, The Republic of Silence, Three Short Novels* (Vercors). / National Council of Teachers of English: "American Books and French Readers" (*College English*, March 1940). / *The New York Times:* "Remembrance of Marcel Proust," "Proust's Earliest Readers," "Gide at the Comédie-Française," "Camus, the Nobel Prize, 1957," "Paris Without Camus," "Writers at Midnight," "Letter from Paris," reviews of *Jean Santeuil, Costals and the Hippogriff, Verdun, Man's Hope, The Reprieve, Troubled Sleep, The Miraculous Barber, The Company of Men, The Castle of Argol, The Voyeur, A Change of Heart, Zazie, Tropisms, The Impostor, The Holy Terrors, Dialogues* (Valéry), *A Barbarian in Asia.* Copyright 1947, 1967, 1951, 1957, 1960, 1945, 1945, 1956, 1940, 1942, 1938, 1947, 1951, 1951, 1950, 1952, 1958, 1959, 1960, 1967, 1957, 1957, 1949, by The New York Times Company. Reprinted by permission. / *Partisan Review:* Reviews of *Les Grands Cimetières sous la lune* and *La Peste.* / *The Reporter:* "Gide's Hamlet," "Letter to Sylvia Beach," "The Style of France's Théâtre National Populaire," reviews of *Marcel Proust: On Art and Literature: 1896-1919, Selected Essays* (Montherlant), *Earthly Paradise, The Delights of Growing Old, The Words, The Art of Poetry* (Valéry). Copyright by The Reporter Magazine Co. / *Saturday Review:* "Proust and Gide Displayed," "French Books, Summer 1939," "French Literature and the War," reviews of *The World of the Thibaults* and *Selected Writings: The Space Within* (Michaux). / *The Symposium: A Critical Review:* "Valery Larbaud: Complete Man of Letters" (July 1932). / *The University Review* (The University of Missouri at Kansas City): "From Dada to Surrealism" (December 1939). / *World Journal Tribune:* "Was Gide a Collaborationist?" "How Gide Translated Hamlet," "Albert Camus, Novelist, Dramatist, Philosopher of the Absurd," "The Renaud-Barrault Company," reviews of *Corydon, Theseus, The Stranger,* Jouvet's production of *L'Ecole des femmes*, 1951, 1952, 1946, 1952, 1950, 1949, 1946, 1951. Reprinted from the *New York Herald Tribune* through the courtesy of the *World Journal Tribune.* / The World Publishing Company: "Imaginary Interview with André Gide" (*The Meridian*, Spring 1959) and Introductions to *Pretexts: Reflections on Literature and Morality* and *From the N.R.F.*, 1959, 1959, 1958. / *Yale French Studies:* "Gide's Fictional Technique" (1951).

To all those, alive or dead, named in the Index of this book, who are continuing to introduce me to the best in French culture.

"What we see on the horizon assumes a mysterious nobility and seems to us to close a whole world that we shall never see again. Meanwhile we progress and soon we ourselves stand on the following generation's horizon; meanwhile the horizon recedes and the world that seemed ended begins anew."

—Marcel Proust, *Le Temps retrouvé*, III, 929

INTRODUCTION

Proust, Gide, and Camus—in this order—have long been focal points for me. And not only for me. The first two belonged to a single generation, the same generation that included Claudel and Valéry and so many other great figures in France. The identical knot in the deep texture of the wood marked them all, like so many planks cut from the same tree trunk. Of the four, Proust was the first to win a vast public and to cross national and linguistic frontiers. He was also the first to die, so that it might be said that he *had* to make his mark early. Indeed, I first read him in Scott Moncrieff's translation while Proust was still alive and his work not yet altogether published in French; hence he appeared to me as a contemporary writer. Claudel was the only one of the four ever to come to America, where he served as Ambassador of France for several years, and yet he is the only one of them who remains almost totally unknown here in translation.

Camus, of course, belonged to quite a different generation—the same one as Sartre and Simone de Beauvoir, of Jean-Louis Barrault and Jean Vilar, of Henri Michaux, Marcel Aymé, Julien Gracq, and Romain Gary. It was also my generation and its members spoke to me directly in my language, even before they were translated. Of all of them, Camus addressed me most urgently.

Between the generation of Proust and that of Camus came a steady flowering, so that hardly a single year or *millésime,* as the French winegrowers prefer to say, failed to earn the designation of "good" or "great"

or even "very great." Such a galaxy of significant writers appeared in France in the twenties and thirties—from Larbaud and Montherlant to Malraux and Cocteau—that it seemed at times as if the *école de Paris* were the only one with new things to say. This is why we Americans expatriated ourselves to sit in the cafés of the Left Bank, to haunt Shakespeare and Company in Rue de l'Odéon, to feed on each monthly issue of the *Nouvelle Revue Française,* and to applaud the daring offbeat theatrical ventures. "Paris was where the twentieth century was," as Gertrude Stein has so aptly said.

Some of us became, almost unintentionally, hyphens in the expression Franco-American, making every effort to introduce to New York our Parisian enthusiasms and, on the rare occasions when someone in France gave us a chance, presenting the best of America to our European counterparts. As France in her most creative periods always shows an openness to foreign influences, she now discovered the new American literature. We *traits d'union,* while we extended Proust's or Gide's public overseas, had the pleasure of seeing Steinbeck and Faulkner and Hemingway taken seriously in Place Saint-Germain des Prés.

At the same time we had the joy of seeing our favorite French writers awarded the Nobel Prize: Martin du Gard and Gide, Mauriac and St.-Jean Perse, Camus and Sartre, while plays by Giraudoux and Anouilh were holding their own on Broadway.

In the midst of such a prolonged love affair with things French, the second war and particularly one black day in May 1940 cut us off from France as if a spell or a quarantine had been cast upon her. Eager to pursue our role and to use whatever talents we had, we volunteered for every para-military service then available: ambulance duty, Red Cross, Voice of America, BBC radio broadcasts, until such day as the luckier were able to get into military intelligence or O.S.S., go overseas and utilize effectively their special knowledge acquired in the cafés and bookshops and salons of Paris.

With the end of hostilities some five years later, we doffed our uniforms as France was suddenly bursting with new talent, too long pent up. Camus and Sartre and Vercors and others came to our shores. Later on,

Introduction

Nathalie Sarraute, Michel Butor, and Alain Robbe-Grillet again brought the breath of renewal. On the other hand, the facility of military transport had taught us to leap the Atlantic with casual abandon for short, refreshing contacts. And now, as we look back, there seems never to have been a break.

This collection records a long, a delightful liaison with the best in French letters of the twentieth century. With but few exceptions, the essays were written on order, some as introductions to books by Proust, Gide, and Camus, and others as critiques of books by someone else. As there was little encouragement to speak of Claudel or Apollinaire or Jouhandeau, for instance, their names hardly figure here. But on occasion I forced my enthusiasm on an unprepared, if not always unresponsive, public—as when New York University's elegant *Symposium* back in 1932 published a study of Valery Larbaud (even now unknown here) or the *Herald Tribune* ran in March 1946, before the American presentation of *The Stranger* and Camus's first visit to America, what was probably the first article on him in this country.

Direct contact with Albert Camus, which took place much earlier in a newly liberated Paris still throbbing with the activities of clandestine publishing and the heroic editorials of his underground newspaper, not only provided a new interest as André Gide's long life was drawing to a close. It also led me to the theater, one of Camus's dearest loves. Had he not invited me to daily rehearsals of his *Caligula* revival in January 1959 at the Nouveau Théâtre de Paris, which he himself was directing with a new cast, I should probably not have adapted that same play for Sydney Lumet's production of it on Broadway in 1960. Indeed, that fatal 4th of January 1960, when Michel Gallimard's car crashed into a tree at Villebleven and suddenly ended Camus's life, I was waiting for him in Paris with the English script and various questions. A year later, Jean-Paul Sartre entrusted his new play, *Les Séquestrés d'Altona*, to me for the same treatment so that it could be played at the Royal Court in London. Next came *The Possessed*, which Camus had brilliantly compressed into a play from Dostoevsky's long novel; it enjoyed a successful run at the Mermaid Theater in murky Blackfriars. Other adaptations from the French followed, with further productions off-Broadway. Every time I enter a stage door, I remember that Albert Camus first opened it for me.

Theater, the newest manifestation of my hyphenated love, would play a larger part in this collection if more and better French plays had found their way to New York over the years. Various considerations limited my reports in this domain to the infrequent visits of French troupes acting in French under the leadership of such inspired *animateurs* as Jouvet, Barrault, and Vilar—all of whom I had the pleasure of introducing in the flesh, between rehearsals, to young and enthusiastic audiences at Columbia University.

To be sure, Columbia has been the true center of my activity for the past thirty-six years, despite an earlier allegiance to Harvard, where my formal studies ended and teaching began. Most of the subjects treated here figured at one time or another in university lectures also—the lectures feeding the printed essays and the essays nourishing and improving the lectures—and many of them provided subjects for M.A. essays and doctoral dissertations. Such essays as these, together with the many translations and the numerous more detailed articles written for learned journals which will have to await another occasion to be collected, form after all but a by-product in a now rather long career of teaching French literature of the twentieth century.

JUSTIN O'BRIEN

Canterbury, Connecticut
January 1967

CONTENTS

Contents

Contents

PROUST

The New York Times Book Review,
December 28, 1947.

REMEMBRANCE OF MARCEL PROUST

Twenty-five years ago, on the eighteenth of November 1922, Marcel Proust died in Paris. Legend has it that, recognizing his last moments, he had his faithful servant Céleste bring him that part of his unpublished manuscript which described the death of the novelist Bergotte. In his final agony Proust presumably added some significant touches to that description, which concludes: "They buried him, but all through the night of mourning, in the lighted windows, his books arranged three by three kept watch like angels with outspread wings and seemed, for him who was no more, the symbol of his resurrection."

In expressing the idea that Bergotte, the imaginary novelist he had created in great part to symbolize himself, was "not wholly and permanently dead" Proust was surely thinking of himself. The volumes of his own great work, *À la recherche du temps perdu,* were already ten in number, and he knew that others were to follow. To be sure, for most of us, he did not even die in the flesh until 1927, when the last section of the work first appeared in French. Consequently, in celebrating the twenty-fifth anniversary of Marcel Proust's death, we are also, we are especially, celebrating the twentieth anniversary of the completion of his work.

Although that single long novel began to inspire critics while it was still appearing, no one was able to judge it definitively until the last volume had come out. Less *Remembrance of Things Past* (as C. K. Scott Moncrieff entitled it in his translation) than an active recapturing of the author's life and his epoch through the action of canceling the effect of time, those sixteen volumes grew out of Proust's discovery of the involuntary memory. According to his theory, the past neither dies in us nor remains faithfully filed like a carbon copy of experience, but rather clings to fleeting sense impressions. A new encounter with such an already-experienced impression involuntarily permits the past to well up within us. Thus it is only when the narrator, a close transposition of the author, tastes a particular cake dipped in tea that he is able to relive his own childhood and youth. This is the magic by which Proust reconstructs *Swann's Way* and the *Guermantes Way,* symbolic of two societies—the bourgeois world and the exclusive world of the Faubourg Saint-Germain. Through his fascinating and detailed account of Swann's love for the unworthy Odette de Crécy in the first volumes he sets the pattern for the narrator's love affairs *Within a Budding Grove,* first with Swann's daughter Gilberte and then with *The Captive* but ever-elusive Albertine. It is in these three prolonged passages that we have the most poignant and perspicacious analysis of the subjective nature of love and of the torments of jealousy in a sensitive mind. The theme of homosexuality—*The Cities of the Plain*—introduced through M. de Charlus passes from a minor to a major position in the work, combining as it does the other themes of love and jealousy, time and decay. Not until some time after the completion of the work did it become apparent how Proust had employed a symphonic composition of interlocking themes. As these themes mature and unfold, the small provincial town cf Combray and the seaside resort of Balbec (both created by Proust out of a tissue of many recollections) and a certain limited section of Paris become alive to us, transfigured in art. Indeed, for Proust the most real things in the world are those which art has transfused by its sorcery, until we truly have *The Past Recaptured.* Consequently, among his numerous characters he has placed three most vivid creative artists: the composer Vinteuil, the painter Elstir, and the novelist Bergotte, who at once transcend ordinary life and symbolize the author and his problems.

4

Introducing us into an entirely original world of his own creation, Proust thus composed a great modern novel, of a flavor so special and of an art so studied and subtle that its acceptance required close reading and even intimate study. He himself did not expect readers to penetrate that world at once, but he must have felt certain that he was writing a masterpiece for the ages.

Proust's untimely death at the age of fifty-one might seem particularly unfortunate as we look back today. Of his three great contemporaries in French literature, all but one older than he, the two eldest, Claudel and Gide, are alive and writing; Paul Valéry, the third, wrote up to his death in 1945. Surely it is footless, though intriguing, to fancy what Proust would have done had he been endowed with more robust health. But, at any rate, whether or not he might have written other works, he would have polished the still unpublished portions of his manuscript which visibly suffer from the lack of his final care. In the light of Albert Feuillerat's findings from a comparison of the galley proofs of 1913 with the postwar volumes, which show that in ten years of reworking Proust added more than 2,500 pages to a finished original of 1,500 pages, we might conclude that he employed a portmanteau method of composition. It is rather dreadful to think of the proportions to which, had the author lived into his seventies, his work might have extended. Only now would the last sections be appearing, and we, instead of forming the posterity somewhat capable of judging Proust's work, should still be its contemporaries.

Proust himself was particularly aware of the difficulty the public experiences in assimilating a new work of art, in painting, in music, or in literature. In a fascinating passage he reflected that some artists, having no faith in their own time, feel tempted to hold their work in reserve and address it only to posterity. But of course, he continued, that audience would not be posterity at all but merely a group of contemporaries living half a century later in time; "And so it is essential that the artist, if he wishes his work to be free to follow its own course, shall launch it, wherever he may find sufficient depth, confidently outward bound toward the future." Willy-nilly, then, by an accident of fate occurring just twenty-five years ago, we are Proust's posterity. We must accept the consequences.

In those years between the death of Proust's body in 1922 and the appearance of the last volume of his work in 1927, he reached the height of his world-wide fame. Read throughout the world in the original French, he was beginning to be translated into various foreign languages. A special volume of *hommage* published in Paris in January 1923 was followed by *An English Tribute* equally impressive in its list of contributors. At first stunned by his wealth of sense-notations and the entirely new world he had created, his readers had eventually come to regard Proust as the creator of involuntary memory and the introducer of the subconscious into literature. From the writer who had conferred a new depth upon the literature of psychological analysis he was rapidly becoming a moralist who had discovered and integrated a new classicism. After various studies devoted to the relationship between Proust and the Bergsonian conception of time-duration, critics were beginning to see his entire work as a metaphor. Such was the general enthusiasm that few even protested against the insistence of his pictures of Sodom and Gomorrah.

Soon after Proust's death the little volume of poems and tales he had originally brought out in 1896 was republished, and in 1927 his occasional contributions to journalism were collected in a volume. The same year he received the same homage that had been paid to Balzac when Charles Daudet brought out an index of his many characters, purporting to list their every action and thought. This was followed by Raoul Celly's similar index of his themes and Pierre Raphael's index to his correspondence. Meanwhile the first complete study of the man and his work, by Léon Pierre-Quint in 1925, inspired others in French and English by Ernest Seillière, by Derrick Leon, and by Ramon Fernandez.

In 1940 a young American scholar named D. W. Alden examined the French criticism devoted to Proust and found as many as seventeen hundred separate items between 1913 and 1938. The parts played by music, by painting, by memory, by the Jews, by high society, etc., in his work have been isolated for study, sometimes several times over.

Literary critics and specialists have analyzed, often superficially and often profoundly, his composition, his aesthetics, his style, his impressionism, his use of intuition, etc. The very scope of Proust's work encouraged detailed studies of specific aspects of that work, and the fact that he was dead made him safe and legitimate prey for the writers of theses. The most recent such theses are, in France, A. Ferré on Proust's geography and Georges Rivane on the influence of asthma on his work, and in America, Philip Kolb on the redating of his correspondence and Maurice E. Chernowitz on Proust and painting. The contribution of America to Proust studies has, indeed, been considerable: from Yale, Columbia, Chicago, Harvard, and many smaller institutions have come significant books and articles. The files of our scholarly journals contain numerous precious discoveries, many of them by such French professors in America as Albert Feuillerat, Robert Vigneron, Germaine Brée, Jean-Albert Bédé, and René de Messières. Other aspects of Proust doubtless remain to be analyzed, but the greatest present need is for a comprehensive synthesis that would take the place of all the incomplete biographical and critical studies now available.

For two reasons the thirties marked a turning point in Proust's reputation, though some of the best studies came out during that decade. First, the appearance of six or seven volumes of Proust's correspondence presented him in an unfavorable light. The instinctive and pervasive insincerity of those letters, their often self-centered complaints, and the futile snobbery they reveal showed Proust as a man apparently out of tune with the noble breadth of his work. That heterogeneous correspondence has now inspired several scholars to work on it, especially in America, and we may hope that, properly edited, it will throw considerable light on *À la recherche du temps perdu,* while portraying an artist in greater harmony with his work. Second, the social consciousness of those years condemned Proust as a writer limited to depicting but one class of society, and that the highest, in an age of class strife and social readjustment. It was chiefly for this second reason that a critic could write, at the end of that decade, that "Proust no longer has a message for the 1930's." That estimate was correct, but the same critic should have seen that its explanation was to be found in the period. Today it is easier to discern that Proust has a message for the ages.

Twenty-five years after his death, the position of Marcel Proust is somewhat hard to realize. In November 1947 the Paris *Figaro* printed eleven replies of writers to the question: "Do you read Proust?" Most of those answering emphasized the fact that *they* read Proust, whereas most people did not. One had the courage to say that he admired the artist but was bored by his characters, adding: "I do not frequent his world." Three of the replies specified that he was read especially by foreigners. This is always an ominous note, where a French writer is concerned, for is this not just what happened to Guy de Maupassant and Anatole France? But perhaps the most significant fact is that probably none of those replying (I am making an allowance for those about whom I know nothing) is now under forty years old. I have yet, in fact, to meet any young French writer who speaks of Proust as a "master," as one who exerted a spiritual or literary influence upon his own work. The young still read Proust, to be sure, but as an earlier generation read Hugo or Flaubert—as a part of their artistic patrimony, but without any conviction that he has anything to say specifically to the present-day reader or that there is anything new to be discovered about him.

The reasons why Proust is thus forsaken are fairly obvious. First, there is the material reason: his complete work is hard to procure in France now and people lack the fecund leisure for reading him. Second, the social consideration still stands in his disfavor, for he reflects a leisured world devoid of the moral problems and specific anguish to which the youth of today is subject. Finally, the aesthetic ideal has changed, substituting for that of Proust a new love of brevity, brutality, and shock. Nurtured on the American novelists and their French counterparts, the young in France feel no special sympathy for the extreme subtlety of Proust.

The fact that Proust has at last been absorbed into the tradition, taken for granted, is perhaps the highest compliment the world could have paid him. He who felt that the public would require decades, possibly generations, to assimilate his originality would doubtless be surprised to return and find that already his influence has been widespread in several languages and that he is known, not only as the creator of unforgettable characters and the memorialist of a world, but also as a psychological analyst, a delicate and original poet, a keen intellect that forced the intelligence to abdicate before the intuition, and a moralist in the classical tradition. Within a few pages of the end of his great work he reflected: "Doubtless my books also, like my earthly being, would finally some day die. But one must resign oneself to the idea of death. One accepts the idea that in ten years one's self, and in a hundred years one's books, will no longer exist. Eternal existence is not promised to books any more than to men." His hopes were not unreasonable and there is no occasion yet to suppose that his survival may not far outlast his own reckoning.

Introduction to *Swann's Way* (*Du côté de chez Swann*), by Marcel Proust, translated by C. K. Scott Moncrieff (New York: The Limited Editions Club, 1954).

"SWANN'S WAY"

If a literary classic can be defined as a work of acknowledged excellence, then Marcel Proust's novel is a classic. If, on the other hand, that term is reserved for the composition which, setting a new standard, is imitated by others and read in the classes of schools, still *Remembrance of Things Past* ranks as a classic. It has achieved that position in less than a quarter of a century, for just that long ago its author died leaving almost half his manuscript to be published posthumously.

Perhaps no writer since Stendhal, unless it be Proust's contemporary and countryman André Gide, has counted less on the readers of his time and more on posterity. Repeatedly he points out—apropos of the composer Vinteuil, the novelist Bergotte, the painter Elstir—that each original genius presents an utterly new vision of the world and hence begins by rejecting the stereotyped image which the public has eventually assimilated from an earlier art. He knows that this process of substitution takes a long time, since the public begins by timidly accepting from the new work what is least original and valuable. Yet little by little the work of art, he claims, creates its own posterity until there exists an ever-widening audience composed of people, such as were unknown when the work first appeared, capable of understanding and loving it.

Proust should consequently have been amazed, though pleased, that his novel received as much recognition as it did during his lifetime. Doubtless the war, coming so soon after the original publication of

Du côté de chez Swann in 1913, helped his reputation by giving the public six years to reread and digest those two volumes before their continuation became available. Since then, thoughtful and subtle critics in all countries have applied themselves to the more than a million words of his masterpiece and brought out, one after the other, its complex characteristics. To some Proust appeared as the scrupulous memorialist of a dead society registering, through his supersensitive nature, a superabundance of sense-impressions; to others he seemed primarily a psychological analyst revealing, by an uncanny method not unlike that of Freud, the motives behind acts and the underlying subconscious intentions of his characters. Others saw in him chiefly the theorist of a Bergsonian relativity in matters of time and the proponent of the involuntary memory identifying past and present. Still others preferred to interpret him as a poet extracting beauty from nature and the realms of art. Individual critics were struck by his classic French qualities and his close relationship to such moralists as La Bruyère and La Rochefoucauld; or by his ultramodern attempt to disintegrate and dehumanize the physical world and refashion it artistically through the metaphor.

If some saw Proust in relation to James Joyce or Picasso, while to others he recalled Saint-Simon or Mme de Sévigné; if some readers took an Einsteinian or Freudian view of his work, whereas others enjoyed seeking in it a filiation from Stendhal or Baudelaire—meanwhile *Remembrance of Things Past* became ever better known and, thanks to such reassuring terms of reference, lost some of that alarming power to shock and repel that belongs to every isolated and original masterpiece. It became apparent that this new work offered something for everyone. In reality all these elements, and others as well, are inherent in Marcel Proust's novel. This is perhaps why it is so early regarded as a classic.

Now, the whole of *Remembrance of Things Past*—in French it has a better title which suggests its author in pursuit of his *wasted* youth and eventually recapturing time itself—tells the story of a literary vocation. Starting in the present, its middle-aged author looks back to the magical and circumscribed world of his childhood, then gradually, with many a parenthesis and excursion down unexplored bypaths, works his way back to the present again, where the novel ends. In the course of this voyage of exploration, besides meeting many people and moving freely from one society to another, he records his infrequent and momentous experiences of the involuntary memory. That memory, over which the intellect and the will have no control, rests upon a vivid sensation identical with some past sensation. It is this identity that opens the sluices through which the otherwise dead past wells up spontaneously until it replaces the present. Through such "privileged moments" (as Proust calls them), with their ability to cancel out the effects of time, the author can truly relive the past. Appropriately his novel ends upon a series of such moments and the consequent resolve to recapture time in an enduring work of art. The circle is complete, for this annunciatory resolution also marks the culmination of the work itself.

Since the privileged moments are for Proust aesthetic experiences which often lead directly to literary creation, it is but natural that he should indulge in aesthetic considerations and confer upon the work of art special privileges. Hence the existence among his numerous characters of three creative artists—a novelist, a painter, and a composer—who are the only ones among his creatures to transcend, in their respective arts, the ravages of time and to escape, again in their art, the ridicule with which he punctures their noncreative contemporaries and even, in their purely social identities, themselves. Since Proust himself, born into an upper-middle-class family, early gained admittance through his charm and intelligence into exclusive *salons* of the aristocracy, he instinctively described the limited world he knew. This is why he depicts snobbery and ambition on every level of society and shows the decay of princely houses, infiltrated by such crass representatives of the bourgeoisie as the Verdurins. Since, furthermore, the author had a personal interest in homosexuality, he saw nothing strange in generalizing his observations on that score to the point where his "abnormal" characters almost constitute the norm. And finally, since Proust had an unfortunate experience of love, he could see love only as a quite subjective emotion felt by a sensitive, anxious individual for an interested and often unscrupulous partner.

These, then, are the principal themes of *Remembrance of Things*

Past, of which the framework is the account of a literary vocation. But what part does *Swann's Way* play in the whole? Roughly one-eighth of the entire novel, it can yet stand on its own—as the war once forced it to do until the appearance in 1918 of the original of *Within a Budding Grove.*

Proust enjoyed thinking of his work—which early alarmed critics by its apparent lack of composition—as rigorously and skillfully composed in the manner of a Gothic rose window fashioned of many thousand small bits of bright, colored glass, each a gem in itself. Most commentators, however, have preferred to see it as a vast symphony with interlocking and recurrent major and minor themes. In this view, *Swann's Way* forms the first movement, which is in an idyllic mood only slightly overcast by somber premonitions. The English translator, C. K. Scott Moncrieff, was not unhappily inspired when he detached the relatively short initial chapter from the section entitled "Combray" and gave it the individual heading "Overture." For it sets the tone and states numerous themes in a brief space while leading up to the first instance of the involuntary memory.

And then, as if miraculously, from that experience of the "petite madeleine" soaked in tea emerges the whole of Combray—that is, the most luminous part of the narrator's childhood. In a traditional bourgeois world, symbolized by his great-aunt's fabulous house, little Marcel grows up surrounded by luxury and affection. Much of his vacation life in Combray centers around the afternoon walks either on "Swann's Way" in the direction of Méséglise, among lilacs, hawthorns, poppies, and apple trees in blossom, or else along the Vivonne with its ever-varied water lilies and gingerly tadpoles on what was called "the Guermantes Way." To the child, as indeed to the entire family, these two walks were mutually exclusive, almost diametrically opposed in character—as indeed they seemed in direction. No one would have dreamed, for instance, of starting out by way of Swann's and Méséglise to reach Guermantes. And yet this is precisely the circuit that Proust is going to make his readers take symbolically in the course of his novel.

Dimly perceived by the young Marcel, just awakening to life with the troubled vision and confused values of childhood, two worlds lie barely outside his comfortable, familiar realm. Little does he suspect how nearly accessible are the seemingly remote domains of aristocracy and of art; for he could not know that his parents' ingratiating neighbor, Charles Swann, provided a link with both worlds. An intimate of the Guermantes and favored member of their inner circle within the exclusive Faubourg Saint-Germain, Swann is also a great friend of Bergotte and an early discoverer of the art of Elstir and the music of Vinteuil. But at Combray Marcel remains unaware of the central position occupied by Swann. He must learn this by reconstructing Swann's past.

Consequently we have, set down in the middle of this first novel of the narrator's awakening, an interpolated novel entitled "Swann in Love." The events described in that long parenthesis having taken place before Marcel's birth, this constitutes a complete flash back which cannot be narrated by Marcel. The tale of Swann's early life is therefore told as directly as any firsthand incident involving Marcel, and in this instance the reader sees through the eyes of Swann—as elsewhere through those of Marcel. Besides providing variety by interrupting the story of a boy's growing-up, "Swann in Love" serves to introduce the Verdurin clan, Odette de Crécy, the Baron de Charlus, etc., and to furnish background for the later narrative. Finally, it is essential as a statement of the principle of love and a foretaste of Marcel's later love for Swann's daughter Gilberte, and for Albertine. Shortly before it begins (and this is significant), Marcel has caught a glimpse of Gilberte over Swann's hedge at Tansonville, and just after it closes, the account of his life resumes as he eventually meets her in the Champs-Elysées.

Indeed, one can go even further in justifying such an interpolation and state that Charles Swann *is* Marcel Proust almost to the same degree that the narrator is. Has he not the same well-born Jewish background, the same sensitive nature, the same connoisseurship, the same unusual social position in which wealth, taste, and charm take the place of noble birth? Several times Marcel, the narrator, speaks of the intimate resemblances between himself and Swann. On one occasion, relating a dream in which Swann found himself consoling a jealous young man in a fez who turns out to be none other than himself, Proust adds:

"Like certain novelists, he had distributed his own personality between two characters." This is just what Proust has done himself. In "Swann in Love" he has given us at once a transposed reflection of the narrator and a microcosm of the whole work.

Like the narrator, Swann circulates through the entire *Remembrance of Things Past*. He belongs to Combray and to Paris as intimately as does anyone; if he never appears at Balbec, he nevertheless knows that resort frequented by "the little clan" and by his aristocratic friends, Mme de Villeparisis, Charlus, and Saint-Loup. His painter is there, his music is there, his ambiguous and provocative Odette is there in an early portrait, so that truly Balbec is full of his memory. The narrator is never far removed from that older *alter ego* who appears to shape so much of his life.

As a boy in Combray, Marcel did not even suspect Swann's crucial position as his only possible contact with the realms of his dream. This is the principal irony of the entire novel—that while the boy was dreaming of the inaccessible, Charles Swann was sitting in the garden below talking to his parents. And not until much, much later—whether figured in years passed or in pages written—does he recognize in retrospect that in fact Swann had been his effective introducer to those realms.

Swann's Way merely *seems* to lead in the opposite direction from the Guermantes Way; yet this is but one of those deceptive tricks of optics in which Proust the impressionist never fails to take an interest. Already in this first part of his work we become aware how fascinated he is by the totally different views of a place or a person afforded by different perspectives. As the narrator matures, then, he gradually discovers that the two divergent paths at Combray, like the two ways of life they symbolize, merge when pursued far enough until they finally fuse inextricably.

By the end of *Swann's Way,* the young Marcel has neither penetrated society nor understood his literary vocation. The domain of art and the elegant world of the Guermantes have both beckoned him obscurely. But, laboring under a series of misconceptions in regard to both of them, he remains outside both—a spectator rather than a participant. His disappointment with Mme de Guermantes seen across the ancient nave of Combray's church parallels his doubts as to his own literary talent. It is characteristic, however, that he instinctively reacts to both unpleasant experiences in such a way as to transmute them into personal enrichment. For he invents an ideal Mme de Guermantes and notes down with joy his fleeting impressions of the towers of Martinville. In so doing he obscurely, and as it were unconsciously, asserts his right to a place in both the worlds which for him were eventually to form but one.

Introduction to *The Maxims of Marcel Proust,* edited with a translation by Justin O'Brien (New York: Columbia University Press, 1948).

PROUST AS A MORALIST

Proust is not generally considered pithy. The vast dimensions of his work with its unbelievable abundance of detail remind one of a Gothic cathedral, which reveals its architectural principle and interrelation of pattern only after long frequentation and study. Upon a first reading, *À la recherche du temps perdu* leaves an impression of enchantment and confusion. But amidst the wealth of apparently disordered elements and through the often tortuous syntax the reader grasps here and there a key to the understanding of the whole. Sometimes he merely senses a relationship, glimpses a theme, momentarily fingers and then loses a tenuous thread leading through the labyrinth.

Such an impression, resulting inevitably from the novelty of his material, is doubtless the one Marcel Proust intended to make at first. In composing his masterpiece he was himself working his way through the maze of his own life. After an idle and frivolous youth spent in the most exclusive society of Paris, during which time he wrote charming light prose and verse and waited for the inspiration of a great subject, a chronic asthma providentially made him withdraw from the world. Shortly before that turning point he had heard his vocation, and it may have been in answer to that call as much as for his health that he cloistered himself.

The voice that eventually called Proust away from the *salons* first sounded in Combray. As he grew older it became more insistent. For instance, upon tasting by chance one day a little biscuit dipped in tea, he felt himself suddenly carried back to his childhood. In one instant the past and the present were suppressed and he stood, a little boy, beside his great-aunt's bed in the very atmosphere of her room as it had not existed since her death many years before. His emotions were precisely those of that day in the otherwise dim past when he had first tasted such a *madeleine* dipped in tea. After a series of similar supra-temporal experiences, in each of which one of the most significant episodes of his childhood or youth was called back to life by some slight sensory perception, Proust formulated a theory. According to him, "Instead of a carbon copy of the various facts of our life always at hand, memory is rather an abyss whence at moments an identical sensation allows us to draw up and resuscitate otherwise dead recollections." The fortuitous repetition of a sensation releases a spring and permits the past to well up within us. What was already known to psychologists as the affective memory, Proust discovered independently and called the involuntary memory. Upon noticing that his most vivid aesthetic impressions always came to him immediately after such experiences, he decided, as he tells us in his last volume, to make his great literary work turn upon such renewals of the past with their power of canceling the effects of time.

Proust's whole work, then, is an impressionistic evocation of a life and of an epoch. Less *Remembrance of Things Past* than a recapturing of his lost youth in its essence, the work rests solidly upon a metaphor which miraculously suppresses the present and substitutes the past for it. As a consequence, his work is thoroughly subjective and highly intuitive. The reason, powerless to reconstruct the past, abdicates before the irrational flood of impressions surging up from the subconscious. From those impressions, free of the contingencies of time and unfettered by stultifying habit, Proust learns the truth about himself and about the world that surrounds him.

This is of capital importance, since Marcel Proust's chief preoccupation is to seize and reproduce the truth. The earliest invitations to write, which he experienced in childhood, invariably came to him as a desire to isolate the essence of things hidden behind their physical appearance. As an example of such impulses, he has recorded for us the few pages he wrote as a boy about the bell towers of Martinville, wherein a series of Proustian metaphors fixes the fleeting impression forever, as surely as if he had set it down in the oils of his beloved Monet. But the essential truths perceived by the senses in an associative flash and later developed by the intellect, like a photographic negative in a darkroom, are not the only ones to interest Proust.

"As for the truths which the intelligence gathers openly and in broad daylight, on its path," he states in the last volume, "their value may be very great. But they have sharper outlines and remain two-dimensional. They lack depth because it was not necessary to plunge through great depths to reach them, because they have not been re-created. . . . I felt, however, that such truths as the intelligence draws directly from the observation of reality are not to be wholly scorned, since they could at once partially intellectualize and also set off (by contrast with a less pure matter) those impressions brought to us, outside the limits of time, by the essence common to sensations of the past and of the present. For the latter, though more valuable, are also too infrequent for a work of art to be made up entirely of them. I felt the presence within me, all ready for this purpose, of a swarm of truths relating to passions, to characters, and to manners."

It is this swarm of truths that has been gathered together in *The Maxims of Marcel Proust*. Carefully picked from among the 4,116 pages of *À la recherche du temps perdu* and disengaged from its context, each of the four hundred and twenty-eight reflections has a definitive quality. They represent Proust's purely intellectual discoveries about man and the world. Though they may not have been drawn painfully from his inner depths, they are nonetheless the fruit of an observant and reflective life. Even if they are two-dimensional by contrast with the subconscious truths that he sets upon a higher plane, they do have the inestimable advantage, from the reader's point of view, of possessing sharper outlines.

Together, these reflections form a corpus which it is not grandiloquent to consider as the statement of Marcel Proust's philosophy. But whether they be read as a series of individual maxims or as a coherent view of life, they present their author in a quite new light. Here Proust is witty, sly, cynical, profound, poetic by turns—and almost always pithy. Though the syntax is often peculiarly Proustian even when he states his thought most succinctly, there is no obscurity in his maxims.

Indeed, no matter how original his thought may be, Marcel Proust appears once again in these extracts as the renovator of an ancient French tradition. He has often been called a classic and likened to those masters of the age of Louis XIV whom he so greatly admired—to Racine for his purity and psychological penetration, to Saint-Simon and Mme de Sévigné as a memorialist of society, to La Bruyère for his clear-eyed view of man's foibles. But here he joins La Rochefoucauld, the misanthropic duke, whose little collection of three hundred and seventeen *Maximes* first appeared in 1665 and contributed as much as any other work, in the opinion of Voltaire, to forming French taste, since "it accustomed the world to think and to express its thought in a lively, precise, and delicate form."

The French have always possessed this gift. Before La Rochefoucauld, to name only the greatest, Montaigne and Pascal knew the value of epigrammatic expression. Even earlier, the rich Middle Ages had abounded in didactic works and seen many collections of pungent proverbs, the maxims of the uncultivated. Since La Rochefoucauld, France has produced Vauvenargues, Voltaire, and Joubert. Sometime in the early nineteenth century the traditional maxim went underground, taking refuge like so many other forms in the novel. Balzac punctuated his novels with rather heavy aphorisms in which the wit is often stifled by the sententious tone. Stendhal, who even made a collection of random thoughts, likewise enjoyed pointing out in his novels the general application of the particular case in such maxims as:

"Misfortune diminishes a man's wits."

"The Russians copy French manners, but they are always fifty years behind the times."

"In Paris love is the son of novels."

But the consummate *moraliste,* as the French call one who concerns himself with the study of manners and morals, remains to the world at large, as well as to his countrymen, François de La Rochefoucauld. He epitomizes the art of epitomizing. Now, the name of Marcel

Proust has already been linked with that of La Rochefoucauld by no less an authority than Aldous Huxley when he wrote: "In a sentence La Rochefoucauld compresses as much material as would serve a novelist for a long story. Conversely, it would not surprise me to learn that many novelists turn to the *Maximes* for suggestions for plots and characters. It is impossible, for example, to read Proust without being reminded of the *Maximes,* or the *Maximes* without being reminded of Proust. 'Le plaisir de l'amour est d'aimer, et l'on est plus heureux par la passion que l'on a que par celle que l'on donne.' 'Il y a des gens si remplis d'eux-mêmes, que, lorsqu'ils sont amoureux, ils trouvent moyen d'être occupés de leur passion sans l'être de la personne qu'ils aiment.' What are all the love stories in *À la recherche du temps perdu* but enormous amplifications of these aphorisms? Proust is La Rochefoucauld magnified ten thousand times" (*Along the Road,* 1925). This remark is certainly true, but is it not extraordinary that so perspicacious a reader should have failed to notice that Proust also rivals La Rochefoucauld in his own *genre*? If the two seventeenth-century maxims quoted by Mr. Huxley seem to sum up much of Proust, how much more so do Proust's own maxims 272 and 293: "L'être aimé est successivement le mal et le remède qui suspend et aggrave le mal." (The beloved is by turns the disease and the remedy that suspends and aggravates the disease.) "À l'être que nous avons le plus aimé nous ne sommes pas si fidèles qu'à nous-même, et nous l'oublions tôt ou tard pour pouvoir—puisque c'est un des traits de nous-même—recommencer d'aimer"? (We are not so faithful to the person we have loved most of all as we are to ourselves, for sooner or later we forget that person in order to begin loving someone else.) Marcel Proust did not have to borrow his texts, and it is noteworthy that the only La Rochefoucauld he mentions in his work is a friend and contemporary, a remote descendant of the famous cynic.

In the passage quoted earlier Proust speaks of "a swarm of truths relating to passions, to characters, and to manners." These are the classic subjects; La Rochefoucauld and La Bruyère could be summed up in those words. And when, after isolating them all individually, one attempts to classify Proust's maxims, one finds that they fall into five categories: Man; Society; Love; Art; and Time and Memory. The first three categories concern characters, manners, and passions. The last two correspond to Proust's chief technical problems; since he held such special conceptions of Art and of Time, it is not surprising that he should have some pointed truths to impart on those subjects. But the greatest number of his aphorisms quite naturally concern man and his ways. It is here that he challenges comparison with his great predecessors. When he states in maxim 10: "Unfortunately our indulgent refusal to perceive our friend's short-coming is surpassed by his obstinacy in yielding to it," he seems to share the disillusioned viewpoint of La Rochefoucauld, who found the key to life in self-love. But Proust attenuates this attitude in maxim 31: "Certain good qualities help us to endure another's flaws rather than making us suffer more from them, and a man of great talent usually gives less attention to another's stupidity than would a fool."

La Rochefoucauld yields parallels to a remark such as 222: "The charms of the passing woman are usually in direct ratio to the speed of her passing"; but, despite the lesson of Descartes, one will not find in La Rochefoucauld a match for the simple and profound maxim 22: "Perhaps the immobility of material objects is imposed on them by our certainty as to their identity, by the immobility of our mind as it looks upon them."

La Rochefoucauld explains most of life by reference to vanity and self-interest; though giving their due to such motives, Proust is neither so specific nor so bitter. Probably the keynote of all his thoughts is the word "subjective": our observations, our loves, our jealousies, our art, even our awareness of the passage of time, are subjective, but this in no way invalidates them. La Rochefoucauld might well have written Proust's maxim 281 ("When we are in love our love is too great to be contained within us. It irradiates toward the beloved, in whom it encounters a hard surface whence it rebounds to its point of departure. It is this ricochet of our own affection that we call the other person's love for us.") but he would have been incapable of maxim 280 ("Probably few people understand the purely subjective nature of the phenomenon love and the fact that it creates a kind of supplementary person, quite distinct from the one who answers to the same name and most of whose elements are drawn from ourselves."). Proust catalogues our illusions, yet without deploring them. In fact he even encourages them (compare maxims 70 to 76). This is because he is a poet. In maxim 71 he observes: "We seek to recapture in things, which have become dear to us for this very reason, the reflection that our soul has cast upon them. We are disappointed to discover that they seem devoid in nature of the charm which, in our mind, they owe to the neighborhood of certain ideas." The antidote for such a disappointment, however, is to continue to contemplate the inner vision.

All the literary types that we are accustomed to find in aphorisms are represented in this collection. The epigrams, such as "To each one of us clear ideas are those which have the same degree of confusion as his own"; and "When we see ourselves on the edge of the abyss and it seems that God has abandoned us, we no longer hesitate to expect a miracle" are, of course, the most striking and most memorable. But the reflections or *pensées,* which often develop a more subtle thought at greater length and without the same witty turn in the expression, are almost as numerous. Good examples are:

"We say indeed that the hour of death is uncertain, but when we say this we imagine that hour as situated in a vague and distant future. It never occurs to us that it has any relation to the day already begun or that death could come this afternoon, which is anything but uncertain—this afternoon every hour of which is filled in advance."

"To a writer as to a painter, style is a question not of technique but of vision. It is the revelation, which would be impossible by direct and conscious means, of the qualitative difference between our various manners of seeing the world—a difference which, but for art, would eternally remain the individual's secret."

The portrait, in which Proust swiftly characterizes human types in a manner reminiscent of La Bruyère's *Caractères,* can be seen here for instance: "A great part of the pleasure that a woman derives from being admitted into a new and different circle would be lacking if she could not let her former friends know of the more brilliant friends by whom she has replaced them. For this purpose she must introduce to that new and delightful world a witness who, like a busy, buzzing insect in a flower, will in the course of her visits proceed to spread the news, the stolen germ of envy and admiration." Others suggest poems in prose as this one does: "Life holds hardly any interest except on the days when the dust of reality is mingled with magic sand—when some ordinary incident of life becomes a springboard for the imagination. Then a whole promontory of the inaccessible world rises from the mists of fancy and enters our life, where, like the awakened sleeper, we see the individuals of whom we had dreamed so ardently that we thought we should never see them except in dreams."

It must be remembered that Marcel Proust never composed any such collection of aphorisms as this. Probably few intentions were more remote from his mind. His maxims have been culled from the many volumes of the French edition of *À la recherche du temps perdu*, where they appear on an average of about one to every nine or ten pages. Actually there is sometimes a run of aphorisms appearing on three, four, or five consecutive pages and followed by twenty or forty pages before another stands out. Proust's love of generalizing has never been hampered by his material, for the maxims occur as readily in the midst of descriptive or narrative passages as they do in the more reflective sections of the work. In this way, either consciously or unconsciously, Proust has truly infused what he calls intelligence into every part of his writing. It is certainly due to the habit of mind from which these maxims spring that Proust's work justly has a reputation for universality.

As for the editing, it consisted of reading Proust carefully and of grouping the aphorisms according to subject. The reader will occasionally notice a pair of maxims dealing with the same subject. It would obviously have been possible to choose the better and to omit the other; but when they have come together from remote sections of *À la recherche du temps perdu* and when each contributes something new on the subject, both have been kept. Furthermore, one even finds such pairs of maxims in La Rochefoucauld and Vauvenargues, who polished their own collections.

Some of the maxims called for a scalpel to disengage them from their context since they came parenthetically in the middle of a long sentence or, on the other hand, were themselves broken by an illustrative parenthetical remark. Others required simply the removal of an initial adverb or conjunction. Three maxims named characters in the book: in one it was advisable to change "Elstir" to "Manet"; in another "Elstir" became "Renoir" and "Vinteuil" became "Debussy"; and in a third "l'artiste" takes the place of "Elstir." By far the great majority of maxims needed no change. Two of the maxims, although they are spoken by characters in the novel (Dr. du Boulbon and Swann, respectively), seemed sufficiently representative of the author's point of view to deserve inclusion.

Since a maxim must be translated as a maxim and not as a sentence in context, the translation was made without reference to C. K. Scott Moncrieff's famous English version of Proust.

The principle involved in isolating individual sentences from their context may strike some readers as indefensible. If Marcel Proust had wished to leave a collection of maxims, they will say, he would have written it himself. It would be footless to answer such critics with arguments drawn from Proust's early death or from the literary fashions of his time. Nor is it more convincing to point out that Dr. Johnson planned making a collection of "Maxims, characters and sentiments, after the manner of La Bruyère, collected out of ancient authours, particularly the Greek, with Apophthegms" and that no less an admirer than Jules Barbey d'Aurevilly grouped and edited the maxims of Balzac.

The fact that *À la recherche du temps perdu* is rich in aphoristic wisdom runs the risk of escaping most readers. To isolate and group together those detachable sentences is to perform the service of presenting a great modern writer in a new light. "To polish commonplaces and give them a new lustre," wrote Logan Pearsall Smith, "to express in a few words the obvious principles of conduct, and to give to clear thoughts an even clearer expression; to illuminate dimmer impressions and bring their faint rays to a focus; to delve beneath the surface of consciousness to new veins of precious ore, to name and discover and bring to light latent and unnamed experience; and finally to embody the central truths of life in the breadth and terseness of memorable phrases—all these are the opportunities of the aphorist; and to take advantage of these opportunities, he must be a thinker, an accurate observer, a profound moralist, a psychologist, and an artist as well" (*A Treasury of English Aphorisms,* 1928). Marcel Proust was all of these; and to deny him the additional title of aphorist would be petty indeed.

La Fontaine, the professionally naïve, once remarked that long works filled him with fear. Proust at first frightened all of us for the same reason. But it is possible to extract from that inordinately long work a series of concise, even lapidary observations. To some readers the maxims may make Proust more palatable. Yet in all justice it must be stated that there is no short cut to his work, for a collection of his maxims omits much that is most essentially Proustian. One of the world's most famous critics wrote: "The critic is simply a man who knows how to read and who teaches others how to read." And Sainte-Beuve would doubtless have conceded that such a collection was an essay in criticism since it merely isolates for our admiration one aspect of Proust that might otherwise have gone unnoticed. As such, it may have the good fortune to lead some readers back again to the extraordinarily rich and ever-varied *À la recherche du temps perdu.*

On *Jean Santeuil,* by Marcel Proust, translated by Gerard Hopkins, with a preface by André Maurois (New York: Simon and Schuster, Inc., 1956). *The New York Times Book Review,* February 12, 1956.

"JEAN SANTEUIL"

When Marcel Proust died in Paris in 1922, the world already revered him for the creation of a new type of novel. Translations of his vast work had begun to appear in various languages, even though but two-thirds of it was as yet available in the original French. During the following six years six more volumes came out, until *The Past Recaptured* closed his special vision of a dead world revivified through the magic of his imagination. By this time, even before having read all of the more than four thousand pages of his masterpiece, critics had discerned in him a poet, a philosopher, and a psychologist, likening him to Bergson for his original conception of time and to Freud for his revelation of the subconscious.

Gradually the conviction grew that the apparently random labyrinth of *Remembrance of Things Past* had been carefully and elaborately constructed by a highly conscious artist, that it had consequently to be read as a whole in the order Proust intended. Looking back to the initial section, *Swann's Way* of 1913, readers saw that all the Proustian themes and techniques had been there from the beginning. But the more they learned—through his voluminous and generally disappointing correspondence and the republication of his early collection of charming prose and verse entitled *Pleasures and Days*—of his idle and frivolous youth spent in the most exclusive Parisian society, the more miraculous it seemed that he should have distilled that past into such a grandiose and universally appealing novel.

How had the snobbish young fop of 1895, friend of princes and fritterer of time, developed into the great novelist of the twentieth century? There grew up an implausible legend of the social butterfly who emerged an eagle after years of pupation in a cork-lined room, of the sufferer from chronic asthma who, bedridden in a fumigated atmosphere, had hastened his death by the feverish pursuit of his wasted youth.

Specialists, to be sure, knew his translations of Ruskin made in the early years of this century, which accounted for some of the intervening time and partly explained the development of his aesthetic theories. Later they learned of the existence of unpublished notebooks, upon which André Maurois drew so effectively in his *À la recherche de Marcel Proust*. And now, just within the last few years, have come the answers to most of their questions with the publication of large sections of those notebooks. *Jean Santeuil*, which appeared in Paris in 1952 (followed in 1954 by *Contre Sainte-Beuve*), was assembled, with the blessing of Proust's niece and under the patronage of André Maurois, by a French scholar named Bernard de Fallois from disordered manuscript folios found in a warehouse after the writer's death. No one can doubt that both manuscripts provide the key to his activity during the period from 1896 to 1913 and the rough draft—hasty and very revelatory—of his unique masterpiece.

Supposedly the unfinished life story of a famous writer, *Jean Santeuil* relates in the third person (though later Proust was to be more at home in the first person) his childhood and young manhood in Paris society and at various attractive vacation spots. The more delightful chapters—pleasing partly because we see in them the first draft of *Remembrance*—recount his loves and social encounters, while the duller ones, without counterpart in the definitive work, trace the Dreyfus affair and government scandals. The whole is so disjointed that, despite the descriptive chapter headings supplied by the editor, one occasionally wonders if the same hero is concerned throughout.

Hardly a novel in itself, *Jean Santeuil* interests by the light it throws on Proust's later work, affording us that special pleasure we take in comparing an original piano score with its full orchestration that we know and love. Again and again the reader feels enveloped in the familiar atmospheres of the Proustian world, whether in the haughty Faubourg Saint-Germain peopled with duchesses or in the quiet provincial town with its Gothic steeple beckoning over the trees by the river. And many of the later themes—from the glamor of nobility to the mysterious resurrection of the past—are already sounded somewhat timidly.

The best of the incidents that we excitedly recognize throughout the book—the mother's good-night kiss, the childish love for a playmate in the Champs-Elysées, the rapture caused by remembered scenes, the mingled joy and anguish at hearing the mother's voice over a long-distance telephone, the thwarted kiss, and the jealous peeking through the shutters of the mistress' window—seem crude here only because they have not been fully integrated with those themes. A word-by-word comparison of parallel passages often separated by a fifteen-year interval is not always to the disadvantage of the earlier one.

For instance, various loves of the hero emerge in some detail, delighting us with episodes and reflections that Proust was later to embody in the love of "Marcel" for Gilberte and Albertine and in Swann's love for Odette. But here we do not feel any particular relationship or progression among those affairs, nor have they any necessary bond with the rest of the hero's life as we are told it. After these first notes were finished and put aside, it occurred to Proust to split up his own personality into three memorable characters: Marcel the narrator, the somber Baron de Charlus, and the urbane Swann. Charlus could stand for Sodom, which only once and discreetly peeks out of this early narrative; whereas Swann, as a rich and cultured commoner who had already penetrated the charmed circle of the Guermantes and lived among the Verdurins, could prefigure the narrator's ascent in society and offer a foretaste of that youth's pathologically jealous loves.

Rarely, if ever, has a great writer been so obviously the author of a single book. Everything in Marcel Proust's life, from his wealth and snobbery to his sexual orientation and providential asthma, served to prepare him for the writing of the particular novel he eventually wrote.

31

His early precious essays, the society chronicles for the *Figaro,* and the clever parodies he made of such classics as Balzac, Saint-Simon, and Flaubert all represent obscure gropings in the direction of his single masterwork.

In *Jean Santeuil* we now have the first nearly complete "dry run" of *Remembrance of Things Past.* Obviously it was too early—these pages were written before he reached thirty—for him to create a system out of his own susceptibility to the involuntary memory. Doubtless he had to reach middle life before seeing that his true purpose, as he tells us in *The Past Recaptured,* was to relive the past in the present and thus to cancel the effects of time through his art. It is chiefly this, however, that makes Proust's finished classic universal.

Yet, in *Jean Santeuil* he is already recording the story of another writer inordinately sensitive to that particular affective memory—in the Paris bells, in the scent of white lilacs and the sight of pink hawthorn, in a sea breeze or the smell of a wooden cottage by the shore, in the buzzing of summer flies or a combination of notes from the piano. Already he can prophetically say, surely without sensing how accurately he was foretelling a part of his mature credo: "I write nothing of what I see, nothing at which I arrive by a process of reasoning, or of what I have remembered in the ordinary sense of remembering, but only of what the past brings suddenly to life in a smell, in a sight, in what has, as it were, exploded within me and set the imagination quivering, so that the accompanying joy stirs me to inspiration."

Undeniably the germ of Proust's later, famous work is here, although he has not yet learned to orchestrate his themes. The greatest value of this volume, in no sense a substitute for *Remembrance of Things Past,* is to make the world appreciate at last the ingenious composition of his more familiar definitive work—the very quality upon which, as it was least apparent at first, he himself most insisted.

On *Marcel Proust: On Art and Literature: 1896–1919 (Contre Sainte-Beuve)*, edited by Bernard de Fallois and translated by Sylvia Townsend Warner (New York: Meridian Books, 1958). *The Reporter,* May 29, 1958.

PROUST ON ART AND LITERATURE

Long after Marcel Proust's death, his achievement remained wrapped in mystery. The more we learned about his frivolous youth, the more miraculous it seemed that he should have managed to distill that uneventful past into such a great and universally appealing novel. To be sure, he had learned why, as he said in the preface to his first book, "invalids feel closer to their souls."

The first hint came from André Maurois' admirable biography, which told of the existence of unpublished notebooks moved from that room to a warehouse at the author's death. Then Bernard de Fallois collated those notes preserved by Mme Mante-Proust, the author's niece and heir, producing first the 1,000-page first draft of Proust's novel, presumably written between 1896 and 1900 under the title of *Jean Santeuil.* Next Fallois issued the present volume, known in France as *Contre Sainte-Beuve,* which, composed in 1908–1909, supplies us the missing link between *Jean Santeuil* and *Remembrance of Things Past.*

Everything that Proust ever wrote is part of the same work. As he himself said in his definitive masterpiece, "Great writers never create but a single work, or rather they consistently refract through different media a single beauty that they bring into the world." It is unthinkable that Proust—even if he had lived into his eighties as his contemporaries Claudel and Gide did, instead of dying at fifty-one—should have followed *Remembrance of Things Past* with another and different book.

Instead, he would simply have postponed the publication of the later volumes while he added new episodes and developments—just as he did when World War I gave him a chance to add 2,500 pages to what had been complete by 1913 in 1,500 pages. The portmanteau construction of his novel seemed designed to accommodate such additions.

By the same token, everything he wrote prior to 1913, when *Swann's Way* first appeared, either found its way into the novel or went into discard as an unsatisfactory first draft, not to be consulted again. Consequently, as we look back now, we can see that from the early 1890's until about 1910 Proust was tuning up for his masterpiece.

Pleasures and Days, that youthful and precious work of 1896, contains many premonitions—in theme, characters, and style—of the mature work. Next came the two translations of Ruskin that clarified Proust's aesthetic theories, taught him much about language, and crystallized his attitudes toward life. Meanwhile, he was sharpening his skill and exercising his critical acumen by writing the delightful parodies of Balzac, Flaubert, Saint-Simon, and Renan eventually collected in *Pastiches et Mélanges,* and chronicling social events, with elaborate portraits of people and costumes, for *Le Figaro.*

This much we could see thirty years ago. But it was not until the recent publication of the notebooks that we entered Proust's workroom and saw him making "dry runs" of his masterpiece. In *Jean Santeuil* (the first of those piano scores without orchestration) a third-person narration presents many of the incidents and characters of the later novel set in the already familiar atmospheres of Proust's world. But the town is not called Combray, the noble family bears an unaccustomed name and has no connection with the hero's province, and—worst of all—several central characters, such as Swann and Charlus and the Verdurins, have not yet come into being. The theme of involuntary memory is there in germ, without forming the basis of the composition, but that of a literary vocation is absent. Indeed, the admirer of Proust, as he reads *Jean Santeuil,* cannot fail to miss the apparently inevitable steps that transmuted these notes into *Remembrance of Things Past.*

But *Contre Sainte-Beuve,* which forms the greater part of *On Art and Literature,* takes many of those steps. Although purporting to be a study in literary criticism, it boldly adopts the first person, which was certainly Proust's most congenial form of narration, and starts off directly with the theory of the involuntary memory, using the famous example of the cup of tea from which all Combray blossoms forth. (The fact that the little *madeleine* served by his mother in the later work is here a piece of toast brought by an old servant only arouses our reflections as to the art of transposition.) Then as it proceeds to other major Proustian themes, we find that the great noble family has finally acquired the name and characteristics of the Guermantes we know, together with a property not far from Combray (which now has *its* rightful name), and that it includes a homosexual Marquis de Quercy who foreshadows the Baron de Charlus and motivates a long generalization about "a race accursed," which will eventually find its place at the beginning of *Cities of the Plain.* Although Swann himself is not yet here, his daughter is, and her description reveals that Swann already existed in the author's mind.

If this book strikes us most significantly as another false start for *Remembrance of Things Past,* then its French title is rather a misnomer. The English novelist Sylvia Townsend Warner, who is obviously steeped in Proustian lore, has translated the volume with that rare combination of knowledge and love that should be indispensable to the translator. Often she boldly and wisely cuts one of Proust's tortuous but beautifully articulated sentences into two or three, and occasionally —as if out of sheer daring—she reverses the process and makes a single sentence out of two or three. Wherever she has changed the order of chapters, identified quotations, and supplied others that had just been hinted at by Proust, her editing is unimpeachable. Yet even she had trouble with the title. The London edition is called *By Way of Sainte-Beuve,* which has the advantage, while reminding us of Proust's two "ways," of suggesting that Sainte-Beuve is merely a pretext for getting on with the novel. The American title, on the other hand, pays more attention to the score or so of brief essays that the French editor appended to *Contre Sainte-Beuve* because he found them among the same papers.

Despite the fact that only a fourth of the volume really concerns Sainte-Beuve directly, Proust used his name in the title because the academic critic, famous for his objective and scholarly method, was his own *bête noire*. Unable to forgive him for failing to recognize the value of his contemporaries such as Balzac, Flaubert, Baudelaire, and Nerval, Proust even thought at one time of writing a history of nineteenth-century French literature according to Sainte-Beuve in which none of the names we now revere would figure prominently.

The critic's blindness, according to Proust, derived from his confusing the writer's soul with the accidental human envelope that clothed it and consequently maintaining that a poet's work can be illuminated by observing the poet and studying his biography. To Proust, on the contrary, "a book is the product of a different *self* from the self we manifest in our habits, in our social life, in our vices." Hence Sainte-Beuve, whom any French literary man constantly encounters in his path, figures for Proust as the complete Philistine. At this point in his career it was essential for him to take issue with his famous predecessor and eject him from his Pantheon, while identifying himself with Sainte-Beuve's victims.

It is also appropriate that at this point Proust should turn critic, after indulging in *pastiches* and translations as a means of forming his aesthetic credo. His beloved Baudelaire once said: "Naturally and fatally all great poets become critics." And Proust's criticism is that of the creator, highly personal and often partial, sympathetic to the point of indulgence, and abounding in flashes of insight. "Every reader reads himself," he tells us toward the end of his vast *Remembrance*. "The writer's work is merely a kind of optical instrument that makes it possible for the reader to discern what, without this book, he would perhaps never have seen in himself."

Thus the subjects of Proust's inquiry here, whether they be Balzac or Dostoevsky, Watteau or Monet, enrich the artist-critic by helping him to find *his way*. Again and again Proust asserts the transcendence of art, the importance of vision and style (which are one and the same to him), and the equivalence of all subject matter. Chardin teaches him that a crude kitchen crock can be as beautiful as an emerald, and Rembrandt that every picture by a single artist reflects a fragment of his peculiar and mysterious world. This is why Chateaubriand constantly sounds for Proust the same lasting, inimitable note; why Gérard de Nerval has *his* note, too, as different from Chateaubriand's as it is from Baudelaire's. While reading or contemplating a work of art, Proust tells us, the poet enjoys a double vision, for he sees at the same time into his own mind.

It is just this double vision, in fact, that persistently draws Proust back to the project of his own novel even when he indulges in criticism. Sainte-Beuve may have been but a pretext for Proust, a way of momentarily escaping the responsibility of getting his creative work under way, yet even Sainte-Beuve leads him to his problems as a novelist. From a discussion of Balzac and the critic's lack of understanding of Balzac he rushes to an image of his own Count de Guermantes reading Balzac in the library of his palatial house, and this in turn evokes the society that frequented that house. By this time Proust is off on his own creation, while Balzac and Sainte-Beuve fade into the distance.

Proust's whole approach to criticism naturally adopts a conversational tone with its attendant ramblings, near-repetitions, and quotations from memory. When he first planned this book, he asked a friend whether it would be better to write an orthodox critical essay or to couch his indignation in the form of a long conversation with his mother, to whom he would outline the article he intended to write. And it is highly noteworthy that he chose the latter form, which permitted seven initial chapters having nothing to do either with Sainte-Beuve or with literary criticism. Many years later—in fact, just a year before his death when he knew himself much better—Proust wrote a friend: "I never do articles; it is like opening a wound from which the rest of my blood will flow." Most cleverly, Sylvia Townsend Warner has quoted this statement in the last footnote she has supplied, as if to suggest to us subtly the chief interest of this fascinating transitional work of exploration and discovery called *On Art and Literature*.

Saturday Review, February 18, 1956.

PROUST AND GIDE DISPLAYED

Probably no nation so tangibly honors a dead writer as does France. Whether or not he has reached the Academy before his death, his posthumous life begins when a Society of Friends and Admirers is formed, a plaque is affixed to his birthplace, or a street is renamed after him. In place of our literary cocktail parties for the living, exhibits organized by libraries and private galleries keep the dead celebrity's memory alive. Recently the Bibliothèque Nationale in Paris has held such shows in honor of the Romantic poet Gérard de Nerval, the sixteenth-century Malherbe, and Emile Verhaeren, born a hundred years ago.

But the most interesting exhibits for twentieth-century literature centered around the persons of Marcel Proust and André Gide. The former, at London's Wildenstein Gallery in New Bond Street, was a thoroughly French manifestation organized by the French Cultural Affairs Office. Besides grouping photographs and paintings of all Proust's relatives and friends, including those who unwittingly contributed something to Swann, Charlus, Gilberte, and other characters, it displayed such mementos of the great recluse as an inkstand, a waistcoat, a lock of hair, and the Ruskin volumes from which he translated *The Bible of Amiens.* A pencil sketch of Oscar Wilde by Boldini showed that controversial figure in a new light, as did an early Jacques-Emile Blanche portrait of a willowy Jean Cocteau that no one would think of looking for in the Carnavalet Museum in Paris, its permanent home. Other paintings by such as Gustave Moreau, Whistler, Monet, and Sisley evoked not only the general atmosphere of Proust's work but even individual scenes and episodes.

The most moving part of the London exhibit, however, was not so much this plentiful iconography, nor yet the impressive roster of great names of France—Gramont, Guiche, Montesquiou, Noailles, Polignac, Greffulhe—borne by the writer's friends, nor even the mass of letters to and from Proust's cork-lined, fumigated room. Rather it lay in the artfully exhibited manuscripts ranging from two schoolboy essays by way of the twenty thick manuscript volumes of *Remembrance of Things Past* to the last note hastily scribbled on the back of an envelope. In those pages, as in the long galley proofs cut and spliced with endless autograph addenda, Marcel Proust distilled his particular vision of the dead world which all the other objects in the gallery strove to reconstruct for us.

Across the channel in Paris, soon after, there opened an equally fascinating Gide exhibit in the small and ultra-rich Bibliothèque Littéraire Jacques Doucet. Inasmuch as that collection covering the best in French literature from Rimbaud to the present was bequeathed by the rich dressmaker Doucet to the University of Paris, it is housed in one large, semi-private room of the Sorbonne library. There the indefatigable and charming Mlle Marie Dormoy and her assistant Jacques Naville (who happens to be one of the literary executors of André Gide) preside over the invaluable collection of manuscripts and first editions, which is constantly growing through bequests and intelligent purchases. In fact, the entire Gide exhibit, but for a few photographs lent by various collectors, was composed of documents bequeathed by Gide himself or given by his daughter, Mme Catherine Lambert-Gide.

In this regard it differed greatly from the Proust show, made up of contributions from all over; and all but the most informed members of Parisian literary circles, who flocked to the opening, were dazzled by the wealth and completeness of the collection. Each showcase covered one aspect of a long and intense literary life: the novelist with manuscripts of the principal novels; the dramatist with neat holographs of *Oedipus* and other plays; the literary critic and influential editor who founded the *Nouvelle Revue Francaise* back in 1908; the public figure who served as mayor of his town at twenty-five, later fought to improve conditions in the Congo, and eventually won the Nobel Prize. To many the most appealing case presented in tumbled disarray, as if an attic trunk had just been opened, the eighty-three pocket notebooks of various formats and colors in which Gide kept his *Journals* from 1889 to 1949.

Almost every showcase bore testimony to Gide's vast correspondence with fellow writers, admirers, and critics through letters carefully chosen from among the ten thousand in the Doucet collection of Gidiana. Letters from Rilke, Valéry, Conrad, and Romain Rolland lay beside others from lesser-known writers, while one small space piquantly grouped handwritten notes on governmental stationery from such disparate political figures as Léon Blum and Charles Maurras, Raymond Poincaré and Edouard Herriot. D'Annunzio's tall stylized hand contrasted with Bergson's neat legible characters and Wilde's loose scrawl. Among the letters and on the surrounding walls, unpublished photographs of Gide at all periods, of his associates and familiar haunts, of his saintly wife and Arab boy Athman, illustrated the eighty years of his full life.

Both these exhibits in London and Paris this winter brought their subjects closer to us, making visitors feel they had penetrated the intimacy of two great modern writers who had much in common and yet lived worlds apart. The obvious differences between the shows reflected the differences between the two men. Whereas in Proust's case the emphasis fell on the brilliant and colorful world in which he had lived, the Gide collection centered rather on the personality and work of the writer. It is also significant—art galleries being more affluent than universities—that this reconstruction of Proust's elegant world will live on in an illustrated catalogue, whereas the Gide material left no record except in the memory.

The New York Times Book Review,
March 5, 1967.

PROUST'S EARLIEST READERS

The fascinating reader's report on Proust's manuscript published in the *Times Book Review* of the 22nd of January 1967 raises the whole question of Proust's first readers and that other problem of any reader's initial impression, at any time, on contact with *À la recherche du temps perdu.* Jacques Madeleine's semiofficial report written in 1912 probably gives heart to some who tried to read Proust only yesterday. Despite the library of books suggesting ways of approaching that vast work, many must have experienced a somewhat similar frustration. Doubtless they are rejoicing now upon learning that the Madeleine bit back.

The beauty of the case lies in the fact that he did not know, as we do, that he was privileged to read one of the greatest masterpieces of the twentieth century. In his place, knowing most intimately the publisher he was advising, should we have acted differently back in 1912? That publisher, Eugène Fasquelle, was a close friend of Gaston Calmette, the editor of the daily *Figaro* to whom the ever-social Marcel Proust cannily dedicated the first part of his work, and it was Calmette who sent the manuscript to Fasquelle out of friendship for Proust. The would-be novelist had already written articles for the *Figaro,* and there was even a possibility that bits and pieces of his novel might appear there.

Calmette had not read the manuscript of 712 pages with many a page numbered A, B, or C added to the total; nor was the busy Eugène

Fasquelle going to be so foolish. After all, he owed nothing to Proust, although Proust consulted his friends about the wisdom of inviting Fasquelle at that time to one of his sumptuous dinners at the Ritz. Instead Fasquelle asked his friend Jacques Madeleine to read the manuscript in his place and advise him.

Now, Madeleine was not exactly a flunky of Fasquelle. Neither a hired reader nor a secretary, he occasionally helped Fasquelle in difficult cases and always with the strictest anonymity. As a young poet enamored of antiquated verse forms, he had had the pleasure of seeing his first volume, *Livret de vers anciens,* listed in an auction catalogue as the work of an unknown poet of the Renaissance. After that start in life, he had been welcomed into the Parnassian school. He it was, moreover, who organized the night vigil under the Arc de Triomphe at the time of Victor Hugo's state funeral in 1885. Without enjoying the reputation of a Zola or a Leconte de Lisle, he was not altogether an unknown.

Faithfully Madeleine strove to record the "plot" of Proust's work, whose thread he naturally failed to discern on the basis of a single part, and to isolate the principal characters among all those that pop in and out among the digressions. Never once did he say categorically that Fasquelle ought not to publish the book. On the contrary, despite his restrictions, he saw that "there is an unusual intellectual performance here."

He also saw certain things of importance that would have been apparent only to a very close reader in 1912. First of all, he noticed that "the little boy is always around." How could we better state today that the narrator's all-seeing eye and all-hearing ear record everything we need to know of the surrounding world, even if he sometimes has to play the part of peeping Tom? Yet he failed to see that the "interminable stories" about apparently minor characters and the myriad "digressions"—but how could there be digressions where there is no central thread of narrative?—are present precisely because of their "influence on the disturbed character of the little boy."

Most perceptive of all is his observation that something ambiguous and perplexing enters the relationship between the boy (who may not be so little now) and the middle-aged homosexual sometimes called

Baron de Fleurus and sometimes Baron de Charlus. Looking ahead with a shudder to the additional 700 pages announced by Proust but not sent with the first 712, Madeleine hazards a very shrewd guess. "If the little boy doesn't become an invert," he writes, "what use is all this monologue? If he does, and one should hope so for the sake of consistency, there is some excuse for the monograph, but it is still monstrously disproportionate."

Today we know that, after the appearance of Charlus, the novel pays increasing attention to homosexuality until some readers have complained that the abnormal becomes the norm. We also know that the little boy never develops in that direction. Furthermore, we also know, thanks to certain items in the prodigous Proustian bibliography, that Proust himself was a homosexual and therefore created the Baron de Charlus largely from self-observation. The "morbid little boy" modeled on the author already belonged to what Proust later called "the accursed race," but the author was never going to reveal this fact if he could help it.

With a shocking disregard of the rules observed by the whole literary world, Proust had submitted his manuscript to two publishers at the same time. The suggestion of Fasquelle had been made by Calmette, but Proust really wanted to be brought out by the young house that developed from the literary monthly founded in 1909 by André Gide and a group of friends, among whom figured Gaston Gallimard. Today the firm is known as Editions Gallimard and each of its publications carries the handsome lower case initials *n r f* designed in the beginning by the novelist Jean Schlumberger for the periodical *Nouvelle Revue Française*. Proust told friends that he really belonged among that austere and dedicated group of writers surrounding Gide, and accordingly he sent part of his manuscript to them.

As the unofficial director of both the review and the publishing house of the same name, André Gide deserved the blame for failing to recognize one of the great books of the era. And such blame as he received throughout the years! Some, totally uninformed, have gone so far as to suggest that there might have been some jealousy in his rejection of the long manuscript. But we now know better, although André Gide never defended himself on this score, for the facts speak for themselves. In Gide's first letter to Proust of January 1914, after Grasset, a third publisher, had finally brought out the book in 1913 at the author's expense, he literally raved about *Du côté de chez Swann* and gave his reasons for rejection. By return mail Proust wrote him that Gide's letter was infinitely more precious than even the joy of being published by the *Nouvelle Revue Française*.

Gide's refusal was motivated by his dim recollection of Proust as a social butterfly of the nineties. The fact that Proust, whom Gide had not seen in twenty years, offered to subsidize the edition of his novel merely confirmed the belief that he was not a serious writer. Yet these are merely extenuating circumstances that by no means exonerate Gide for having failed to read the manuscript carefully and discern in it the qualities of genius. After all, Gide knew as well as anyone that great works of art always come as a surprise.

Even without reading the manuscript carefully, Gide did more than merely leaf it over with his mind on something else. The passage concerning the *madeleine* dipped in tea, for which he was not prepared, gave him pause, to say the least, and then two pages later he stumbled definitively on a sentence in which the ubiquitous little boy kissed his grandmother's forehead marked with salient and visible vertebrae. "Vertebrae on a forehead!" the naturalist in Gide thought, and he closed the book until someone else had published it.

That sentence has stopped everyone of an observant turn of mind. Much as I love every line Proust wrote, it used to bother me frightfully —until a student in my graduate seminar on Proust who had spent a year in Aix-en-Provence as a lodger in the ancient house of a ninety-year-old French dowager explained it. She, like Marcel's Aunt Léonie, wore a wig which Nicholas had seen in the early morning when the Countess had clapped it on hastily, failing to tuck in the little dangling devices in front which probably served to anchor the false hair. With a badly drawn sketch on the blackboard, Nicholas convinced us all that *these* were the frontal vertebrae.

No wonder that André Gide, whose aged relatives were far more tidy, stopped reading. And what a pity that no editorial reader told Proust to change or clarify the sentence!

GIDE

Introduction to *The Journals of André Gide*, Volume I: 1889–1913, translated with an introduction and notes by Justin O'Brien (New York: Alfred A. Knopf, Inc., 1947).

ANDRÉ GIDE: THE JOURNALS I

When, at the age of eighteen or nineteen, André Gide began keeping his first journal, he already intended to be a writer. Indeed, he was even then elaborating his first literary work, a symbolic prose poem interspersed with poetry, which in recounting the conflicts of his awakening to life was to draw heavily upon that journal. His often-interrupted formal education was drawing to a close, for he had left the strict and pious Protestant school that had once mortified his family by expelling him, and had even signed up at the university with a vague intention of working for an M.A. He was living in his native Paris with his widowed mother and Aunt Claire, who still treated him as an irresponsible child. Once a week he lunched with Miss Anna Shackleton, the Scottish spinster who, after tutoring his mother as a girl in Rouen, had become her lifelong companion, and with her he practiced his faltering German. Every day he played his beloved piano for hours. The summers he spent at the family estate not far from the sea in Normandy walking with his cousins, perfecting his technique at the piano, patiently herborizing with Anna Shackleton, and voraciously reading. Already versed in the French classics, he was during the next few years to discover Baudelaire and Verlaine, Dante and Goethe and Shakespeare, and the German philosophers.

But his inseparable companion—even more frequently opened than his piano, even more essential to his spiritual life than his cousin Emmanuèle, whom he was already planning to marry—was the Bible. All

49

his thoughts were interpreted in the light of the Scriptures. If he "anointed his literary style with music," if he even dreamed of "writing in music," that style had already received its basic form from the Bible.

A tall, well-built youth, André Gide was inordinately austere and painfully shy. His upbringing had developed in him an excessive sensitivity and feminine grace. His hair fell below his ears, almost touching his stiff collar; his cheeks were covered with a soft down that was soon to become a full beard. Hypnotized by his keen dark eyes, everyone but Oscar Wilde failed to notice his full sensual lips and fine aquiline nose. He dressed with a somewhat antiquated elegance, preferring soft, flowing bow ties, a loose cape, and a broad-brimmed soft hat.

Such was the young man whose uncompromising intellectualism and devout faith rather embarrassed the other disciples at Mallarmé's charmed gatherings each Tuesday evening in the early nineties or in the more social *salon* of the poet José María de Heredia, where, amidst literary discussion, his friends Pierre Louÿs and Henri de Régnier courted their future wives among the poet's daughters. The symbolist movement was at its height: the poetry of Baudelaire, Rimbaud, Verlaine, Laforgue, and the teachings of Mallarmé were forming the taste of a generation; little reviews and new theories of versification were rapidly multiplying; Schopenhauer was the rage and Nietzsche was beginning to be discovered; Wagner's music (against which Gide was perhaps the only one to revolt) made the young swoon at concerts and led to endless discussions of new art forms; painters like Gustave Moreau, Puvis de Chavannes, and Odilon Redon were producing literary allegories and painting symbolic visions; the art theaters were stirring audiences to ecstasy and indignation with novel and ambitious works that were most often singularly undramatic. From Paris the electric current flashed to *avant-garde* groups everywhere: in Italy Gabriele d'Annunzio recognized the call and subscribed at once to the new *Mercure de France;* Oscar Wilde, Whistler, George Moore, Aubrey Beardsley, and others came over frequently from London and took back ideas for their own *Yellow Book;* the young Maeterlinck came down from Brussels and was hailed in Paris as a second Shakespeare; in provincial Montpellier Louÿs met the young Paul-Ambroise Valéry and sent him to Gide in Paris.

In this world André Gide moved stiffly and cautiously. With his friends he started several little reviews and contributed to others, sometimes as far away as Liège. He shared Mallarmé's conception of the nobility of the artist and the sacrifice of everything to the work of art. His first works were poems in prose and in verse, symbols in limited editions and without name of author, legible only to the initiate.

Most appropriately, his journals for these first years are concerned principally with himself. Notes on his reading, travel diaries, and records of conversations with friends (which play such a large part in the later journals) occupy but few of these pages devoted almost exclusively to self-scrutiny and dreams, to philosophic hesitations and emotional unrest, to gropings after a rule of conduct and amorphous plans for future creation. The will figures importantly in those early years and he seems never to have faltered in his intention; in January 1890 he notes:

"My pride is constantly being irritated by a thousand minute slights. I suffer absurdly from the fact that everybody does not already know what I hope some day to be, what I shall be; that people cannot foretell the work to come just from the look in my eyes."

Fifty years later, when for the first time André Gide made his complete *Journals* widely accessible, the text (despite the passages removed for incorporation into other works, and the suppressions) ran to over 1,300 pages. The author had become a great figure of European letters, and his reputation as novelist, dramatist, literary critic, and essayist was equaled only by the immense legend built about his name by unscrupulous critics and uncritical admirers. The *Nouvelle Revue Française* he had founded in 1908-09 had for thirty years occupied the forefront of modern literature, serving as a model for literary reviews in England, Germany, and America and molding literary taste more effectively than had publicity, prizes, and academies. The fifteen volumes of André Gide's *Œuvres complètes,* though they did not include anything published since 1930, still bore impessive testimony of a full literary life. His influence, perhaps the most widespread in France since that of Baudelaire, had been deeply felt by such Academicians as

Jacques de Lacretelle, François Mauriac, and André Maurois and eagerly accepted by the Nobel Prize-winner Roger Martin du Gard, besides contributing significantly to the formation of such younger writers as Julien Green, Malraux, Saint Exupéry, and Giono. Outside the frontiers, it had touched Aldous Huxley and T. S. Eliot, Rilke, Thomas Mann, and a host of younger writers.

And yet he was not a member of the French Academy; nor did he wear in his buttonhole any of the little ribbons symbolic of national distinction that are so much appreciated in Europe. Honors had begun by fleeing him early in life, he said once, and later he had learned to flee them.

In appearance, too, André Gide had changed considerably from the æsthete of the early nineties, and this transformation corresponded to his growth in intellectual stature. In 1939 he was a vigorous, large-boned man who seemed much younger than his age. Long ago, like the hero of *L'Immoraliste,* he had sacrificed first beard and then mustache because they masked his emotion. The long hair had likewise yielded to a more modern style and had receded to reveal a noble brow. The firm, attentive eyes were still the striking feature of his face. His long stride and lithe step were those of a young man who would rather walk than ride. His deep, modulated voice, conforming to his precise diction, made one think of an actor or singer. The *lavallière* necktie had given way to the familiar four-in-hand, and the formal black suit to tweeds of excellent British quality. In fact, his appearance no longer had anything about it specifically marking him as an artist—save perhaps the long rough cape loosely thrown on his shoulders.

The man himself was as devoid of affectation as was his external appearance. André Gide had traveled widely both throughout the world and within himself, and he had come, oh, what a long way from the fervent, sentimental André Walter he had created to serve as the author of his first two books! In the interval he had identified himself with a great many characters, as any creative artist must, but the critics (and his legend) had narrowed that crowd down to but a few: the cynical hedonist Ménalque of the *Nourritures terrestres,* the cruel and bewildered superman Michel of *L'Immoraliste;* the seductive Lafcadio of *Les*

Caves du Vatican, curious of the world and of himself, whose self-expression extends to committing a gratuitous murder; the Corydon of the four Socratic dialogues named after him; and the amoral novelist Edouard of *Les Faux-Monnayeurs.* For these writings, with a few others, were the ones that had created scandals periodically throughout the first fifty years of André Gide's career.

Like any original thinker and artist, he early began to scandalize. His contemporaries were shocked when he returned from his first trip to Africa in 1895 and mocked them in the first of his ironic works, *Paludes,* that brilliant satire on banality and moral stagnation written with special reference to the literary circles he knew so well. But already before he started out in the autumn of 1893, André Gide sensed—as is evident from his leaving behind his familiar Bible—that this trip was to effect more than his conscious break with symbolism; indeed, that it was to mark the great turning point in his life. Doubtless this would have been so even if he had not fallen ill at Biskra and approached so close to death that his long convalescence seemed a resuscitation. For without the resultant discovery of the value of life and of that ardor which gives life its zest, he would nevertheless have learned the secret of his tormented nature. But the escape from death, the self-identification with Lazarus, helped form the resolve not to stifle his unorthodox inclinations.

"In the name of what God, of what ideal, do you forbid me to live according to my nature?" he cries in his memoirs. "And where would that nature lead me if I simply followed it? Until now I had followed the rule of Christ or at least a certain puritanism that had been taught me as the rule of Christ. My only reward for having striven to submit to it had been a complete physical and spiritual upset. I could not agree to live without a code, and the demands of my flesh required the consent of my mind. But then I began to wonder whether God himself called for such coercion; whether it was not blasphemous to resist constantly, and whether it was not against him; whether, in that struggle which was dividing me, it was logical to decide against the other. Eventually I sensed that this discordant dualism could perhaps be resolved into a harmony. And immediately it occurred to me that that harmony was to be my sovereign aim and seeking to achieve it the evident justification of my life."

Uprooting himself then from his entire past, he attempted to resolve his vital conflict by suppressing all that education, in the broadest sense, had added to nature. But how difficult this was for such a man one can realize from the capital entry in his journals for 10 October 1893 with its revealing remark: "Yet the habit of asceticism was such that in the beginning I had to force myself toward joy. . . ."

After such an experience it is but natural that the work that followed *Paludes,* entitled *Les Nourritures terrestres,* is a handbook of revolt and a hymn to freedom. Breaking forth from the cloistered walls within which French literature was becoming ever more hermetic, André Gide instinctively voiced the message of Nietzsche and Walt Whitman and expressed more emphatically than had Pater or Wilde the doctrine of supreme individualism. While the very popular Maurice Barrès was teaching the need of rooting oneself firmly in one's native soil and keeping close contact with one's traditions, André Gide exhorted his reader: ". . . and when you have read me, throw this book away—and go out. I should like it to have made you want to get away—away from anywhere, from your town, from your family, from your room, from your thought."

As the *Journals* clearly indicate, the *fin-de-siècle* combination of persuasive prose and ejaculatory verse that made up *Les Nourritures terrestres* failed to reach a large public in 1897, when the work first appeared. But the fact remains that, in addition to marking the turning-point in its author's career, it struck the note of the future since, twenty years later, this little book preaching the cult of unrest and ardor with the attendant glorification of desire and spontaneity came to be the chief agent of that Gidian influence which to conservative critics has seemed nothing less than diabolical. It is dangerous indeed to describe "the savage and sudden savor of life" and to urge people to "act without *judging* whether the deed is good or evil." Many youths found in this volume a justification for indulging their worst instincts, but this is perhaps the inevitable result of freeing people. Had they shared the author's background, they would have been aware also of a more sober current in the book and noted the exhortation: "Let everyone follow his inclination . . . provided he go upward." In recent years André Gide himself has judged the work harshly on the basis of style and because of the misunderstandings to which it has given rise. But as the journal entry for 18 April 1928 states: "My writings can be compared to Achilles' spear, with which a second contact cured those it had first wounded. If one of my books disconcerts you, reread it; under the obvious poison I took care to hide the antidote; each one of them aims less to disturb than to warn."

Paludes in 1895 had showed Gide's associates to what an extent they were prisoners of their habits, their ideas, and even their emotions; two years later *Les Nourritures terrestres* was an urgent call to freedom. But as if the author felt that on this occasion the antidote deserved more attention and better labeling, he was for some time to devote himself to clarifying his message—as much in his own mind as in that of the reader.

"To free oneself is nothing; it's being free that is hard," says Michel of *L'Immoraliste*. This is the problem that André Gide examines from all sides during the next thirty years. The overgenerous Candaules and the too receptive Saul (heroes of the beautiful dramas *Le Roi Candaule* and *Saül*), together with the protagonist of *L'Immoraliste,* end tragically because of breaking with conventional morality in their search for self-realization and thus offer a commentary on the doctrine of *Les Nourritures terrestres.* In the philosophic dialogue couched in dramatic form *Philoctète,* the debate between two opposing systems of ethics ends with the victory of self-fulfillment. The heroine of the tale *La Porte étroite* (counterpart of *L'Immoraliste,* published seven years later, in 1909) illustrates the dangers of the other extreme, renunciation, and her very different form of selfishness leads to just as tragic a conclusion. In *Le Retour de l'enfant prodigue* the prodigal, while admitting his own errors, yet helps his younger brother to escape as he had done. And the attractive young hero of *Les Caves du Vatican,* born and educated without any reference to tradition, yet finds himself the prisoner of a free, unmotivated act he has committed simply to prove his own liberty.

André Gide

During his period of full maturity between the two wars, André Gide constantly returns to the problem of personal freedom: in his memoirs entitled *Si le grain ne meurt;* in his dialogues on the subject of homosexuality (*Corydon*); in his studies of criminology (*L'Affaire Redureau* and *La Séquestrée de Poitiers*); in his drama of *Œdipe,* which enacts the struggle of the individualist against religious authority; and finally—because of all Gide's works it is the best known abroad —in *Les Faux-Monnayeurs.*

The Counterfeiters (as this novel is known in English) is another break with the past. The earlier works of fiction, which most critics would be willing to classify as novels were it not for their author's insistence that they are tales, are all marked by a concentrated action performed by but three or four characters, a personal form of narration by one of the interested individuals, and a distinct simplicity of style. But now, obsessed with the example of Dostoevsky, whom he had been re-reading and analyzing in a series of lectures, André Gide set out to write a *summum* of modern life encompassing many plots and simulating the confusion of life itself. "What should I like this novel to be?" he asks in the *Journals* in 1923 and immediately replies: "A crossroads—a meeting of problems." This is why, within his own work, he has reserved the designation of novel for this single book. The four principal themes of the novel—the adolescent revolt against the older generation, the decay of the family, the creation of the work of art, and the counterfeit of life to which we all contribute—are interlocked in a contrapuntal composition inspired by Bach's *Art of the Fugue.*

All the problems raised and stylistic innovations attempted in *Les Faux-Monnayeurs* had occupied André Gide's mind for some time. Often the *Journals* are a revelation in this regard. For instance, before 1902 Gide notes his inability to find a single sentence spoken by Christ that authorizes the family, and again in 1921 he records his observation that of some forty families he knows particularly well there are hardly four in which the parents' actions do not make it desirable for the child to escape their influence. Likewise in the case of the novel within the novel (a complication that Gide had already broached in seven earlier works), the *Journals* contain a revealing passage dated 1893 about the transposition of the subject of a work into the work itself (as in the play scene in *Hamlet* or in certain Dutch paintings).

However fascinating the composition of the novel may be and however complicated the interweaving of themes, *Les Faux-Monnayeurs* strikes the reader most forcibly as a study of the free individual in opposition to the institution of the family. Once again André Gide's long preoccupation with self-realization fuses with his equally permanent concern with the nature of virtue. As we watch the evolution of the numerous characters, particularly the young Bernard and Olivier, we are reminded of the author's own early search for a rule of conduct that should combine expression and restraint. His particularly admirable form of equilibrium has nothing static about it.

The definition of virtue and the problem of self-realization are so fundamental in Gide's work as to make of him a *moraliste* or moral philosopher in the best French tradition. "The only drama that really interests me," he wrote in his *Journals* in 1930, "and that I should always be willing to depict anew, is the debate of the individual with whatever keeps him from being authentic, with whatever is opposed to his integrity, to his integration. Most often the obstacle is within him. And all the rest is merely accidental." This is a capital text for the understanding of *Les Faux-Monnayeurs* as of all his literary work. Bernard Profitendieu is not the only protagonist to wrestle with the angel, nor Prométhée the only one upon whom an eagle feeds.

But this text is also—since the obstacle is not always within the individual—a key to André Gide's social preoccupations. Having from his earliest years enjoyed an enviable economic independence permitting a life devoted wholly to disinterested art, he could have ignored such concerns. Had he remained faithful to the doctrines of pure art current during the nineties, he would have done so. But with his discovery of life beyond the confines of the *cénacles* came also a sense of responsibility and solidarity. His keenly sympathetic nature and anxiety for freedom caused him to become increasingly a champion of the oppressed. As mayor of a commune in Normandy (1896), later as a juror in Rouen (1912), and finally as a special envoy of the Colonial Ministry (1925–26), he had ample opportunity to observe social injustice. His

Voyage au Congo and *Retour du Tchad,* in fact, led to legal reform and eventually to curbing of the industrial concessions in the colonies.

He had done for the exploited Negroes of central Africa what he had earlier done for the homosexual instinct in his *Corydon.* Indeed, in a public debate that took place in 1935 André Gide emphasized the essential relationship of such literary "campaigns" when he said: "Enthusiastically and almost systematically I become the advocate of whatever voice society ordinarily seeks to stifle (oppressed peoples or races, human instincts), of whatever has hitherto been prevented from or incapable of speech, of anything to which the world has been, either intentionally or unintentionally, deaf."

The periodic scandals that punctuated André Gide's career have been alluded to in passing. Restricted in the earlier years by the voluntarily limited editions he issued and the correspondingly small public he reached, their repercussions were greater in the twenties and thirties. Naturally the chief scandals centered on *Corydon* and on what Gide now calls, with a slightly apologetic smile, his "honeymoon with Communism." In the early thirties when he announced his admiration for Soviet Russia and his sympathy toward Communism, he shocked even his most faithful admirers and raised another barrier between himself and official honors. At about this time, on the other hand, the *Soviet Encyclopedia* hailed Gide's abandonment of "the world outlook of the middle-class *rentier*" in favor of a realization "together with the best representatives of Western intelligentsia" of the collapse of the capitalist system.

But those who were more sophisticated than André Gide could appreciate the extent of his misunderstanding when they read the text of his enthusiastic message to the first Congress of Soviet Writers in August 1934 with its statement that

"The Communist ideal is not, as its enemies declare, the 'ideal of an anthill.' Its task today is to establish, in literature and art, a Communist individualism. . . .

"Communism cannot assert itself without taking into account the peculiarities of each individual. A society in which each man resembles all others is not desirable; I shall even say it is impossible; and this is even more true of a literature. Each artist is necessarily an individualist, however strong his Communist convictions may be and his attachment to the party. Only in this way can he create a useful work and serve society."

And when, in 1936, he undertook a trip through Russia to observe the realization of Utopia at close hand, he was quite naturally shocked by the lack of personal liberty, the intellectual regimentation, the "depersonalization," the continued existence of poverty he found there, and the reconstitution of social classes that he had hoped were forever abolished. In his *Retour de l'U.R.S.S.* and *Retouches à mon Retour de l'U.R.S.S.* he did not hesitate to say these things at the risk of another scandal, this time in other quarters. In addition to embarrassing those whom his influence had led into the ranks of Communism, he lost the handsome royalties that he had begun to receive from Russia.

Thus in his devotion to truth André Gide first refused to rely on second-hand evidence; and when he had seen for himself, he hastened to revoke his adherence to a cause he could no longer approve completely. He even warned the French Communist party against dangerous errors and thus brought upon himself the attacks that have not ceased even now. In this whole episode, however, André Gide remained true to his own evolution. After its close he could truthfully repeat the statement he had made before his trip to Moscow:

"I believe that the value of a writer is linked to the revolutionary force that drives him, or more precisely (for I am not so foolish as to recognize artistic value only in leftist writers) in his force of opposition. That force can be found in Bossuet, Chateaubriand, or, even today, in Claudel as well as in Molière, Voltaire, Hugo, and so many others. In our form of society a great writer or great artist is essentially nonconformist. He swims against the current."

Once again Gide was ahead of his time. In Soviet Russia, as in the new Germany or Fascist Italy, he now discerned a current that he instinctively resisted. At considerable personal sacrifice and at the risk of losing his vast prestige with the young of the world, he once more resolutely took an independent attitude.

That the *Journals* throw new light upon his creative work is indubitable. In 1931 he himself expressed the hope in these pages that the *Journals* might help to prevent the misinterpretation of his works, which are so often misunderstood. Though Gide has frequently warned his reader that he writes to be reread, that he writes for posterity, that one work must be read in the light of another, it is still helpful to discover here his secret intentions and intimate hesitations. One is more inclined to give his creative writings the deep attention they deserve when one learns how carefully, almost painfully, many of them were elaborated. Often the reader is amazed to find out how long a certain subject has haunted the author—sometimes for ten or fifteen years before publication or even before composition. In fact, the *Journals* constantly bear out the rather presumptuous-seeming letter, written at the age of twenty-four, in which André Gide claimed that he could already see his unwritten works, so real they appeared to him, taking their preordained places *among* (rather than after) the already written works in such a way as to form a complete whole only when everything should finally be written.

Yet if the *Journals* merely provided marginal notes for Gide's works, they would interest only specialists. They represent considerably more than a notebook filled with confessions, acts of literary repentance, and raw material for future works. In an atmosphere which had so little use for real life that Mallarmé was shocked when he mistook Gide's imaginary description of a trip to Spitzbergen for the account of an actual voyage, the *Journals* were begun as a literary exercise. But little by little—the evolution can be traced in their pages—they assumed more importance until, as André Malraux says, they became almost an obsession with their author, gradually drawing him from art to life, away from Racine toward Stendhal. In their present form the *Journals* record a half-century of full and varied life—and not only that of André Gide. The period covered by these fifty years includes the Dreyfus case, the First World War, and the spread of Fascism and Communism. André Gide, though in each case a noncombatant, has significant things to say about these and other historical moments. In literature and art, however, he has occupied a position on the front line during the whole of this period and, in fact, still does so today.

But the interest of any journal remains essentially autobiographic; ultimately the journal is worth no more than the personality of its author. If this work is to have permanent value for us, we must feel as François Mauriac felt when, interrupting his reading of the *Voyage au Congo,* he exclaimed: "And suddenly I am seized, not by Africa, but by this Gide so different from what the journalists have written about him. . . ." Until we have finished the whole of the *Journals* we should remember the words Gide so often quotes: "Judge not." Even then, his "esprit ondoyant et divers" will make it difficult to seize the real personality of André Gide, for never has a writer seemed to hesitate, to contradict himself, and to complicate his thought as he has done—not even the great Montaigne, who first used these words about himself. But whatever we decide about the many temperamental conflicts that produce those antinomies on which his dynamic equilibrium rests— the soul and the flesh, life and art, expression and restraint, the individual and society, ethics and æsthetics, classicism and romanticism, Christ and Christianity, God and the devil—we cannot fail to admire his genuine modesty, all-embracing sympathy, and proud independence. Nor can we fail to note, through all his transformation and growth, an unusual fidelity to his youth.

There is not one of André Gide's works that does not raise, over and above the particular destinies it unfolds, considerations of the most general and most basic kind. From his earliest writing to his latest André Gide has been consistently concerned with man's relation to man and especially with man's relation to himself. Despite his own periodic spiritual debates (of which the most sustained gave the deeply moving *Numquid et tu . . . ?* written between 1916 and 1919), his most constant attitude is that of the broadest humanism. It is perhaps as much for this reason as for any other that he deserves his position as one of the leading spokesmen of our age.

His Oedipus tells us that he knew his answer to the Sphinx long before the question was put to him, for every youth encounters an enigma to which the only solution is Man. Furthermore, for each one of us, says the King of Thebes, that man is necessarily himself. Again in the recent *Thésée* (1946) Gide has brought together toward the end of their lives blind Oedipus, the victim of the gods, and Theseus, the conqueror of the Minotaur and builder of Athens. In this supreme confrontation Oedipus vaunts the inner world he has discovered by blacking out the visible universe and releasing the divinity within, whereas the materialistic Theseus feels confirmed in his philosophic naturalism. This capital dialogue (has not the author told us he was a creature of dialogue?) receives light from a supplement to the *Journals* written in June 1942: "As soon as I understood that, instead of existing already, God was *becoming* and that it depended on each one of us that he should become, my ethical sense was restored." Gide refuses to see any impiety in this statement since it is also true that man culminates in God, and creation, which culminates in man, starts from God. Hence there is no question of blindly obeying God. Rather, one must infuse life into God, "demanding him of oneself through love and obtaining him through virtue." These words were written in Tunisia during some of the darkest days of the recent war. It is fair to consider them as representative of Gide's mature philosophy. It is characteristic of the author, as of the times, that he should add less than a week later: "But how slow God is in becoming!"

As a stylist, André Gide has always been admired even by those of his countrymen who are least sympathetic to his "message." The apparent paradox of his basing his æsthetics on the very classical austerity that he had fled on the ethical plane has been pointed out by commentators. One even suggests that his original puritanism simply deviated into literary purism, since if the puritan is a purist in morals, the purist is also a puritan in taste.

In the *Journals* can be seen Gide's deliberate forging of a style at once classical and personal until the slightest thing he writes bears a peculiar mark. He tells why he purified his language of metaphors in his first book and then longed for an even poorer, nuder style, for which he sought inspiration in Stendhal. Later he confesses his desire to achieve inimitability by dint of the secret perfection of his sentences. On the other hand, he often sees the *Journals* themselves as an exercise in spontaneous rapid composition, since, disliking to write rapidly, he must force himself to do so here. Nothing could be more characteristically Gidian, as his adolescence and African experience abundantly illustrate, than this need of constraining himself to cast off constraint.

However difficult it may be to define his personality and credo, it is certain that the *Journals* of André Gide, like Goethe's *Conversations with Eckermann* and Montaigne's *Essays,* reveal a moral philosopher struggling with the fundamental problems of humanity. The comparison with those two giants of modern letters is not fortuitous, since they have been Gide's constant companions from his earliest years. Complaining at the age of fifty-nine that he had waited too long to write certain things, he comments that Montaigne's strength comes from distrusting his memory and writing on the spur of the moment rather than waiting until he had better organized his thought; "I have always counted too much on the future and had recourse to too much rhetoric," he adds. This reproach, just or unjust in the case of the other writing, cannot be addressed to the *Journals.* It may be simply because of their spontaneity that they will endure, for, more than any other work, they show us André Gide himself and prove that, like Montaigne and Goethe, he is first a man and secondly a writer.

Introduction to *The Journals of André Gide,* Volume IV: 1939–1949, translated and annotated by Justin O'Brien (New York: Alfred A. Knopf, Inc., 1951).

ANDRÉ GIDE: THE JOURNALS II

"I heartily scorn," André Gide wrote at the age of sixty-one in his *Journal* for January 1931, "that sort of wisdom which is attained only through cooling off or lassitude." We must not then expect to find him, even twenty years later, soothing himself or his reader with the maxims of senility. In this, the fourth volume of his *Journals,* written between his seventieth year and his eightieth, his mind has lost neither its incisive vigor nor its vital warmth. We find here the same disciplined intelligence freely expressing itself, equally removed from facility and dryness, in a constantly maturing thought as far from smugness as from feverish restlessness. Ever in contact with life, that intelligence has maintained a perpetual ardor—the hard, gemlike *ferveur* that his *Nourritures terrestres* extolled over fifty years ago. This is doubtless the secret of Gide's perennial youth and of his undiminished favor with the young.

Rich with the lessons of experience, a man in his eighth decade must of necessity take many a backward glance. The Second World War naturally suggests parallels with the first one; voluntary exile from France and loved ones recalls the past and even the dead. Problems encountered in writing and fresh attacks launched by his enemies cause him to review his judgments of earlier works: in 1942, for instance, and again in 1946 he reconsiders the significance, effectiveness, and artistic achievement of his *Corydon* and again returns to that book through an interviewer's indiscreet question at the time of the Nobel Prize.

Several times he turns back to the period of his flirtation with Communism, the better to define the misunderstanding that led to his position of the early thirties. And the postwar emphasis, largely among the existentialists, on the necessity of committing oneself and writing a "littérature engagée" leads him to re-examine his past commitments and eventually to issue, in 1950, under the ironic title of *Littérature engagée* a collection of his tendentious and polemical writings, all of which he considers as extra-literary. Indeed, he had already noted here in mid-1940:

"The social question! . . . If I had encountered that great trap at the beginning of my career, I should never have written anything worth while."

But, like his own Theseus venturing into the unknown while unwinding, in the form of Ariadne's thread, his tie with the past and tradition, André Gide finds it more natural to look forward. Even in the early stages of the war he foresees with remarkable clarity the postwar plight of France; elsewhere he reflects on the literature and art of the future. Despite his extensive travels and those he undertakes the moment Tunis is liberated, he deplores the fact that the map is still studded with territories unknown to him. Finally, but without dread or false solemnity, he frequently meditates on death and the possibility of an afterlife. Some of the finest pages of this last *Journal,* in fact, reflect a serene contemplation of his own—of everyman's—future.

Nothing is perhaps more characteristic of André Gide than this consistently healthy forward-looking attitude. Not altogether lightly, he early identified himself with Prometheus, who revolted against the gods and communicated to man "the devouring belief in progress." That active belief has never left him. Recognizing his inaptitude for contemplative stagnation, he can state at seventy-three that "Real old age would be giving up hope of progress." Thus it is that, smiling at his impulse to improve himself so late in life, he continues the study of German, exercises his memory by learning hundreds of lines of French verse by heart, and, rediscovering Virgil, devotes three or four hours a day to the arduous and delightful deciphering of Latin. His mind always open and alert, he rereads the French classics and Shakespeare and Goethe and Euripides, often revising his impressions with startling results. And, leaving the main highway, he explores such diverse writers as Cyril Tourneur, Eichendorff, Grimmelshausen, James Hogg, Dashiell Hammett, Pearl Buck, Jorge Amado, and Ernst Jünger. In his eightieth year we find him discussing the latest volume by Sartre, catching up on the contemporary dramatists, disputing with Koestler and James Burnham. Simultaneously he can become captivated, as in the past, by a new treatise on radioactivity, a study of the metamorphoses of sea animals, a history of Moslem customs, or a revolutionary approach to surgery. A lively curiosity has always been one of his dominant characteristics.

Because these last ten years cover the period of the Second World War, the reader might justly expect that conflict and the occupation of France to play a large part in André Gide's reflections from day to day. In the beginning, however, he deliberately planned to omit events, noting that thought was most valid when it could not be modified by circumstances. In September 1940 he reflected that "The number of stupidities an intelligent person can say in a day is not believable. And I should probably say just as many as others if I were not more often silent." In contrast to the invasion of the timely, to the anguish resulting from current events, there is always the timeless, to be found in the classics of art and literature. In an article dated 1936, he had written: "I have a great need to maintain in myself the feeling of permanence; I mean a need of feeling that there are human products invulnerable to insults and degradation, works on which temporal changes have no influence." But viewed without perspective, the timeless often appears to be merely the untimely; to some it may seem shocking that only a month after the French defeat of 1940 Gide could momentarily forget his country's tribulation by reading Goethe in the original. Throughout the *Journals*, to be sure, from 1889 to 1949, thoughts out of season abound: *Unzeitgemässe Betrachtungen,* to borrow from Nietzsche a title that Gide obviously likes. Almost equally frequent are statements to the effect that the artist is "out of harmony with his time" and that this constitutes his *raison d'être:* "He counteracts; he initiates.

And this is partly why he is so often understood at first by but a few"
(6 July 1937).

Yet, whether in the south of France for the first two and a half years
of the war or in North Africa for the duration, Gide is unable to maintain here such an ideal aloofness. Never do his *Journals* come so close
to journalism—"I call 'journalism' everything that will be less interesting tomorrow than today," he wrote in 1921—as during the long siege
of Tunis in 1942-43. In those pages we have a marginal history of events
recorded by an eyewitness whose vision was necessarily limited, a sort of
Journal of the Plague Year with all the dispassionate, flat reportage of
Defoe's document. There is, indeed, for us who were on the outside,
a fascination in sharing the intimate feelings of a particularly sensitive
person on the inside of the vast concentration camp set up by Hitler.
Despite Gide's effort to heighten and enliven that account by a running
description of little Victor, a portable microcosm of all that was dis-
tasteful in the world around him, none the less this is the part of the
Journals that will doubtless age least well. Several times in recent years
André Gide has expressed the desire for simultaneous publication of
those pages in French and English, in the naïve hope, unshared by his
French publisher, that such a delicate attention would somewhat miti-
gate the sting of his remarks about the American forces in Tunisia. But
Americans are hardly so susceptible as not to appreciate such frankness; the men who took part in the North African campaign should be
interested in the way they looked to those they were about to liberate,
especially as that view changed so drastically upon contact.

During the decade from 1939 to 1949 André Gide's creative activity did not slacken, for he wrote (in addition to this *Journal*) the
Interviews imaginaires, a play entitled *Robert ou l'intérêt général,* a
book on *Paul Valéry,* his *Feuillets d'automne,* and *Thésée,* of which
the last would soon come to be considered as one of his major works.
Meanwhile he finished his inspired translation of *Hamlet,* compiled
an *Anthology of French Poetry,* wrote several prefaces, including that
for the collected edition of Goethe's drama, and with Jean-Louis Barrault adapted to the stage Kafka's *The Trial*—besides working on still
unrealized film-scenarios of his novels *Isabelle* and *Les Caves du Vati-*

can. One of the last entries in this volume (4 June 1949) states: "Some days it seems to me that if I had at hand a good pen, good ink, and good paper, I should without difficulty write a masterpiece."

An index of Gide's continuing vitality can be found as readily in the attacks directed against him as in his own production. Throughout his long career he has been the object of frequent, often savage assaults. If they are remembered at all in literary history, some of his accusers, such as Henri Béraud, Jean de Gourmont, René Johannet, Camille Mauclair, Eugène Montfort, and Victor Poucel, will receive mention only for the crude shafts they aimed at Gide. Others, like Francis Jammes and Henri Massis, have sullied their reputations by contributing to the picturesque and fanciful Gide legend. But, despite the intention of such critics, they did not bury their enemy very deep. During and after the recent war the weight of his years did not keep him from serving frequently as whipping-boy. As early as July 1940 an anonymous journalist in *Le Temps* accused him of exerting a baneful influence on youth and contributing to form a "deliquescent generation." A year later, in California, Fernand Baldensperger blamed such demoralizers as Gide and Proust for the French defeat. In January 1942 René Gillouin echoed in Geneva an unfounded accusation of Gide's having led a susceptible young reader to suicide. Hardly had Paris been liberated when Louis Aragon, the literary spokesman of the French Communist party, which cannot forget Gide's return from Moscow, repeated the charge of antipatriotism and defeatism made in the Provisional Consultative Assembly in Algiers by a certain Giovoni. Soon thereafter Julien Benda and Edmond Buchet separately accused Gide of anti-intellectualism and Alexandrianism, somewhat as Arthur Koestler was to do in English. Probably the most categoric crushing of Gide was found in an interview with the Catholic poet Paul Claudel, a contemporary and early friend, published in March 1947. "From the artistic point of view, from the intellectual point of view, Gide is worthless," said Claudel.

Gide himself is more equitable toward his former friend, for in February 1943 he noted in the *Journals:*

"There is and always will be in France (except under the urgent threat of a common danger) division and parties; in other words, dialogue. Thanks to that, the fine equilibrium of our culture: equilibrium in diversity. Always a Montaigne opposite a Pascal; and, in our time, opposite a Claudel, a Valéry. At times one of the two voices prevails in strength and magnificence. But woe to the times when the other is reduced to silence! The free mind has the superiority of not wanting to be alone in enjoying the right to speak." If there could have been any doubt before, it must now be recognized, since the publication last year of the correspondence between Claudel and Gide, that to the world at large the name of Paul Valéry is less appropriate in the foregoing passage than would be that of André Gide.

Another important Catholic writer, François Mauriac, who has never ceased to admire and to acknowledge his debt to Gide, seems to have recognized this when, writing in the *Figaro* about certain pages detached from the latest *Journal,* he finds Gide's thought "serenely aggressive as on his finest days" and regrets that "this elderly Faust, who is so dear to us, should fix himself permanently in the definitive affirmation that man must be put in the place of God."

Coming from the pen of Mauriac, the expression "serenely aggressive" is most appropriate. In his eighth decade André Gide *has* achieved a measure of serenity, manifest in his *Theseus* and *Autumn Leaves* as well as in this *Journal*. One thinks of the Olympian serenity of Goethe, Gide's lifelong companion, and notes with pleasure that during the ten years covered by this volume Gide reread both the *Conversations with Eckermann* and Boswell's *Life of Samuel Johnson,* as if recognizing the company in which he belongs. In fact, the complete *Journals,* representing sixty years of a varied life, form one prolonged intimate conversation, a single, often interrupted dialogue of the author with himself. Such a document precludes the necessity of any other interlocutor; after all, Montaigne had neither Boswell nor Eckermann. The serenity to which Gide has attained is that of a dynamic equilibrium between opposing tendencies within him, the classic balance toward which he has tended since youth. Yet, even today, there is nothing static about this condition; as the author notes in this

Journal: "The sole art that suits me is that which, rising from unrest, tends toward serenity."

On the last page of this installment of his *Journals,* André Gide has scribbled a note implying that he has forever ceased to keep a journal. If this is the end of his long and rich self-scrutiny, the final distillation of his reflections on man and the universe, what definitive revelation or ultimate message does it contain for his readers? Those who have followed him this far know him better than to expect such a thing or be surprised by his note of 15 December 1948:

"*Last words* . . . I do not see why one should try to pronounce them louder than the others. At least I do not feel the need of doing so."

On *Corydon,* by André Gide, translated by Hugh Gibb, with a comment on the second dialogue in *Corydon* by Frank Beach (New York: Farrar, Straus and Young, Inc., 1950). *New York Herald Tribune,* March 12, 1950.

"CORYDON"

In recent years André Gide has expressed his opinion that *Corydon* is the most important of his books. His readers agree that he is wrong. But he is in good company, for even the greatest writers—such as Petrarch, Voltaire, Wordsworth, and Flaubert—mindful of the effort occasioned by this or that composition, have put forth similar judgments that have not been ratified by readers.

It is easy to understand why Gide feels as he does. Having discovered his own sexual anomaly as a young man, he followed with great interest the trial of his friend Oscar Wilde shortly thereafter and the homosexual scandals in the German aristocracy in 1907–08. He then began writing these Socratic dialogues in defense of homosexuality, which he had printed in 1911 and again in 1920, with both author and publisher remaining anonymous. In 1922 Proust's fictional treatment of the same subject came out at about the same time that Freud was made available in French. Two years later *Corydon* was issued openly under its author's name and was followed by an even more courageous work, Gide's personal confessions entitled *Si le grain ne meurt.* Most of the attacks launched at André Gide during the 1920's and 1930's were inspired by these two books, and he is not wrong in thinking that they set up a barrier between him and official honors. But the Nobel Prize in 1947 seemed to consecrate, and the Kinsey Report to document, his theories, the expression of which had already begun to strike him as unnecessarily timid.

That the book springs from a profound conviction there can be no doubt. Gide has here treated a very serious theme in what seemed to him the simplest manner, avoiding all appeal to the emotions. As early as 1911 he noted in his *Journals:* "I do not want to move to pity with this book. I want to embarrass." *Corydon* ought to embarrass those who glibly decide what is natural and what is "unnatural." Gide achieves this effect by a clever and ironic technique in which he has excelled since the early years of his career and which achieves its finest examples here and in *The Fruits of the Earth* and *The Prodigal's Return.* Has he not said that he is a creature of dialogue? The progression within the dialogues of *Corydon* from exposition of the problem through natural history to its various solutions in human history skillfully illustrates the author's intention to persuade logically rather than to stir emotionally. All his life Gide has been an accomplished naturalist, and the testimony of Professor Frank Beach, of Yale, to the validity of his arguments after thirty years proves his soundness. It is unfortunate that Professor Beach comments only on the second dialogue and reproaches Gide for not including the related subject of lesbianism, about which he had no special competence. Furthermore, if the "straightforward definition" of homosexuality which the commentator misses does not emerge by implication from this book, he should turn to *The Journals of André Gide,* Volume II, p. 246, under date of 1918.

The translation of *Corydon,* attributed solely on the jacket to Hugh Gibb, is "honest" as he often says in rendering the French deceptive cognate; in other words, it is notably free and reads easily though not always preserving the tone of the original.

The publishers might have, now that we have the mass of Gide's work available, used as an epigraph the following lines from *If It Die . . .* : "We always have great difficulty understanding the loves of others, their way of making love. . . . And doubtless this is why we are so lacking in understanding on this point and so ferociously uncompromising."

Introduction to *Madeleine* (*Et nunc manet in te*), by André Gide, translated with an introduction and notes by Justin O'Brien (New York: Alfred A. Knopf, Inc., 1952).

"MADELEINE"

Rarely has a writer confessed himself more intimately in public than André Gide. Having no confidence in posthumous publications and fearing the zeal of parents and friends for "camouflaging the dead," he long ago stated his belief that "it is better to be hated for what one is than loved for what one is not."

Yet, even to those who had studied his work most attentively, the entire chapter of his conjugal life remained a mystery. Years after Mme André Gide's death on 17 April 1938, the most enlightened commentators did not even know her real given name and had to call her by the symbolic name Emmanuèle, which Gide had consistently given her in his writings. Until today, no photograph or portrait of her has ever been published to place beside the myriad images of her photogenic husband. No indiscreet friend, so long as André Gide lived, provided impressions of her in print with which to fill out the muted sketch emerging from Gide's discreet prose.

The memoirs entitled *Si le grain ne meurt* . . . furnish the largest number of trustworthy details about "Emmanuèle." There we first see her and her two younger sisters spending the summers at their father's estate of Cuverville near the Norman coast, where their little cousin André shared their games and studies. In the beginning she was too quiet for his taste, always quitting the noisy games for a book, forever yielding her turn or her share with smiling grace. As the years passed, he came to prefer her for that very reserve and gravity, and finally, when

75

he was about twelve and she fourteen, occurred the startling event that suddenly revealed her secret sadness and gave his life a new orientation. For, upon realizing that the discovery of her mother's adultery had struck the child with unbearable grief, he decided at once to devote his life to her happiness. "I hid in the depths of my heart the secret of my destiny," he later wrote. "Had it been less contradicted and crossed, I should not be writing these memoirs."

From this point onward, his cousin was to be in his thoughts constantly. She was, indeed, the dominant influence of his adolescent years, open to such varied influences. Each step in his intellectual and spiritual development had to be taken, not only in full view of her, but even in unison with her. While reading, he would write her initials opposite every sentence that he wanted to share with her. Away from her, he wrote her innumerable letters, which later struck him as odiously artificial.

Thus what André Gide always maintained was the only love of his life began in childhood. When her father died, in 1890, Madeleine Rondeaux (as we now know her real name to have been) became the responsibility of her aunts, and particularly of the widowed Mme Paul Gide. Although he was not yet twenty-one and she was his first cousin, young André already planned to marry Madeleine. The following year his first published work, *Les Cahiers d'André Walter*, crystallized that youthful love and constituted, at least in the author's mind, a bid for her hand. Made up in part of extracts from his actual diary kept during his seventeenth and eighteenth years, it depicts a pure, intellectualized love rather like that of Dante for Beatrice, divorced of the carnal, impossible of fulfillment, and in any case thwarted by Emmanuèle's marriage to another. By making his hero succumb to madness as a result of losing his beloved, the writer hoped to convince his family of the intensity of his love. But with its frank recognition of the body's demands and its typically adolescent insistence upon the necessity of dissociating the spiritual and the physical, the book formed a disturbing document from the hand of so austere a youth brought up in the strictest Calvinist tradition. That Madeleine never told her cousin what she thought of his work and rejected the proposal that followed its publication is not altogether surprising.

Two years later, in the autumn of 1893, came the great turning point in André Gide's life when, in Tunisia during his first extensive journey from home, he first indulged in pederasty. At the same time that he thus discovered his anomaly, a serious illness and long convalescence taught him the value of a life of sensation, so that he returned to France in the summer of 1894 a different man. In the total change he had undergone, the precise orientation of his sexual impulse, which he could neither believe nor accept, doubtless seemed but one manifestation of a general awakening. So changed was he, indeed, that of the former self there remained only his literary vocation and his ethereal love for Madeleine Rondeaux.

Another sojourn in North Africa the following winter and a decisive encounter with Oscar Wilde on the eve of his scandalous trial must have contributed greatly to Gide's self-knowledge. But his recall to Paris in the spring of 1895 and particularly his mother's death at the end of May suddenly stifled the new man in him. The systole-diastole of his young life, outwardly figured by the lure of an exotic Africa and the attachment to a sheltering home, was brusquely interrupted. Years later he wrote in his memoirs: "That very freedom for which I panted, while my mother was still alive, stunned and choked me like a gush of fresh air, perhaps even frightened me. Like the prisoner abruptly set free, I felt dizzy—like the kite with its string suddenly cut, like the boat cast adrift, like the derelict about to be tossed by the wind and the waves."

The one fixed point in his life remained his deep affection for his slightly older cousin. As family concern about his way of life grew during his early literary career and his first trips to Africa, the relatives in general had gradually come to look upon his eventual marriage with Madeleine as a possible steadying influence. While doubting that such a union would be happy, his uncle Charles Gide (not yet the internationally famous economist he was to become) had written the youth's mother with a scholar's instinctive caution: "Yet, if it does not take place, probably both of them will be surely unhappy, so that there remains only a choice between a certain evil and a possible one." Finally, during their last hours together, Mme Gide, foreseeing her death and perhaps fearing to leave him alone, had admitted to her son that she wished him to marry the niece whom she had long considered as her daughter-in-law.

André himself was convinced that his cousin needed him to be happy, and when, shortly after his loss, he asked for her hand he was thinking less of himself, he asserts, than of her. Intoxicated by the sublime, he was ready to give himself away as he had just distributed among indifferent relatives the jewels and mementos belonging to his mother. As the mature Gide says most meaningfully in the last lines of his memoirs: "Our most sincere acts are also the least calculated; the explanation one looks for later on is useless. Fate was leading me, perhaps also a secret need to challenge my nature; for was it not virtue itself that I loved in her? It was heaven that my insatiable hell was marrying; but at the moment I was omitting that hell; the tears of my grief had extinguished all its fires; I was as if dazzled with azure, and what I refused to see had ceased to exist for me. I believed that I could give myself to her wholly, and I did so without withholding anything."

On 8 October 1895 the young cousins were married at Etretat, a few miles from Madeleine's estate of Cuverville, with a Protestant minister from Rouen, named Roberty, officiating; the best man was Elie Allégret, himself a minister and missionary, who later became director of all French Protestant missions.

The very conception of a "marriage of Heaven and Hell" (which must have been suggested to Gide by his translation in 1922 of William Blake's prophetic work with that title) already divulges much of the truth, while surely explaining the name that Gide consistently gave his wife in his writings. He might have satisfied her natural discretion and fear of the limelight by adopting one of the unused given names of Louise-Mathilde-Madeleine Rondeaux. It would be quite unlike Gide ever to have explained, yet it is strange that no one else has ever pointed out, that the name Emmanuel is interpreted in the Bible as "God with us." Throughout life his wife appeared to André Gide as his refuge, his anchor to windward, his link with tradition and the past, his protection against everything in himself that he feared, and his possible salvation. It is for this reason that her simple headstone in the little cemetery at Cuverville-en-Caux bears a verse from the beatitudes: "Blessed are the peacemakers: for they shall be called the children of God." In the French version of Ostervald, which Gide chose for the stone-carver, the wording is even more appropriate, for it reads: "Heureux ceux qui procurent la paix. . . ."

Immediately after the marriage, the young couple set out on a protracted journey that was to last until May of the following year. After two months in Switzerland and another two in Italy, they reached North Africa in February 1896; there they visited Tunis, El Kantara, Biskra, and Touggourt. This was André Gide's third sojourn in the desert and its oases; it seems as if a fatal attraction, which he will later attribute to the Michel of his *Immoralist,* drew him back to the scene of his awakening. From Neuchâtel a fortnight after the wedding, he wrote to a friend: "Now I am beginning an indefatigable rest beside the calmest of wives." But only three months later he wrote from Rome: "Here it is madly beautiful weather and my senses and soul are stampeding; I am drinking in the sunlight like an over-warm wine and my wisdom is confounded." The systolic rhythm was re-established.

Instead of tying him down to Paris and the two Norman estates that he and his wife had now inherited, marriage was not to influence his restless roving—as his next and seventh work, with its praise of the nomadic state, was to prove. But Madeleine could not have felt the same interest in Africa as he did. It was not long, in fact, before she renounced accompanying her husband on his many travels and settled into the retired life to which she was faithful until her death in 1938 at the age of seventy-one.

That life centered in the château of Cuverville, in which she had grown up. The long three-story house with its fourteen master bedrooms dates from the eighteenth century, of which it has the typical mansard roof and small-paned windows. The pale yellow, white-shuttered dwelling is ornamented solely by the precision of its proportions and its central pediment, bright against the slate roof. It stands in a seventeen-acre park surrounded by over three hundred acres of farmlands. In front of the stone steps extends a vast lawn shaded by a giant cedar planted one hundred years ago by the grandfather. On the left runs an avenue of tall beeches. Behind the house, protected by a thick curtain of trees, a flower garden basks in the sun, its winding paths outlined by espaliered fruit trees. As is customary in such houses, the common rooms extend from front to back, receiving light from windows at both ends; both façades command a broad view of the wild, monotonous landscape of the Caux region, intersected by beech groves for shelter against the Channel winds.

Gide's love for Cuverville is apparent from many descriptions in his work, such as that of Fongueusemare in *Strait Is the Gate;* but perhaps the most evocative one occurs in his *Journals* for May 1906: "The grass of the lawn is deep like the grass in a churchyard. Each apple tree in the farm yard is a thick mass of blossoms. The whitewashed trunks prolong their whiteness right down to the ground. Every breath of air brings me some perfume, especially that of the wistaria, on the left, against the house, so loaded with blossoms that one can hear its bees from here. . . . Yesterday before sunset I had just time to visit the garden thoroughly. The big apple tree leaning toward the tennis court, smiling and rustling in the last rays of the sun, was becoming pink. A frightful shower, a few hours before, had submerged the countryside and purged the sky of all clouds. Every bit of foliage was brimming as with tears, particularly that of the two big copper beeches, not yet copper-colored, but transparent and blond, which fell about me like soft hair. When, going out by the little door in the bottom of the garden, I saw the sun again and the luminous cliff in front of it formed by the grove of beeches, everything struck me as so affectionately beautiful, so new, that I could have wept with joy."

The interior of the large dwelling possesses the same charm as the sober exterior. On the right of the entrance hall, one enters a white-paneled drawing room with windows at both ends. Its mahogany furniture and petit-point armchairs harmonize with the gay draperies and honey-colored parquet floor. On the left of the hall opens the dining room, with its three wicker armchairs by the wood fire, each sheltering a majestic Siamese cat. Meals are served with an Anglo-Saxon simplicity at a round table by one of the windows. Near the table a door leads to Mme Gide's domain: the pantry, milk room, storeroom, and vast kitchen with its gleaming coppers. "There Mme Gide spends hours at her daily tasks in a stifling odor of kerosene, wax, and turpentine. For the religion of polish reigns at Cuverville. Everything that can be rubbed shines like a mirror," writes Roger Martin du Gard; and, faithful to the technique of his *World of the Thibaults,* he gives a striking example: "The staircase is a model of its kind: according to an unalterable rite at least fifty years old, every morning patient servants with wool cloths tirelessly caress all its surfaces, all its flat spaces, all its reliefs—from the red tiles of the steps and their oak borders to the least projections of the iron balustrade. As an alluvium of several generations, a thick layer of hardened wax, transparent like a topaz-colored varnish, makes the whole staircase look as if carved out of some precious, polished, indefinable material, a block of dark amber."

This was the world of Madeleine André Gide, within which she willingly circumscribed her life. In summers, and often at other times of the year, she was surrounded by her sisters Jeanne and Valentine— the former married to Professor Marcel Drouin, and the latter the widow of Marcel Gilbert—and their children. Her best friend, Agnès Copeau, the wife of the great theatrical director, frequently came with her children also. Mme Gide hardly lived at all in the rambling house that André Gide had built in Auteuil and never learned to like; there is no evidence that she ever set foot in the rue Vaneau apartment that became his Paris headquarters in 1928 and where he died in 1951.

In the last years of Gide's life the rumor circulated that he had an illegitimate daughter who had grown up in the south of France. Reference to the *Journals* showed frequent mention, from 1926 on, of "little Catherine." After the war she began to be seen in his company—an attractive young woman with a marked resemblance to her father. By the time of the Nobel Prize, their photograph had appeared in newspapers, and the writer was known to be a grandfather. In the ensuing years the date of Catherine Gide's birth has been given as 1923 and her mother has been several times identified in print as Elisabeth Van Rysselberghe, the daughter of the painter Théo Van Rysselberghe.

So much could be gleaned during Gide's lifetime. By implication one got the impression that the poet Francis Jammes summarized when he referred to his friend's wife as "Madame Sainte Gide." Nonetheless, the intimate drama of Gide's conjugal life remained a mystery, as did the personality of the wife who had never shared his fame.

With what keen curiosity and excited anticipation, then, did we note a passage in the last *Journals* in which Gide, blocked in German-occupied Tunis in March 1943, wondered if he would ever see again the private papers he had left in Paris—among which, he says, "the manuscript relating to Em., in which I had transcribed the unpublished parts of my *Journal* and everything concerning that supreme part of my life which might explain and throw light upon it." On his return to Paris he found the precious documents intact and was thus able to have them printed in Neuchâtel by his friend Richard Heyd under the strange title of *Et nunc manet in te,* in a private edition of but thirteen copies, each bearing the name of the recipient. That was in 1947 at the time of his receiving the Nobel Prize. But even then, to all but a handful of most intimate friends, the bibliographical entry of a new Latin title for the year 1947 remained a tantalizing mystery until a few months after Gide's death, when, according to the author's wishes, M. Heyd issued the text publicly. The present translation, with annotations added as for the American and English editions of the *Journals,* has been made from that publication of 1951.

Now we *know.* At last all our questions are answered—as well as it was in André Gide's power to answer them, and in a prose as vibrant as anything he ever wrote. In this letter to his dead wife, which he could never have addressed to her in her lifetime, the ring of sincerity is unmistakable. At once self-accusatory and self-excusing, it fully presents the husband's side of the case. As for her whose life was sacrificed to the cruel needs of genius, we now know that she was forever unable and unwilling to defend herself. As Roger Martin du Gard noted at the time of her death (but published only in 1951): "She left nothing in writing, no intimate note, no message for him. No one will ever know precisely what a cross she bore, what she grasped, what she suspected, what she refused to know, what she knew despite herself, what she forgave or did not forgive. She carried her secrets with her."

Yet now we are able to grasp the tragedy of André Gide's life and to recognize, as we had suspected, that his wife stood at the very heart of his life and work.

Introduction to *So Be It, or The Chips Are Down* (*Ainsi soit-il ou Les Jeux sont faits*), by André Gide, translated with an introduction and notes by Justin O'Brien (New York: Alfred A. Knopf, Inc., 1959).

"SO BE IT"

In late 1947, about the time he received the Nobel Prize, André Gide noted in his *Journals:* "I shall be able to say: 'So be it' to whatever happens to me, were it even ceasing to exist, disappearing after having been." Indeed, the serenity of his last years found its perfect expression in the oft-repeated words *Ainsi soit-il* which he was to use as the title for his final manuscript.

But, despite his resignation to the inevitable, there was one thing Gide could not forgo even on the threshold of death: the inveterate habit of probing into himself and setting down his impressions. The very last page he wrote, six days before his death, forms a most revealing confession in this regard. Although still quite recognizably his, the hand is shaky at first, becoming firmer as it continues. In the first two or three lines, certain words, through the repetition of a syllable, seem to stammer; but visibly the mind clears as the hand gains in suppleness. There is something infinitely pathetic in the observation that the old man, at the end of a literary career extending over more than sixty years, is tormented, between two periods of coma, by the thought that he may not have said all he had it in him to say, that he may want to add something, he knows not what. And, sure enough, after letting his pen run on for a few minutes, he does succeed in recording as his *novissima verba,* before again sinking into unconsciousness, a beautiful ambiguous sentence, stylistically perfect like the best of his prose.

The whole of this ultimate work from the hand of Gide is motivated

83

by the same desire to leave nothing essential unsaid. In mid-1949, shortly before his eightieth birthday, he had deliberately closed up his vast *Journals,* begun before the age of twenty. But soon he must have missed the pleasure of setting down his daily reflections in a little notebook, for by the following summer—despite the absorbing work of polishing his own theatrical adaptation of an early novel, despite the organization of various voluminous collections of his correspondence, despite the declarations he was constantly called upon to write for different groups from Venice to Tokyo—he had begun the manuscript of *Ainsi soit-il ou Les Jeux sont faits.*

When I saw Gide again in the last two months of his life, after a year's interruption in our conversations, he spoke at length of this work, frequently opening the fat folder on his table to show a page or two. Refusing to consider those pages as related to his *Journals,* he insisted rather on their difference from everything he had ever written and likened them more than once to the *Essays* of Montaigne. Their originality for him lay in their rapid, spontaneous composition, without retouching or even rereading. He admitted that he had often striven for such a free-and-easy manner in the *Journals,* as a protest against his innate concern for form, but each time he had soon given up. "This time," he said, "I am going through with it to the very end." It was impossible to tell whether he meant the end of the manuscript or the end of his life. Probably he thought of the two as synchronous.

But he did not, for all his eighty-one years, necessarily think of them as imminent. Having become atttached, for instance, to the American fountain pen and its special ink that I had given him thirteen months earlier, he found in late January 1951 that he was on the point of running out of the ink, which was not then available in Paris. Through friends I found him a fresh bottle, which he planned to take to Marrakech with him. Only his fatal illness a fortnight later canceled the trip and put an abrupt end to his manuscript.

The unpremeditated manner of writing naturally gives this work a conversational flavor—that is, the flavor of André Gide's conversation, of which his close friend Roger Martin du Gard noted:

"Gide seems to be continually playing hide-and-seek with himself, and with his interlocutor. His conversation—broken into by parentheses,

reminiscences, anecdotes, and bursts of delicious fooling—has the gratu-
itousness, the unconcern, of a game; it is full of turns and returns, details touched and retouched, pauses and hesitations, brusque advances
and brusque retreats; it is a mixture of modesty and cynicism, reticence
and candor, unexpected avowals and the discreetest of allusions. Sometimes as plain as a straight line, sometimes as baffling as the convolutions
of a maze, it makes its way—regretfully, one might suppose—toward
its final precision. That it is always aiming at this precision is clear;
but it never seems in any hurry to get to it, so great is its pleasure in the
long twilit pauses, which culminate in that blazing moment when the
whole question is resolved in a few astonishing phrases. But whether
these phrases are the result of some lightning flash of happy inspiration
or of an opportune verbal accident, or whether they are the fruit of experience, the outcome of lengthy meditation—all this one cannot say"
(*Recollections of André Gide,* 1953).

As Gide was well aware in writing *So Be It,* the inevitable hazard of
such a carefree form, which aims not to "sort out the spontaneous run
of the mill," is repetition. Hence we are not surprised to find here certain incidents and reflections that he had recorded years before in his
Journals. Beside them, however, as the octogenarian's mind ranged over
the fullness of his past, stand pages containing revelations even for
readers most familiar with André Gide and his work. In a voluminous
and exhaustive study of the writer's youth, for instance, Dr. Jean Delay
cites a passage from *So Be It* as the most revealing of Gide's many confessions. He refers to the page in which Gide tells how the image of
his mother and that of his wife fuse in his dreams into a single person
playing an inhibitory role. Other numerous comments here about his
sexual preferences—even though they come after so many calculated
indiscretions—are equally valuable for an understanding of his psychology.

Whether he is discussing such matters, indulging in futile regrets,
analyzing his untrustworthy memory or his strange disbelief in reality,
developing his thoughts about Molière or social injustice or the art of
acting, or simply adding to his recollections of his travels in the U.S.S.R.
and in the Congo, Gide continues here his lifelong work of destroying
the legends that had grown up about him and presenting himself as

he really was—or at least as he saw himself. In order to complete the image he had already built up in his many works, he had at the end of his life to show us the effects of age, the physical infirmities, the doubts and hesitations, the waning appetite for life. And to his credit it must be said that such lucid admissions are almost without precedent in literature. As he notes here, "I had not made arrangements to live so old"; but, having lived on, he quite naturally took advantage of his reprieve to record and analyze the feelings of an old man in order to throw further light on the image of himself that he intended to leave behind.

Soon after Gide's death, V. S. Pritchett wrote of him in *The New Statesman and Nation*: "One went to him as one goes to an interpreter who is familiar with several spiritual tongues; for the spell of a clear beguiling voice speaking the truth about himself. He was a natural traveller; but his best journeys were through his own life, which he displayed like some candid and figured landscape." Just because *So Be It* constitutes one more journey through his own life, it belongs, whatever the author himself thought, together with his monumental *Journals*, which Mr. Pritchett found "likely to rank as one of the great autobiographies of the West."

So Be It, or The Chips Are Down—the alternate, rather flippant title reflects Gide's lack of solemnity about himself and his fate—represents the author's first truly posthumous work. For if *Et nunc manet in te* (known in America as *Madeleine*) reached the world only after André Gide's death, he had nevertheless caused it to be issued as early as 1947 in a private edition. Yet it is significant that both these messages from beyond the grave, as Chateaubriand would have called them, are closely related to the *Journals*, which they prolong. It is fitting, therefore, that the present translation of *Ainsi soit-il* should be annotated as were the American and English editions of the *Journals* and of *Et nunc manet in te*. At least until such time as his many creative and critical works are universally accorded their due, Gide survives through his personal confessions—as he does also in the already numerous memoirs, eyewitness accounts, confessions, and indiscretions written by his close friends and bitter enemies who suffered the contagion of those *Journals*.

New York Herald Tribune Book Review,
April 29, 1951.

WAS GIDE A COLLABORATIONIST?

Now that André Gide is dead, perhaps this is the time to examine
the facts behind the frequent criticism that during the German occupation of his country Gide envisaged the plight of Europe with serenity
and even wrote for collaborationist periodicals. In France such accusa-
tions bear weight in certain circles because they are made chiefly by such
as Louis Aragon, chief spokesman of the French Communist party, and
echoed by sundry scriveners, the theory being that anything that is
repeated three times automatically becomes true.

Soon after France declared war on Nazi Germany in September 1939,
Gide entered his seventy-first year. Sometime in mid-winter, as was his
wont, he went south. In early May he longed to return to Paris and
even went so far as to reserve a seat in the train. He would have reached
the capital on May 10, just in time to learn of the invasion of the Low
Countries; but fortunately at the last moment something made him
stay near Nice.

On 14 June 1940, two days after the fall of Paris, Gide wrote in his
Journals: "We are at the mercy of Germany, which will strangle us as
best she can. Despite everything, we shall shout very loud: 'Honor is
saved!' resembling that lackey in Marivaux who says: 'I don't like people to show disrespect for me,' while receiving a kick in the rear. . . .
How can one deny that Hitler played the game in masterful fashion,
not letting himself be bound by any scruple, by any rule of a game that,
after all, has none; taking advantage of all our weaknesses, which he had

87

long and skillfully favored. In the tragic light of events there suddenly appeared the deep decay of France, which Hitler knew only too well. Everywhere incoherence, lack of discipline, invoking of fanciful rights, repudiation of all duties. What will the well-intentioned young men who yesterday were concerned with remaking France do with the miserable ruins that will remain? I am thinking of Warsaw, of Prague. . . . Will it be the same with Paris? Will the Germans let the best of our energies breathe and recover themselves? They will not limit their attention solely to our material ruin. Today we cannot yet envisage the frightful consequences of the defeat."

It was courageous, if unusual, to note such thoughts at that moment. The dreadful armistice followed with its division of France into occupied and unoccupied zones and its myth of a "loyal collaboration" with the enemy. Meanwhile, Pétain had become Chief of State and proclaimed the "National Revolution" of Vichy.

In January 1941, Gide wrote: " 'Neither victors nor vanquished!' I do not much like that slogan. It implies on both sides a pretence so flattering for our self-esteem that I am suspicious. A 'collaboration' such as is proposed to us today could not be 'loyal' when it is thus based on a lie. . . . And, indeed, nothing saddens me more than seeing France at present expecting her salvation to come only from an attachment to everything about her that is oldest and most worn out. Their fine 'National Revolution' gives me a pain in the neck. If our country is to be reborn (and I firmly believe that it will be), it will be in spite of that and against that. I expect our salvation to come from what is getting ready in the shadows and cannot emerge into the light of day until tomorrow."

This should suffice to show an utter refusal, lucid and realistic as always with Gide, to accept the conditions of defeat cheerfully—as well as an early faith in the Resistance.

André Gide never wrote for a collaborationist journal. Two extracts from his *Journals* appeared in the December 1940 and the February 1941 issues of the *Nouvelle Revue Française*. The June 1940 issue appeared under its regular editor, Jean Paulhan. Immediately the *N.R.F.* was suspended by the Nazis; Gide was in Nice, whereas Paulhan and

Gallimard, the publisher, were in another remote part of France. A plan was made to revive the review and many of the regular contributors sent manuscripts to Paris. But the new editor, Pierre Drieu La Rochelle, favored collaboration, and when Gide read the first part of his own journal extracts in the December 1940 issue (the first to come out after the suspension), he wrote: "I ought at least to have dated these *Feuillets* taken from my *Journal*, which I have just reread with displeasure in the issue of the resuscitated *N.R.F.* I am no longer in the same state of mind that made me write them, a mind still filled with the defeat. Furthermore, my reflections on the lapses and intermittences of the patriotic sentiment no longer seem to me quite fair. There is nothing like oppression to give that sentiment new vigor. I feel it re-awakening everywhere in France, and especially in the occupied zone. It assures and affirms itself in resistance like any thwarted love."

On 8 January 1941, Gide returned to the subject: ". . . a shift of which it is already impossible to be completely aware. My contributing to the review, the *Feuillets* I gave to it, the very plan of resuming publication—all that goes back to the period of dejection immediately following the defeat. Not only was resistance not yet organized, but I did not even think it possible. To fight against the inescapable seemed to me useless, so that all my efforts at first tried to find wisdom in submission and, within my distress, to right at least my thought."

On 30 March 1941, after reading Jacques Chardonne's *Personal Chronicle of the Year 1940* and receiving a letter from Drieu La Rochelle trying to persuade him to put in an appearance in Paris, the seventy-one-year-old Gide telegraphed Drieu: "Appreciate your cordial letter and regret comma after reading last pages of Chardonne's book clarifying your positions comma having to ask you remove my name from cover and advertisements in our review."

Thus André Gide had contributed in good faith to his own *Nouvelle Revue Française,* which, under a new editor, was to turn collaborationist in the very issues that contained Gide's writing; furthermore the editor had broken up Gide's manuscript to spread it over more than one issue.

As soon as Gide was aware of the review's new orientation, he broke with it, most vigorously acknowledging his mistake.

The only other periodical that published Gide during the German Occupation was the *Figaro,* which no one has ever shown to have been collaborationist. In fact, it moved from Paris to Lyon in order not to have to submit to German censorship. There it was that Gide's initial article came out on 12 April 1941 in the form of a protest against Chardonne's collaborationist book. From then until 30 August 1942 his articles continued to appear in the *Figaro,* many of them containing covert encouragement to resist the enemy. Most of them can be read in his *Imaginary Interviews,* translated by Malcolm Cowley. Meanwhile, warned by friends to get out of France, Gide had sailed from Marseille for Tunis on 5 May 1942.

When his *Pages de Journal, 1939–1942* were first published in a liberated Algiers and in New York in 1944, they contained the following warning in the Foreword: "In these pages from the journal that I kept, quite irregularly by the way, during the somber months following our defeat, I do not recognize that I have any right to change anything. I am not pretending to be any more courageous than I was: it was not until about March 1941 that I began to hold up my head somewhat again, and again took heart. A certain book by Chardonne that I read at that time contributed to this opposition and acted on my mind like a reagent. Then only did I realize just where we stood, and in the first article I wrote on this subject for the *Figaro* I made clear what I would not accept being. . . . I should like these pages, and especially those of the beginning, to be granted but a relative value: if all together they contain a lesson, let it be in the manner of an intellectual itinerary by marking the stages of a slow progress out of darkness into light."

Yale French Studies, No. 7, 1951.

GIDE'S FICTIONAL TECHNIQUE

André Gide, though he is more widely known for his fiction than for his drama, journals, essays, or literary criticism, claims to have written but one novel. Yet to the world at large he has written no fewer than nine other novels, each of them shorter than the famous *Faux-Monnayeurs* or *Counterfeiters* of 1926, for which he has reserved that designation. The author has preferred to label eight of those works as *récits* or "tales" and one of them as a *sotie* or "satirical farce."

Historically it is easy to understand why Gide took so long to overcome a prejudice against the novel form. He belonged, after all, to the generation of young symbolists who in the 1890's sat at the feet of the hermetic poet Mallarmé and who, in reaction against the excesses of naturalism, fled everything that smacked too much of life. For such men the novel appeared as a vulgar form not susceptible of great literary development or worthy of very serious literary consideration. It must not be forgotten, however, that even in the mid-nineties Gide was one of the first, if not the first, of the aesthetes to revolt against the narrow conventions of symbolism and turn fearlessly to a glorification of life. In 1897 appeared *Les Nourritures terrestres* (*The Fruits of the Earth*), his little handbook of revolt preaching the necessity of uprooting oneself and pursuing sensation for its own sake. Already it should have been apparent to any member of Mallarmé's circle that Gide's trip to Africa had taken him out of the ivory tower. And indeed, five years later was to appear his first work of fiction somewhat timidly classed as simply a "tale."

Just what does Gide mean by a *récit?* The word signifies merely a narration and is by no means so exact a designation as *conte* or *nouvelle.* It is vague and not very committal. All his tales have certain elements in common: (1) concentration of action, (2) limitation to two, three, or four characters with almost no incidental figures, (3) a personal form of narration by one of the interested parties, and (4) a directness and simplicity of style. In other words, the tale as Gide conceives it is a narrative of crisis, an active type of fiction, close in form to the famous seventeenth-century novel *La Princesse de Clèves* or even to the French classical tragedy of Racine. It is highly dramatic because of the concentration of action and because of the narration by one of the actors. It is noteworthy that *L'Immoraliste* (*The Immoralist*) is told entirely by the chief protagonist to a group of friends who may be able to help him. On the very first page he says: "I am going to tell you my life simply, without modesty and without pride, more simply than if I were talking to myself." *La Porte étroite* (*Strait Is the Gate*) is again a direct narrative made by the principal actor Jérôme, who begins: "Some people might have made a book out of it; but the story I am going to tell is one which it took all my strength to live and over which I spent all my virtue. So I shall set down my recollections quite simply. . . ." But at one point in Jérôme's account he is obliged to describe the most intimate emotions of his beloved, which he could not possibly have known. Hence Gide has him discover her journal after her death and that journal is incorporated verbatim into the novel. *La Symphonie pastorale* (*The Pastoral Symphony*) is entirely in the form of a journal kept by the principal male character, the Pastor himself. On the very first page the Pastor notes: "I will take advantage of the leisure this enforced confinement affords me to think over the past and to set down how I came to take charge of Gertrude." The use of direct narration and especially of the diary form has obvious advantages and disadvantages. Its appearance in so many of André Gide's works—even in *The Counterfeiters* he will have a novelist character commenting on events in his own diary—suggests that the journal is Gide's form *par excellence* and that his imaginative works might almost be considered to be extracted from his own *Journals.* It would be more just to say that the habit of spiritual self-scrutiny contracted during his pious childhood and reinforced by the fairly regular keeping of his own diary has caused him to make his characters indulge in the same practice.

Thus Gide repeatedly risked the dangers of narration in the first person singular. By the time *The Immoralist* appeared Oscar Wilde had already warned Gide never again to use the pronoun "I," but Gide was to flaunt that advice so consistently that in 1921 Marcel Proust had to repeat it to him. It would be hard to imagine, indeed, what his work would be like were it less personal—and one might even say less confessional. Autobiographical elements in *The Immoralist* are so numerous that the author has suffered ever since from the identification of his hero with himself. Ignoring for the moment the close parallels between the character of Marceline and that of André Gide's wife, and the manner in which so many incidents in the novel correspond to the author's life, let us look rather at the essential problem of Michel as it is found in the life of Gide himself. He, too, awoke to his true nature at Biskra in North Africa, striving thereafter to cast off the effect of his puritanical education. In April 1893 he had already noted in his *Journals:* "And now my prayer (for it still is a prayer): O my Lord, let this too narrow ethic burst and let me live, oh, fully; and give me the strength to do so, oh, without fear, and without always thinking that I am about to sin!" Again, in October 1894 he had reflected that "All education tends to negate itself. Laws and rules of conduct are for the state of childhood; education is an emancipation. . . . The wise man lives without a rule of conduct, according to his wisdom. We must try to reach a higher immorality." Yes, Michel was torn from the very heart of his author but this does not mean that Michel is Gide. In one of the most significant letters written by that great letter-writer, whose entire correspondence will doubtless not become known for many years yet, he stated his theory of the creation of a character. It so happens that he related that theory to this particular novel, stating: "That a germ of Michel exists in me goes without saying. . . . How many germs or buds we bear in us which will never flower save in our books! They are 'dormant eyes' as the botanists call them. But if one intentionally suppresses all of them *except one* how it grows! How it enlarges, immediately monopolizing all the sap! My recipe for creating a hero is quite simple; take one of these buds and put it in a pot all alone, and one soon has a wonderful individual. Advice; choose preferably (if it is true that one *can* choose) the bud that bothers you the most. In this way you get rid of it at the same time. This is probably what Aristotle called katharsis." Others have expressed the same theory, even going so far as to see works of imagination as safety valves preventing the writer from indulging in the excesses which symbolize his characters. Bergson, for instance, remarked that "Shakespeare was not Macbeth nor Hamlet nor Othello but he would have been those various characters if circumstances and the consent of his will had brought to a state of eruption what was but an inner urge."

Gide's theory of katharsis holds of course not only for Michel but also for his other characters. In general, each of the short tales presents a single protagonist who represents the monstrous flowering of one of the buds in the author. Has not Gide said of himself: "I am a creature of dialogue; everything in me is at war and in contradiction"? In *Strait Is the Gate* a very different bud is produced: the heroine Alissa, who is so close in many ways to Mme André Gide that we tend to forget she is a projection of the author. Alissa is the excessively pious young person afraid of life whom Gide might have been had he never transcended his adolescence. In its briefest possible form the story is one of two sisters in love with the same man and each nobly striving to sacrifice herself for her sister's happiness. But it is Juliette, the younger sister, who takes the drastic step of marrying another. Henceforth, no obstacle stands between Alissa and Jérôme. Yet Alissa continues to refuse to marry Jérôme, giving as a pretext that he will achieve spiritual salvation better without her. In this way, she ruins both his life and hers; for they might have been happy together. By a series of subtle touches, Gide unfolds the obsessive character of Alissa and reveals her motivation. At one point she asks her diary: "Was that sacrifice really consumed in my heart? I am, as it were, humiliated to feel that God no longer exacts it. Can it be that I was not equal to it?" From such a doubt it is but a step to the decision to make the sacrifice anyway, simply to prove that she is capable of it. Commenting on his novel years later, Gide noted that whenever she thought of Jérôme, there welled up in Alissa a sort of unconscious and irresistible burst of heroism. And he adds: "Absolutely useless heroism."

In *The Pastoral Symphony,* still a third bud reaches fruition. Here it is the Pastor with his lamentably good intentions, his sanctimonious hiding behind the Scriptures, and his blind self-deception who reflects a facet of his creator. André Gide's grandfather was a Protestant minister and he himself grew up in the strictest possible religious atmosphere. His entire childhood was marked by his teachers and private tutors, who were either ministers or closely identified with the church. Some of his playmates were the sons of ministers, and the best man at his wedding was a minister. The atmosphere was, therefore, familiar to him. He had, furthermore, spent the winter of 1894 at La Brévine, the scene he chose for the novel. All his life he has had a passion for teaching—like the Pastor who admits in an unguarded moment that he had promised himself great pleasure from educating his blind charge.

Thus it was easy for André Gide to put himself in the position of the hero of his *Pastoral Symphony.* Around this figure he constructed a parable of blindness in which the spiritual blindness is so much more dangerous than the physical blindness. Subtly and yet emphatically by repetition Gide established a parallel between Gertrude's actual blindness, her state of innocence, and the Gospels on the one hand, and on the other, lucidity, the state of sin, and the Epistles of St. Paul.

It is important to note a variation of the diary form in *The Pastoral Symphony.* Obviously the Pastor would not and *could* not have recounted the whole story after the final tragedy. Or if he had, he would inevitably have transferred to its beginning the state of mind with which he witnessed its end. Hence Gide makes him begin to keep his notebook in the middle of Gertrude's evolution, recording at the start events that began two and a half years before. On 10 February he makes his first entry and on 30 May, his last. Meanwhile, on 8 May events catch up with his diary, and from that point on the Pastor is recording the *present* as it unfolds. This skillful technique gives to the tale an extraordinary mounting intensity that could have been achieved in no other way.

André Gide

La Symphonie pastorale was written in 1918. To anyone, then, who does not share André Gide's scrupulous regard for the *genres,* he was already an accomplished novelist when he sat down in June 1919 to write what he calls his first and only novel. Judging his work from the inside, Gide is pleased to emphasize the differences between his *Faux-Monnayeurs* and all the rest of his fiction. In an ironic and unused preface for that novel he declared that he had not classified his earlier works as novels for fear they might be accused of lacking some of the essentials of the *genre,* such as confusion, for instance. In the novel itself he makes his novelist Edouard reflect that his earlier tales resemble those basins in French parks, precise in contour, but in which the captive water is lifeless. "Now," he says, "I want to let it flow according to the slope, at one moment rapid and at another slow, in meanders that I refuse to foresee."

Between *The Pastoral Symphony* and *The Counterfeiters,* Gide gave a series of lectures on Dostoevsky in 1921 and 1922. Rereading the great Russian, he noted certain similarities between Dostoevsky and himself; he found the same type of irresolute, half-formed, contradictory characters to which he has always been drawn himself; he recognized his own familiar themes: the relation of the individual with himself or with God, the demoniacal role of the intelligence, the challenge to conventional ethics and psychology, the value of an audacious deed, the opposition of thought and action and of carnal and emotional love, the influence of convention in counterfeiting us. He became aware that Dostoevsky, too, invariably expresses ideas in relation to individuals, depicts the particular to achieve the general, intentionally interrupts action at its most intense, and creates a painting with a specific source of light rather than a lifeless panorama.

But the break at this point in his career is less abrupt than he implies. In actual fact *The Counterfeiters* covers less ground both spatially and temporally than most of the tales. *The Immoralist* includes scenes in Paris, North Africa, Italy, and Normandy; *Strait Is the Gate* is laid in Rouen, Fongueusemare, Paris, Havre, and Aigues-Vives (near Nîmes); only *The Pastoral Symphony* with its limitation to La Brévine and nearby Neuchâtel rivals the economy of *The Counterfeiters,* which takes us out of Paris only for a brief stay at Saas-Fée in Switzerland. It is equally surprising to note, in view of the novel's complexity, that the action of *The Counterfeiters* is concentrated within a few months, whereas *The Immoralist* records three years, *Strait Is the Gate,* twenty years, and *The Pastoral Symphony,* two years and nine months of life. Furthermore, for all their precise contours, not one of the tales is as balanced in composition as *The Counterfeiters* with its eighteen chapters and 220 pages of the first part exactly paralleling the eighteen chapters and 225 pages of the third part.

The complexity and "confusion" of the novel must be attributable, then, to the number of characters or rather to the number of plots, since the twenty-eight characters are necessitated by the multiple plots. Now, André Gide has noted most loyally in his *Journals* for 1928 that his friend Roger Martin du Gard gave him "the advice to gather together the various plots of *Les Faux-Monnayeurs,* which, had it not been for him, would have formed so many separate 'tales.'" Eight years earlier in the *Journals,* Gide had noted a conversation with a third novelist, Georges Duhamel, who "protests that I was not wrong to write *first* those monographs which Martin du Gard regrets not seeing fused together and confused in one thick cluster; and that those little purified tales that Martin du Gard criticizes have more hope of enduring than the complex novel that I now long to write." Interesting as it might be to attempt disentangling the various plots of *The Counterfeiters* and isolating the separate tales, this is not our purpose here. Just now—after noting in passing that even more than the example of Dostoevsky was required to renew Gide's fictional technique—it is more important to emphasize the persistence, nevertheless, of certain elements within that technique.

From June 1919 to June 1925—that is, during the actual writing of *The Counterfeiters*—Gide kept a separate notebook in which to record "inch by inch," as he said in English, the progress of his novel. That fascinating and invaluable *Journal of "The Counterfeiters,"* which has never been a part of Gide's monumental *Journals,* was first published in French the same year as the novel and will soon be available in English as an appendix to *The Counterfeiters.* In it the author presents the problems encountered in composition, his hesitations and false starts, and the solutions he has found to his difficulties. The novelty of his approach throughout and his little youthful thrill of triumph at each new problem overcome prevent the reader from noticing how many of the apparent technical innovations had already found their place in the earlier tales. For instance, the first entry in *The Journal of "The Counterfeiters"* reads: "For two days I have been wondering whether or not to have my novel related by Lafcadio. Thus it would be a narrative of gradually revealed events in which he would act as an observer, an idler, a perverter." Is this not again the first-person narration of the tales? To be sure, a month later Gide abandoned this plan after writing some pages of Lafcadio's journals; yet in doing so he added: "But I should like to have successive interpreters: for example, Lafcadio's notes would occupy the first book; the second book might consist of Edouard's notebook; the third of an attorney's files, etc." Surely this is the same technique as in *La Porte étroite* where, at a certain point, Jérôme's account is broken to admit the diary of the dead Alissa.

In fact, it was not until much later that it occurred to Gide—possibly as a result of rereading *Tom Jones*—to resort to impersonal narration with frequent interventions of the author. As late as May 1924 he noted: "The poor novelist constructs his characters; he controls them and makes them speak. The true novelist listens to them and watches them function; he eavesdrops on them even before he knows them. It is only according to what he hears them say that he begins to understand *who* they are. I have put 'watches them function' second—because for me, speech tells me more than action. I think I should lose less if I went blind than if I became deaf." Without question, this is still the author of the tales speaking. Again he states: "I should like events never to be related directly by the author, but instead exposed (and several times from different vantages) by those actors who will be influenced by those events. In their account of the action I should like the events to appear slightly warped; the reader will take a sort of interest from the mere fact of having to *reconstruct*. The story requires his collaboration in order to take shape properly." But this is already true of the tales. That there are two points of view in *Strait Is the Gate*—

thanks to Jérôme's account and Alissa's diary—is obvious. In *The Immoralist,* although there is but one narrator (Michel) who is trying to report himself objectively, he is nevertheless judged by his wife, Marceline, and by his friend, Ménalque, not to mention the Arab youth Moktir; and Michel strives to record those judgments—with the inevitable result that the reader has to re-establish the truth. Likewise in *The Pastoral Symphony* where the lamentable Pastor is judged by his wife, his son, and the blind girl he loves.

After *The Counterfeiters,* when Gide writes *L'Ecole des femmes* (*The School for Wives*) and its two sequels, *Robert* and *Geneviève,* he somewhat mechanically presents three views of the same family conflict, one to a volume, much as he had toyed with doing in *The Counterfeiters.*

Perhaps the most generally acknowledged originality of *The Counterfeiters* is that of a novel within the novel. As the author noted in *The Journal of "The Counterfeiters":* "Properly speaking, the book has no single center for my various efforts to converge upon; those efforts center about two *foci,* as in an ellipse. On one side, the event, the fact, the external *datum;* on the other side, the very effort of the novelist to make a book out of it all. The latter is the main subject," he continued, "the new focus that throws the plot off center and leads it toward the imaginative. In short, I see this notebook in which I am writing the very history of the novel, poured into the book in its entirety and forming its principal interest—for the greater irritation of the reader." With Edouard's journal this is precisely what Gide has done. It was a brilliant idea to set Edouard the novelist at the center of the novel, both an observer and an actor in the events, engaged in grappling with the problems posed by the translation into art of those events. Yet this was far from a new idea with Gide. His very first work, published in 1891, shows a young romantic hero writing the novel we are reading. And in his *Journals* for 1893, Gide has noted: "I wanted to suggest, in the *Tentative amoureuse,* the influence of the book upon the one who is writing it, and during that very writing. . . . Our acts exercise a retroaction upon us. . . . In a work of art I rather like to find transposed on the scale of the characters, the very subject of that work.

Nothing throws a clearer light upon it or more surely establishes the proportions of the whole. Thus, in certain paintings of Memling or Quentin Metzys a small convex and dark mirror reflects the interior of the room in which the scene of the painting is taking place. . . . Finally, in literature, in the play scene in *Hamlet,* and elsewhere in many other plays. . . . In *The Fall of the House of Usher* the story that is read to Roderick, etc. None of these examples is altogether exact. . . . What would be much more so . . . is a comparison with the device of heraldry that consists in setting in the escutcheon a smaller escutcheon *'en abyme,'* at the heart-point." The *Journal* entry of 1893 is capital, for Gide was to use this device of *composition en abyme* in most of his imaginative writings from 1891 to 1926, with the notable exceptions of *The Immoralist, Strait Is the Gate,* and *The Pastoral Symphony.*

In *The Counterfeiters* this apparent narcissism reaches its height when Gide puts a novelist resembling himself at the center of the novel, engaged in writing a novel to be entitled *The Counterfeiters* and recording and commenting the action in his diary as it unfolds. Such a device offers the incalculable advantage of narration by indirection, for "a character may well describe himself wonderfully while describing someone else or speaking of someone else—according to the rule that each of us really understands in others only those feelings he is capable of producing himself"—as *Journal of "The Counterfeiters"* points out. Thus it is that the progress of Michel in *The Immoralist,* or of the Pastor in *The Pastoral Symphony,* becomes apparent to us through his wife's attitude toward him *as reported by him himself.* In the latter novel, for instance, the Pastor sets down his wife's remarks which he does not fully understand but which tell us that she knows he loves Gertrude, and this long before he recognizes the fact himself. Hence, Gide is stating a principle that has always been his when he says in *Journal of "The Counterfeiters":* "It is appropriate, in opposition to the manner of Meredith or James, to let the reader get the advantage over me— to go about it in such a way as to allow him to think he is more intelligent, more moral, more perspicacious than the author, and that he is discovering many things in the characters, and many truths in the course of the narrative, in spite of the author and, so to speak, behind the author's back."

Many of us have long admired the ending of *The Counterfeiters* with Edouard's suspensive remark: "I am very curious to know Caloub." And indeed, in his workbook the author notes: "This novel will end sharply, not through exhaustion of the subject, which must give the impression of inexhaustibility, but on the contrary through its expansion and by a sort of blurring of its outline. It must not be neatly rounded off, but rather disperse, disintegrate. . . ." This too is less new than Gide would have us think. Do not the earlier novels likewise blur off, leaving the reader to reflect at length on the situation and emotions of the chief protagonist? Particularly in *The Immoralist* and in *Strait Is the Gate,* when the end is reached, the reader feels better informed—thanks to the technique of indirection—than does the bewildered narrator. Consistently André Gide has allowed the reader the illusion of getting the advantage over him.

It is by no means necessary, or even advisable, to attempt to diminish *The Counterfeiters* in order to build up the earlier tales. That there is a difference is only too apparent. The example of Dostoevsky and the capital advice of Roger Martin du Gard suffice to explain Gide's new orientation in the years 1919 to 1925. But three points must not be forgotten: (1) that as early as 1908 Gide had already sketched a portrait of *Dostoyevsky According to His Correspondence,* (2) that between 1909 and 1914 in the newly formed group of the *Nouvelle Revue Française* the conversation and writings of such intimate friends as Jacques Rivière, Roger Martin du Gard, Jean Schlumberger, and Albert Thibaudet had centered about the aesthetics of the novel, and finally (3) that in 1914—directly between *Strait Is the Gate* and *Isabelle* on the one hand and *The Pastoral Symphony* on the other—Gide had brought out *Les Caves du Vatican* (badly titled in one English language edition as *Lafcadio's Adventures*). That thrilling novel—for it is a novel despite the author's timid and misleading classification of it as a *sotie*—has more in common with *The Counterfeiters* than with the tales that precede and follow it. Comprising almost the same multiplicity of plots and contrapuntal composition as the later novel, it is narrated in the third person by a very conscious writer who even indulges in Fielding-esque or Sterne-like apostrophes and asides to disclaim omniscience and responsibility; and it unfolds swiftly with all the complexity and compulsion of a novel of adventure. Furthermore, it comprises a microcosmic novel within the novel, which Julius is writing almost at the dictation of Lafcadio. Clearly it is a tryout of the techniques to be used ten years later in *The Counterfeiters*. Nothing is more natural than that Gide should have begun *The Counterfeiters*, in his first draft, with the journal of Lafcadio, the charming and elusive hero of the earlier novel. His later rejection of Lafcadio reflects his characteristic desire not to take conscious advantage of momentum acquired in an earlier work.

Yet, as we have seen, it was impossible not to benefit from unconscious momentum in the form of the fictional techniques patiently elaborated over the preceding twenty-five years. Some readers will always prefer the concentrated, gemlike tales of Gide's early maturity, whereas others will choose the exasperatingly living, Dostoevskian qualities of *The Counterfeiters*. But, whatever their differences, the men and women who have the good fortune to read those works a century from now will doubtless not hesitate for a moment to recognize the same hand in all of them.

The Nation, November 28, 1942.

"THE COUNTERFEITERS" AND "POINT COUNTER POINT"

It has been said that the classics of only yesterday do not bear rereading. But of three such books I have recently reread, two stood the test; if that is an average, it is not a bad one. Probably it is quite fortuitous that those two books were French novels, André Gide's *Counterfeiters* and Proust's *Remembrance of Things Past.* The other was *Point Counter Point* by Aldous Huxley.

For years Proust's work has suffered from the short-sighted attacks of the socially conscious critics, blinded by its almost exclusive preoccupation with aristocratic society to the bitterly ironic view it takes of that society.

Proust revisited still charms: his vision of the world is still new, and Combray and Paris and Balbec live in even fuller detail than on the first reading. The poet who sees and creates by metaphor becomes more apparent, as does the classic observer of men's foibles, and when I was not admiring the universality of the maxims and reflections, cast in the manner of La Rochefoucauld, I found myself pausing on almost every page to savor the beauty and variety of the imagery. Time only helps the Baudelaire and the La Bruyère in Proust to emerge.

Gide maintains that he writes to be reread, hoping to win his case on appeal. What stupid things we have all said of him on a single reading! No one should ever talk about Gide—in print at any rate—

without having read all of his major works at least twice. *The Counter-feiters* bears a third and fourth reading even better than it does a second. The ideal is to approach it afresh after a lapse of a few years, with the action still fairly clear in one's mind and the characters still answering to their names. Then the multiplicity of plots and the corresponding abundance of characters cease to be elements of confusion, and one can fully appreciate the art of the novelist. Then only does one see, in spite of Gide's explicit desire never to take advantage in one chapter of the impetus carried over from the preceding chapter, the subtle balance of chapter against chapter and incident against incident. One comes to understand the role of such characters as La Pérouse, Armand, Sarah—half-effaced by their more dazzling neighbors. And finally, through the confusion caused by the initial critics back in 1926 who disagreed as to the primary subject of the novel, Gide's purpose becomes clear. *The Counterfeiters* gives, first of all, a picture of the struggle between the generations: this is the reason for the introduction of little Gontran de Passavant, of the many members of the Vedel family, and of the old musician's misunderstandings with his son and grandson. This is why Edouard, who belongs by age to one generation and by temperament to the next, stands at the center of the action. But *The Counterfeiters* is also the story of a novel's creation in its author's mind, the very novel we are reading, in fact. And since the one subject is a story of flux—the decaying of one generation and the growing up of another—what is more appropriate than that the novel itself should be in a state of becoming? Beneath this double subject lies the conflict between reality and its representation, its counterfeit, both in social life and in art.

For full enjoyment—let it be said at the risk of making Gide appear discouragingly difficult and thus incurring the just rebuke that Joseph Wood Krutch addressed to modern criticism—the rereader of *The Counterfeiters* should also read both the little daybook kept by Gide during the composition of the novel and certain pages of Gide's *Journal* of the last fifty years. Those supplementary texts will greatly enlighten him as to the novelist's problems and will correct any false impressions he may have formed from identifying Edouard too closely with Gide.

In the *Journal*, for instance, he will find under the date of August 1893
—Gide was then not quite twenty-four—this significant note:

"I wanted to suggest, in the *Tentative amoureuse*, the influence of
the book on the one who is writing it, and during that very writing.
. . . In a work of art I rather like to find, transposed on the scale
of the characters, the very subject of that work. Nothing throws a better
light upon it or more surely establishes the proportions of the whole.
Thus, in certain paintings of Memling or Quentin Metzys a small
convex and dark mirror reflects the interior of the room in which the
scene of the painting is taking place. Likewise in Velázquez's painting
of the Meninas (but somewhat differently). Finally, in literature, in the
play scene in *Hamlet* and elsewhere in many other plays. In *Wilhelm Meister* the scenes of the puppets or the celebration at the castle.
In *The Fall of the House of Usher* the story that is read to Roderick.
None of these examples is altogether exact. What would be much more
so and would explain much better what I strove for in my *Cahiers,*
in my *Narcisse,* and in the *Tentative,* is a comparison with the device
of heraldry that consists in setting in the escutcheon a smaller one '*en
abyme,*' at the heart point."

This *composition en abyme,* which like the triple mirrors at the
tailor's opens a staggering abyss before our eyes, has preoccupied André
Gide from the first; in addition to the very early works he mentions,
he has used it in *Paludes,* in the *Caves du Vatican,* and most effectively
in *The Counterfeiters*—where the novelist within his novel is himself
writing a novel with a novelist as the central character.

Huxley does much the same thing. And his novelist, Philip Quarles,
sees this form of composition in terms of the Quaker holding a box of
oats pictured on the Quaker Oats box. This is why the rereader of
The Counterfeiters should also read *Point Counter Point* if only to
enhance his admiration for Gide's achievement. Despite Ruth Temple's
easy dismissal of Gide in her very full study of Huxley's debt to
France (*Revue de Littérature Comparée,* January 1939), Huxley's best
novel is directly inspired by, not to say frankly imitative of, Gide's.
Nor is his use of the novel within the novel at all effective. Unlike
Edouard, Quarles does not stand at the very center of the action. Out

in India at the beginning of the novel, he never catches up with events, knowing nothing directly of Burlap's seduction of Beatrice, of his father's affair with Gladys, of the satanic evolution going on within the Baudelairean Spandrell, or even of Walter Bidlake's abandoning of Marjorie for Lucy, which is to figure in his novel.

To be successful, the novelist used thus as a character must be a meeting point for all the currents—a fuse box, as Edouard is—and hence preserve the real author from the necessity of omniscience. Gide can afford to let his creatures get out of hand, even—in the eighteenth-century English manner—to interject ironic comments on their antics. But Huxley, who has hurriedly seized upon an original discovery and badly used it, must maintain the Olympian attitude of the traditional novelist. Like his prototype Edouard, Quarles keeps a notebook, but, unlike Edouard's, his jottings neither advance the story nor reproduce from another angle events already related in the form of action or conversation. Quarles' notebook most often serves simply as an excuse for the essayist to elaborate ideas set forth by Rampion. Just as Gide did, Huxley wants to seize all the layers of reality—"multiplicity of eyes and multiplicity of aspects seen." Nevertheless, he attempts only rarely, and then quite mechanically, to view the same problem or event through different eyes, as, for instance, when Webley's fascist speech is reported directly by the author, described in terms of Elinor's emotions, and noted by Quarles in one of his little essays.

Gide, who calls for the reader's collaboration and expects him to remember what he has read, is a master of indirection. As in life, his characters often remain ignorant of details that appear clear to us outsiders, but Gide has permitted us to make the deduction ourselves. When Olivier becomes enthusiastic over Passavant's knowledge of marine biology, we know that the latter has simply handed on facts he had learned from Olivier's brother Vincent. Likewise, the moment we learn of Strouvilhou's sojourn at Saas-Fée we guess the source of Bernard's counterfeit coin. But even when Huxley has a chance to let the reader add two and two, he steps in and shouts the answer—as when Molly d'Exergillod thinks Elinor a fool for not noticing how much Philip is attracted to Molly. Forgetting that the preceding chapter has told us how Elinor regularly pushed her husband into other women's arms to humanize him, Huxley tells us all over again.

Does Huxley really forget? On the contrary, it would seem deliberate, this unwillingness to permit the reader that little thrill of recognition akin to creation. Like the old-fashioned schoolteacher, Huxley must always show himself more intelligent than his readers, and this he does by always being painfully explicit. In consequence his novel is repetitive, wordy even.

Even Huxley's contrapuntal composition ("All you need is a sufficiency of characters and parallel contrapuntal plots") comes directly from Gide, whose Edouard claims that he wants to write a novel based on Bach's *Art of the Fugue*. Indeed, many of the characters and the situations they find themselves in have their parallels in *The Counterfeiters*. In addition to the Quarles-Edouard parallel, Lucy Tantamount corresponds to Lady Griffith, Walter Bidlake to Vincent Molinier, Marjorie Carling to Laura Vedel, Spandrell to Strouvilhou, John Bidlake to La Pérouse, Burlap to Passavant, and so on. Finally, both novels—which opened with a family "scene" and with the novelist character traveling to the point of action—close with scenes of violence abruptly related in the Dostoevskian manner. With a similar group of characters Gide depicts the decay of the bourgeois family; Huxley, a society that is rotten to the core. But in Gide's novel, so much of which deals with the young who are aiding the dissolution of their families, there is hope in youth. Huxley's world shows no element of hope.

Both works have frequently been classified as immoral. A moralistic and myopic critic early called *The Counterfeiters* the novel of uranism and onanism; *Point Counter Point* offers a society in heat in which adultery is the normal practice. In Gide's work there is a greater dosage of positive evil, creative evil—which Gide would attribute to the collaboration of the demon—whereas Huxley's world from Burlap to Spandrell is shoddily immoral. But as for the immorality that lies in the attitude of the author, and that D. H. Lawrence particularly castigated in *Point Counter Point*, no comparison is possible.

In his *Journal* for March 18, 1931, Gide recorded: "For the third time I gather my strength to read *Point Counter Point*, for I have been told that you must get beyond the beginning. But what can I think of a book whose first seventy pages I read attentively without finding a single line rather firmly drawn, a single personal thought, emotion, or sensation—not the slightest bait for the heart or the mind which might invite me to continue?" And later that day he drops the book definitively at the one hundred and fifteenth page. Imitation may be the sincerest form of flattery, but André Gide has never been susceptible to flattery.

On *Theseus* (*Thésée*), by André Gide, translated by John Russell and illustrated by Massimo Campigli (New York: New Directions, 1949). *New York Herald Tribune Book Review,* October 30, 1949.

"THESEUS"

Throughout his career André Gide has shown a remarkable predilection for Greek mythology; characters such as Narcissus, Oedipus, and Prometheus figure as heroes of individual works and many others enter occasionally. As early as 1911, he began reflecting on Theseus as a subject, but did not write the story of that virile hero who slew the Minotaur until his North African exile during the recent war. Following its first publication in French by Pantheon Books in 1946, the book was reworked and shortened before it appeared in Paris later the same year. Beautifully translated by John Russell, it now appears in a sober and handsome volume hand set in Garamond by Hans Mardersteig at Verona and illustrated in twelve lithographs by the Italian painter Massimo Campigli.

The text deserves such special treatment, for it is a gem of ironic story-telling, which may well become one of the classics of our time. Written when Gide was in his seventy-fifth year, it assembles many of his favorite themes. As Theseus narrates in the first person his deeds of prowess in overcoming monsters and dominating women, one recognizes the early fervor of the *Fruits of the Earth* and the insistence upon self-knowledge in order to achieve self-realization. It is equally characteristic of Gide that the famous labyrinth should be psychological in nature and that Icarus should have gone mad through attempting to escape it upward.

In his "Reflections on Greek Mythology" Gide sees myths as rational explanations of natural phenomena. What, consequently, is more logical than to point out that Theseus forgot on purpose to change his sail or that bulls are not carnivorous or that, though a native of Attica, Theseus was out of his element in sophisticated Crete?

After the Cretan adventure and the rape of Phaedra, Theseus becomes the assembler of cities and builder of Athens. At this stage Gide arranges for this unrepentant materialist a supreme encounter with blind Oedipus, now become a symbol of spirituality. Few things could be more revelatory of Gide's essential dichotomy—his Goethian humanism and his longing for the metaphysical—than their conversation.

As has happened with most of Gide's works, early readers, misled by the use of the first person, identified Theseus with Gide. It is more nearly true to see all of the characters as personifications of various aspects of this so complex writer. Every word of this little tale, indeed, is charged with meaning. This is why it had to be translated with consummate skill and, for full appreciation, has to be read more than once.

New York Herald Tribune, November
30, 1952.

HOW GIDE TRANSLATED "HAMLET"

André Gide once reflected that if he had been Napoleon he would
have instituted a sort of prestation for writers, imposing on each worthy
writer the task of enriching his own literature with the translation of
some foreign work offering an affinity with his own talent.

Gide made the statement in 1928, after he had already distinguished
himself as a translator from English into French. By that time he had
given his compatriots vivid re-creations of a play by Rabindranath Ta-
gore, Joseph Conrad's novel *Typhoon,* a group of poems by Walt
Whitman, Shakespeare's *Antony and Cleopatra,* which Ida Rubinstein produced in 1920, and William Blake's *Marriage of Heaven and
Hell.*

The variety of these works bears witness to the complexity of his
own nature, because, for one reason or another, he felt a keen affinity
with each of them.

Some of his admirers have deplored the fact that instead of leaving
such translations to less gifted pens he took time away from his own
creative writings to do them. But such a view overlooks the consummate
skill in the use of language that he perfected through those exercises;
it also forgets the moments in any artist's career when the creative
stream flows sluggishly and he might better devote himself to re-
vivifying another's conception than to twiddling his thumbs or playing
canasta.

Having already dared to tackle Shakespeare, doubtless the greatest challenge to any translator, André Gide felt naturally drawn to the greatest and most difficult of Shakespeare's plays. In July 1922, he took time out from the arduous composition of his *Counterfeiters* to write a version of the first act of *Hamlet*.

After three uninterrupted weeks at five hours a day, he finished the act and abandoned his plan of doing the whole tragedy, convinced that to write good French one had to get too far from Shakespeare. His version of that single act was published seven years later, after considerable polishing, in the bilingual Parisian review *Echanges*.

Presumably Gide had abandoned *Hamlet* to the professional translators. But in May 1942, with the Nazis occupying more than half of France, he was in Marseille ready to leave for the relative calm of North Africa, which did not then look like a future battlefield. On the day before he sailed he lunched with Madeleine Renaud and Jean-Louis Barrault, whom he described in his *Journals* as possessing a "wonderful face, instinct with enthusiasm, passion, genius."

With his characteristic alertness to everything concerning the theater, Barrault had read Gide's partial version buried away in a periodical that had appeared when the actor was still a schoolboy. He urged the writer to complete his *Hamlet* (begun twenty years before) so that Barrault could present it on the stage.

As soon as he reached Tunis, the seventy-three-year-old Gide returned to the task "with an adolescent's zeal," as he recorded in his *Journals,* "and an old man's patient equanimity." This was apparently just the combination required, for he finished the work by the end of August 1942 and felt satisfied with it.

Thanks to events that Gide could not have foreseen, French Africa was liberated long before the mainland; and the writer was able to ship the manuscript of his *Hamlet* to New York, where his friend Jacques Schiffrin, at Pantheon Books, brought out the first edition, a handsome bilingual printing, in 1944. The Parisian edition, without the English on facing pages, followed two years later—at just the time that Jean-Louis Barrault and Madeleine Renaud, having left the Comédie-Française, opened their new theater at the Marigny with a beautiful and triumphant presentation of Gide's adaptation of *Hamlet*.

In a letter to a friend Gide expressed the regret that he had not kept a workbook of his *Hamlet* translation, as a pendant to the *Journal of the Counterfeiters*. In such a special journal he would have cited passages from his predecessors in the arduous undertaking—such as François-Victor Hugo, Marcel Schwob, Guy de Pourtalès, and Jacques Copeau—all of whom seemed to "sacrifice rhythm, lyrical power, cadence, and beauty to mere exactitude." They all share the shortcoming of being too bookish and hence utterly unsuited to the stage.

Unlike them, Gide aimed to preserve "certain poetic qualities, most often untranslatable," he admitted, "but for which it is not always impossible to find a sort of French equivalent."

This is precisely what André Gide has succeeded in doing. For his translation in sensitive, poetic prose is not only the most vivid acting version in French; it is also the French *Hamlet* that most faithfully reflects the qualities we love in the original.

Perhaps no adaptation of that play into another idiom will ever wholly please Anglo-Saxons. Yet we should not want Shakespeare to be our exclusive property any more than we should want Sophocles to belong solely to the Greeks, or Dante to the Italians. In seeing Jean-Louis Barrault's thoughtful interpretation of Gide's *Hamlet,* we shall enjoy a rare and broadening experience in the theater.

GIDE'S "HAMLET"

Hamlet has survived all manner of interpretations—stylish modern dress, a bare rehearsal stage, an all-Negro cast, even a woman in the title role. As John Barrymore, Sir John Gielgud, Richard Burton, and many great actors have agreed, the play can be rediscovered and re-created every decade or so. Indeed, no performance of the past is ever definitive—not even in the career of a single actor who is fortunate enough to play it in several revivals. Each novel production throws new light on that perennially fascinating masterpiece.

Similarly, *Hamlet* has survived translation into most modern languages, being played to foreign audiences who may often have wondered what English-speaking people saw in the play and why it stood in a category by itself. And just as any translation, even of a paragraph of prose or four lines of verse, cannot but be an interpretation, each new version of *Hamlet,* in whatever language, is bound to provide a personal commentary. Within a single language, no translation can be final, for in such matters, thank heaven, there exists no "authorized version" or "exclusive rights." André Gide's *Hamlet* is necessarily as different from those of his friends Marcel Schwob and Jacques Copeau as Maurice Evans' *Hamlet* is from Laurence Olivier's. Each provides a new and personal interpretation.

But why should we, who know and love Shakespeare's *Hamlet,* be concerned with André Gide's *Hamlet?* A translator's work, made to inform his compatriots and to enrich the literature in his own tongue, is rarely of interest to readers of the original. But Gide was a great creative writer in French, a tremendous force in modern letters who left, and will continue to leave, his mark on generations of Frenchmen. Let us reverse the situation for a moment and try to imagine what would result. No one in France would bother collecting and comparing English versions of Molière, except a scholar-specialist who might thereby draw interesting conclusions about Anglo-Saxon attitudes toward France's great dramatist or about changing tastes across the Channel or the Atlantic. But if a T. S. Eliot suddenly issued his translation of *Tartuffe* after a lifetime of reflecting on Molière, his interpretation would interest all literary-minded Frenchmen with a knowledge of English.

The analogy is not farfetched, for throughout his long life Gide revered Shakespeare as few Frenchmen do. References to Shakespeare abound in his voluminous *Journals* from their beginning in 1889 to their end in 1949. His translation of *Antony and Cleopatra* was published in 1921, and he was fifty-two when he interrupted his writing of *The Counterfeiters* to begin the translation of *Hamlet*.

Then at the height of his literary career, with more than twenty books to his credit, he was just beginning to enjoy a widespread reputation as a disturber of youth and a controversial figure in modern letters. He had not yet taken up the defense of homosexuality in *Corydon*, confessed publicly in *If It Die . . . ,* or become converted to Communism. But his monthly *Nouvelle Revue Française* was already setting the literary tone throughout Europe; his early novellas, *The Immoralist, Strait Is the Gate, The Pastoral Symphony,* were winning new readers; and his enigmatic creature Lafcadio was becoming a sort of model for many restless postwar young men.

It was at Jean-Louis Barrault's insistence, in the darkened France of 1942, that Gide in his seventy-third year returned to the thorny task of translating *Hamlet,* begun and abandoned in 1922. After three months of labor at six to eight hours a day, he finished his full version, which was first published in 1944 in New York by his friend Jacques Schiffrin under the imprint of Pantheon Books.

GIDE AT THE COMÉDIE-FRANÇAISE

Delighted to find in André Gide the same charm and enthusiasm he has always had, I plunged into conversation with him just as if eleven months had not elapsed since our last meeting. No one is easier to talk with; he shows neither pose nor concern for the figure he cuts. Gide began by saying of Faulkner: "My admiration for him, which is often very great, is not without nuances. His work, and especially his short stories, strike me as very uneven in quality."

Naturally he asked for news of "our book," as he calls his *Journals* in my translation, and was pleased to hear that volume four was to appear in New York in April.

However, I was eager to discuss his new play, *Les Caves du Vatican,* which I had just seen at the Comédie-Française. I should have liked to ask how it felt to be played in the state-subsidized theater of Molière for the first time at the age of eighty-one. But I could not quite think how to formulate the question in any language.

"If I were to adapt your farce for Broadway," I told him, "I should not keep either of the titles used for the novel when it appeared in English: neither *The Vatican Swindle* (which could only shock a certain element among American readers) nor *Lafcadio's Adventures* (the definitive title in English). No, I should use *The Roman Underground,* which permits an allusion both to the idea of the Pope's subterranean prison and also to the ramified network of Protos and his confidence men."

117

"That strikes me as excellent," said Gide, "since the word 'underground' took on a new significance during the war. But tell me whether the characters of the novel seemed to you faithfully preserved in the play?"

"Yes, despite the greater importance given to the novelist Julius, so wonderfully acted by Henri Rollan, they all ring true. Lafcadio is sufficiently seductive, as all the critics have said, and the lamentable Amédée with his preposterous purity and suspicious pimple becomes the complete puppet we have always imagined him to be."

"Some of the critics accused my play of being too long and too complex," said Gide, "and indeed the final curtain on the opening night was after midnight. But since then I have cut out two scenes."

"Even though there are still seventeen tableaux, the action unfolds with the same precipitation as in the novel," I volunteered. "I have never seen such rapid changes of scene in a French theater."

"Did you notice any weak points?" he asked, leaning eagerly forward as he nervously stamped out his cigarette in an overflowing ashtray. I risked the observation that the last scene had disappointed me.

"Why, of course! Lafcadio falls to pieces in the last few lines. I have been rewriting that scene, which has given me no end of trouble. Here is the new version that finally satisfies me," Gide said, handing me two typewritten pages. "I have just given this to Jean Meyer, the director, who will use it beginning tomorrow."

I am not surprised to learn that the actors who play the young people are delighted with the change, for Lafcadio—who now interrupts packing his suitcase to fall onto the bed with Geneviève—remains true to his nature.

"Just now, however," Gide said as he lighted another Chesterfield, "I am less interested in what I have already written than in what I am writing." He then read me a fascinating and flattering appeal from a group of Japanese intellectuals devoted to his writings. I was amazed to hear that even before there was a complete French edition of his works there was a twenty-volume set in Japanese. Yet quite ignorant of the true political situation in the Orient and of the Japanese state of mind in particular, Gide is somewhat embarrassed to know how to reply.

"Consequently I have decided to express myself in general terms and to say what I could say to the entire world. Tell me what you think of this." Whereupon he read me a four-page manuscript written in his characteristic, clear hand on pink foolscap. He had taken as text the last words of his 1946 lecture in Syria—"I have confidence in the chosen few: the world will be saved by a handful of individuals."

Introduction to *Pretexts: Reflections on Literature and Morality (Prétextes: Nouveaux Prétextes, Incidences, and Divers)*, by André Gide, selected, edited and introduced by Justin O'Brien; translated by Angelo P. Bertocci and others (New York: Meridian Books, 1959).

"PRETEXTS"

The ancient opposition between creator and critic no longer prevails in tutored minds. The examples of Goethe, Coleridge, Poe, Baudelaire, and, more recently, of Valéry and Eliot have shown conclusively that the creative and critical faculties can cohabit harmoniously. Today no one contests the justice of Baudelaire's statement in his *Art romantique* that "It would be an unheard-of event in the history of the arts for a critic to become a poet, a reversal of all psychic laws, a monstrosity. On the other hand, through a natural development, all great poets eventually become critics. . . . It would be stupendous for a critic to become a poet, and it is impossible for a poet not to contain a critic. Hence the reader will not be shocked that I look upon the poet as the best of all critics." As Baudelaire's application of the term "poet" to Wagner and Delacroix makes clear, he called any maker, any creator in whatever art, a poet, always careful to spell the name with a diaeresis rather than a grave accent to indicate its particular nobility.

In the same spirit, André Gide—who quoted part of Baudelaire's statement as an epigraph to his essay on Paul Valéry—could confidently state elsewhere: "Criticism is at the base of all art." Partly because Gide himself produced so much critical work and partly because, like every great artist, he never failed to temper his lyricism with an almost infallible critical sense, Gide belongs in the tradition of the Goethes, Baudelaires, and Eliots—in the tradition of the creator-critics.

Indeed, Gide's voluminous work counts no fewer than fifteen volumes of criticism. Besides, his *Journals* and the eight published collections of his letters are brimming with additional critical comments. His second published book, which appeared before he was twenty-two, was already a work of literary and artistic criticism, for the *Traité du Narcisse* of 1891 with its "theory of the Symbol" stated better than had Gide's elders the theoretical bases of symbolism. Six years later, when his own volumes of poetry and imagination already numbered six, he brought out discreetly in an anonymous edition of a hundred and twelve copies his first *Réflexions sur quelques points de littérature et de morale* and began contributing his incisive literary criticism to periodicals with the brilliant review of Barrès' novel *Les Déracinés* in *L'Ermitage*. The controversy which that single review called forth from the best established (Emile Faguet) and the most thoughtful (Charles Maurras) of French critics led Gide to reply in 1903 with "The Poplar Tree Quarrel," which established him as one of the keenest polemicists in a nation of keen polemicists. But in the meantime he had written his series of ironic "Letters to Angèle" for *L'Ermitage* between 1898 and 1900, followed up the question of nationalism in his lyrical "Normandy and Bas-Languedoc" in *L'Occident* for 1902, and brought out three major essays on aesthetics in *L'Ermitage* between 1900 and 1903. In addition, he had succeeded his friend Léon Blum in 1901 as regular reviewer for *La Revue Blanche* and held the post for several months. And somehow he had found time—while issuing his first plays and his first novel—to write for still other periodicals in Paris and Brussels.

In 1903, then, as a thirty-four-year-old writer who already had to his credit an impressive list of titles representing the different *genres* of poetry, satire, fiction, drama, aesthetic theory, and travel impressions, André Gide brought out his first volume of collected essays, *Prétextes,* with the subtitle that he had used before and was to use again: "Reflections on Some Points of Literature and Morality." When the volume reached the poet Paul Claudel in distant China, where he occupied a diplomatic post, he wrote Gide enthusiastically: "Why don't you write criticism deliberately and out of preference? It seems to me that you have to a very high degree the critical sense, which is as rare as the poetic sense and perhaps rarer. Not everyone knows what a man or a tree means. At least I know of only two critics who really deserve the name: Baudelaire and Poe."

Obviously Gide liked the title *Prétextes,* sufficiently vague so that it suited equally the literary, moral, and social problems that he treated with the same urgency. Eight years later he brought out his *Nouveaux Prétextes* and still later a third collection of essays, which he called in his *Journals* "a third volume of *Prétextes*" until he hit upon the title *Incidences (Angles of Incidence).*

Most of the essays in those collections of 1911 and 1924 had first appeared in the *Nouvelle Revue Française,* or *N.R.F.,* which Gide had founded in 1908–09 with a group of friends and disciples. For he had eventually tired of writing for others' journals, in which he could never feel altogether at home. To be sure, he shared many ideals with Adrien Mithouard, the editor of *L'Occident,* and with the young groups in Brussels that had launched *La Vie Nouvelle* and *Antée.* In Edouard Ducoté's *Ermitage,* to which he had begun contributing at the age of twenty-five, he had his greatest chance to influence editorial policy, but even there he had to get along with his fellow editor Remy de Gourmont, whose theories and attitudes were often at variance with Gide's. The moment he could set the policy for his own monthly review, he revealed, as St.-John Perse wrote of Gide the editor, "a sense of values that has never failed; an innate sense of the mainsprings and, as it were, the very essence of French genius; a predilection for the human in the written word and for the universal in the individual work; the perception, in everything, of its quality, urgency, veracity." From 1909 until 1940 the *N.R.F.* illustrated, in its choice of authors as in its rigorous standards, the Gidian critical spirit through which it influenced several generations of French writers.

Like Baudelaire, Gide had early "resolved to inquire into the *why,* and to transform into knowledge the pleasure he took in art." It is in this way that the creator who questions his art and that of his predecessors and contemporaries inevitably becomes a critic. When the young novelist Jean Prévost wrote: "André Gide could have been the greatest of French critics; he probably knew this, and yet he preferred to be a creator," Prévost subscribed to the outmoded distinction between creation and criticism. More recently, Albert Camus implied the necessary fusion of the two activities by stating: "When Gide criticizes, he creates."

Gide himself, who never tired of quoting Oscar Wilde to the effect that "the imagination imitates, whereas the critical spirit creates," would have liked Camus's remark. Commenting on Wilde's paradox and thinking more of self-criticism than of the criticism of others, he once pointed out that "among the multiple phantasms that the imagination offers us in disorder, the critical spirit must choose. Any drawing implies a choice—and it is a school of draftsmanship that I admire most in France." But the exercise of that choice in one's own work leads inevitably to judging the work of others, and that Gide considered his critical essays no less important than his "works of imagination" there can be no doubt. The critical spirit persisted in him to the very end. Late in life he took pride in the fact that many of his "judgments of still unclassified works were premonitory." During his last ten years he brought out no fewer than seven volumes of literary and art criticism, and his *Ainsi soit-il* (*So Be It*), which he left in manuscript, abounds in literary judgments.

The qualities that made André Gide a good critic are simply those that are doubtless essential to any good critic. From early in life, to begin with, he was a voracious reader in many domains, and a critical reader. From the first part of his *Journals* we have some indication of this, but we shall know far more if ever anyone publishes the "Cahier de lectures" that he kept between the ages of twenty and twenty-three and that Dr. Jean Delay has drawn upon so effectively in his *Jeunesse d'André Gide*. There he not only listed his readings but also commented on them at length; for instance, this is what he noted with adolescent punctuation at twenty about Turgenev's *Virgin Soil:* "Infinite charm—one of the most beautiful books read—mysterious psychology, quite intimate though without analysis—monochrome poetry —odd feeling of life, personal vision of things, even at times somewhat upsetting just because of his great personality. . . . How I should like to have said all that; I should have said it at less length, with, if I could, less mystery in the external life and more (but I should have been wrong) in the inner life."

Secondly, Gide always read with an open mind, free of prejudices. Some of his keenest critical remarks are found in a little volume he entitled *Un Esprit non prévenu* (An Unprejudiced Mind), which opened with the statement that there is nothing rarer than such a mind ("or one that has managed to get rid of its prejudices"). It was this quality that allowed Gide to note the flaws of his close friends Francis Jammes, Henri Ghéon, Paul Claudel, and Jacques Rivière, and the virtues of those he did not in general admire. It was this that kept the *N.R.F.* from ever becoming the organ of a school, because it chose its contents according to their quality rather than according to the tendencies they manifested. Claudel could fulminate periodically when he found *his* contribution beside one that he considered shockingly revolutionary by Proust or Valéry or Paul Léautaud, but the review continued to maintain its eclecticism by just such juxtapositions.

Thirdly, and this is perhaps but an illustration of the same independence, Gide commonly looked upon the past and the present with the same eye. No *laudator temporis acti,* he never revered the past merely because of its venerability. Rather, he sought occasions to reread and to revise his scale of values. "Originality," he said, "is perhaps never so rare as in matters of judgment; and never less noticeable, for an opinion, though it is original, does not necessarily differ from the accepted opinion; the important thing is that it does not try to conform to it. I can admire Bossuet, La Fontaine, or Voltaire for the same reasons as the most banal literary handbook and not suffer at all from this. But I can perceive later that some of my admirations were not altogether sincere and that my judgment on that point was merely conforming." He knew as well as anyone that, to the classics as to mythology, each generation brings a different thirst.

Surely it was that same independence of judgment, free from the shackles of fashion, that gave Gide such an extraordinary ability to judge his contemporaries. At the height of their popularity he saw the shallowness of Catulle Mendès and Edmond Rostand and was willing to risk his reputation on his apparently untimely condemnation of such dramatists as Henri Bataille and Henry Bernstein. On the other hand, he stood among the first to applaud the genius of Claudel and Valéry, of Perse and Proust, of Valery Larbaud and Giraudoux and Romains, of Malraux and Camus. Instead of being shocked by such manifestations as dada and surrealism, he hailed them as healthy signs of youth in revolt and helped them to express themselves fully.

When the poet Heredia died, whom he had known and frequented, Gide refused to force his voice and exaggerate his grief as is the custom. Keeping his usual intonation, he dared to say: "Conservative minds scarcely like innovators, who are inclined to look upon the conservatives as useless and tedious tardigrades and profess a scorn for them. It is essential, however, that neither that right nor that left should cease to be represented in our literature. I shall even go so far as to say that the innovating element owes its strength to the excellence of the conservative element, and the soundness of its forward thrust is in direct ratio to the solidity of its purchase. Many an error of the Romantic drama is due perhaps to the lack of firmness of Ponsard, and I do not think it really paradoxical to assert that those who owe the most to Heredia today are not his imitators but, on the contrary, the practitioners of free verse and Symbolists, those, it so happens, who, repulsing him, find in his work a smooth, hard, vibrant surface from which to spring forward."

In this case Gide sacrificed the conventional, ceremonial praise of the famous poet who had died to a truthful evaluation of his place in modern letters. And this is doubtless why we can still read today with profit his few pages on Heredia written in 1905.

Gide's attitude toward Heredia might suggest that he was always on the side of the innovators. To be sure, he did consistently show a particular understanding for the artists "who ever fight [as Apollinaire says] on the limitless frontiers of the future."

But, on the other hand, for those who do not see classicism as he did, Gide's lifelong preoccupation with classicism might belie a view of him as a champion of the *avant-garde*. Probably no other question, not even that of nationalism or the glorification of individualism, returns more insistently in his critical writings than the question of classicism.

Indeed, that concept subsumed for Gide the idea of individualism and that of universality, which he opposed to the doctrine of such nationalists as Barrès, Maurras, and their followers. Whether he is composing a lecture on "The Limits of Art" in 1901, writing his answer to Faguet's criticism of Baudelaire in 1910, prefacing the *Fleurs du mal* in 1917, jotting down his fragmentary "Reflections on Greek Mythology" of 1919, indulging in one of his ironic "Notes to Angèle" in 1921, or compressing into a few lines his reply to a periodical's inquiry in 1923, André Gide constantly returns to the concept of classicism, ever refining and sharpening his definition, as if it provided the solution to all critical problems.

First of all, he sees classicism as "the demonstration of a hierarchy" in which the word is subordinated to the sentence, the sentence to the page, the page to the work, and the writer's individuality to the work he is writing. In other words, individuality must be sacrificed to achieve true individualism. The really classical writer becomes human to the point of banality (what Baudelaire called *"la forme banale de l'originalité"*), thus achieving a truly personal form by dominating his inner romanticism. Just as Valéry spoke of a prior romanticism that all classicism presupposes, so Gide stated that "the classical work will be strong and beautiful only by virtue of a romanticism brought under control." As late as 1940 Gide summed up this whole argument in his *Journals* by saying: "The sole art that suits me is that which, rising from unrest, tends toward serenity."

Even though, France being the last refuge of true classicism, the terms "classical" and "French" are almost equivalent to Gide, he refuses to reject romanticism—which such great writers as Ronsard, Corneille, and Hugo manifest in their writings. Upon reading Pierre Lasserre's attack on romanticism, Gide applauds because he has always had a horror of romanticism and artistic anarchy—not so much, as he ironically notes, because they are un-French as because their inaesthetic character shocks his French sensitivity. But Hugo, Michelet, and so many others have enriched French literature, and he would not reject them. In another essay he loyally points out that Pascal, Rabelais, and Villon are often as far as possible from classicism, that

Shakespeare, Michelangelo, Beethoven, Dostoevsky, Rembrandt, Dante, and Cervantes (all of whom he admires) are not by any stretch of the imagination classical.

The classicism that Gide admires—an art of delicate understatement which consistently expresses the general through the particular—embodies a whole ensemble of moral qualities, the first of which are modesty and reserve. Here Gide's strict Protestant upbringing and his refined aestheticism combine to harmonize an artistic ideal with a way of life. Hence the struggle between classicism and romanticism takes place in every individual mind and "the greater the initial revolt of the object brought under subjection, the more beautiful is the work of art," as he says. And one might add: the more beautiful is the personality. This is the sense in which true classicism is not conservative, but creative.

By constantly returning to the consideration of classicism, which he frequently discovers in the most unlikely men and works, André Gide takes the concept out of the musty atmosphere of the classroom and revivifies it as a perennially young and robust force operating upon art. His own deep interest in such non-French writers as Shakespeare and Dostoevsky, Blake and Browning and Nietzsche (to mention but a few of those on whom he wrote), made him keenly conscious of French classicism's narrowness, its distrust of the foreign. In the same comprehensive and basically optimistic spirit, he never ceased to combat La Bruyère's idea that we are born too late, when everything has been said by our predecessors. On the contrary, alert to the present and curious about the future, he could never have taken the side of the ancients in any new quarrel of the ancients and the moderns. Once he called on his readers to try to imagine a Balzac, a Walt Whitman, or a Dostoevsky among the Greeks, and then proposed a new definition of genius: "Genius is an awareness of hidden resources."

Delacroix alluded ironically to "that immutable concept of the beautiful, which changes every twenty or thirty years." It might be said that at the basis of Gide's thought also lies the belief that beauty is not one but many, not stable but changing. This it was that allowed him, while entertaining standards and an intimate set of criteria, to keep an open mind before new manifestations in the arts. In his last piece of writing, at the age of eighty, Gide wonders whether he would be capable of recognizing at once an utterly new form of beauty at variance with all tradition. He shudders to think that a new Rimbaud or Lautréamont might strike him as a madman. Aesthetic judgments continued to be important to him until the day he died, and he longed for the elasticity of mind and eye that he had known in youth. Despite such regrets, however, he had remained throughout life, as St.-John Perse said of him, "more—and how much more!—than a man of culture or a man of taste. A writer of the noble French type well known to old Europe, who according to his needs extended the uses of every literary form, freely transcending the implications of the occasion." Indeed, the moment we go beyond his provocative and highly personal study of Dostoevsky (the one purely critical work by Gide that has hitherto been available in English) to his occasional literary and moral essays, we find that he was equal to every passing pretext— a lecture before a literary society, a preface, an imaginary interview, a memorial tribute, an open letter, a book review, or a mere answer to a periodical in need of copy—because he had simply to refer to a whole background of serious thought on the subject.

IMAGINARY INTERVIEW WITH ANDRÉ GIDE

"Is it true, *cher ami,* that since my death you have been translating my young friend Albert Camus?" André Gide asked as he teetered backward in his old wooden chair and stared at me with his piercing dark eyes. We were facing each other in the musty little reception room of his sixth-floor apartment known among his friends as "the Vaneau," where everything was just as it had been on my last visit eight years ago. Gide was wearing the same heavy jacket and gray flannels, the same black béret and felt slippers, and the ashtray on the table before him had, as usual, been full of cigarette butts when I entered.

"Yes. I hope you don't mind."

"Not all! Not at all! I simply remember how you used to insist on being an occasional translator, when the spirit moved you. . . . But Camus is an excellent writer who has much to say to the world, and I am happy that you are making him available in America. He deserves to be known abroad. Moreover, word has reached me where I now am of his winning the Nobel Prize just ten years after I received that honor. Some of those who share my exile were deeply shocked because of his relative youth; but they were the same ones, I have no doubt, who were similarly shocked, for other reasons, when the award came to me."

"In any event, Monsieur Gide, most of your works are now available in English. Why, you are even about to become known in America as a literary critic. . . ."

"But I thought my *Dostoevsky* had had an American edition long ago."

"To be sure, it did; but it was the only one of your critical writings to be known there. Here is what we are doing now." And I handed him the jacket of *Pretexts,* which Meridian Books is to bring out in September.

"*Mon Dieu!* What have you done to my photographs?" was his first reaction.

"Not I, but Elaine Lustig, one of the most original book-designers in our country. Do you approve?"

"On second thought, I do approve: after all, other photographs of me have been widely enough circulated so that everyone knows what I really look like. Why not distort these three slightly for the sake of design? Please convey my congratulations to Miss Lustig. By the way, *mon cher,* you were here the day these photographs were taken, do you remember? It was about a year before I died. I recall protesting against the artificiality of having a cameraman follow me about the apartment and making me look too solemn; I asked someone to tell a joke just to relieve the atmosphere and you told a very funny story about a taxi driver. The middle one of these photographs was snapped just as I started to laugh. . . ."

"What do you think of the title itself?"

"Why should I think anything about it? It's my own title, isn't it, that I used back in 1903?"

"Yes, but I have generalized its application by including in this volume the best essays from four of your collections of criticism."

"That seems quite defensible. After all, I used it a second time in 1911 with *Nouveaux Prétextes* and should have repeated it in 1924 instead of *Incidences* if there had been a convenient way of doing so. As for *Divers.* . ."

"Let me say it for you, Monsieur Gide. It's a nondescript title like the subheading 'Miscellaneous' at the end of a budget. If it hadn't been followed by your name no one would have bought the book, I'm sure."

"You gave me a little shiver just now, *mon cher* O'Brien, when you referred to selecting the best essays from four of my books. Did you really choose only the best and all the best ones? What about 'Nationalism and Literature'?"

"It's here. But your lack of confidence surprises me. Be assured that had you been alive I should certainly have consulted you. And allow me to point out that I know America and the tastes of my fellow Americans a little better than you do."

"Don't take amiss what I said simply out of curiosity, and let me see the table of contents, which I am sure you have in your pocket."

"You are right; here it is. Don't you think I did right by starting off the volume with those four brilliant lectures you gave early in your career?"

"Perfectly right. Because of their length and the seriousness of the problems they treat, they belong together. And they set the tone admirably for all my critical writing; I have often thought that the lecture on influence was one of the best things I had ever done. Not long ago, I saw Oscar Wilde over yonder, who expressed his delight at my basic agreement with the essays of his *Intentions*. I am so glad that you include my memorial essays on Wilde and on Mallarmé; I couldn't face those two old friends if you hadn't, and some of the best conversations I have these days. . ."

"Do you notice any glaring omissions?"

"Nothing glaring or even regrettable. My *Journal sans dates* and *Feuillets* really belonged to the *Journals* and you have already translated them in those volumes. The brief book reviews, which I so much enjoyed doing in the early years of this century, dropped out, I suppose, because Americans don't know the books I was treating. . . ."

"Good for you! That's just the point. And for the same reason I reluctantly omitted the brilliant 'Lettres à Angèle,' which. . ."

"What! You left out those little gems? I thought you admired their sprightly wit and offhand manner."

"Indeed I do, but I find the same qualities in your review of Barrès and subsequent quarrel with him and Maurras about the poplar tree, in your exploding of Senator Bérenger's statement regarding immorality, in your taking Faguet to task for his judgment of Baudelaire, in your 'Open Letters' to Cocteau and Jammes, and in those later 'Billets à Angèle' which, you have to admit, deal with subjects of more general and more current interest, such as classicism, Proust, and the *N.R.F.*"

"All right, all right. You have convinced me. Too bad for poor, shadowy Angèle. Yet she is there in the 'Billets' at any rate. Before you start again proving to me that I am living in the past, let me say at least how happy I am that you are ending the volume with my 'Characters' and 'An Unprejudiced Mind.' Whatever else may be said of me—and God knows that my critics have stopped at nothing—it has to be granted that I maintained an open mind throughout life."

"Yes, ever ready to greet the new, to explore the trackless underground of human psychology (that's an expression from my introduction) and, at the same time, to check and revise periodically, if need be, your past judgments. This is why I look upon you as one of the truly great critics of our literature and civilization, a writer in the tradition of the best creator-critics such as Goethe, Baudelaire, and. . ."

"I shouldn't go that far myself, *cher ami.*"

"But this is an imaginary interview, the kind you wrote back in 1905 as represented in this volume. Hence I can make you say anything I want."

"In that case, I refuse to play. *Au revoir, cher ami.*"

CAMUS

New York Herald Tribune Book Review,
March 24, 1946.

ALBERT CAMUS: NOVELIST, DRAMATIST, PHILOSOPHER OF THE ABSURD

"The entire foreign policy of General de Gaulle is now in question. We have never shown any indulgence toward that policy. In fact, we have constantly emphasized its dangers. And, again today, it strikes us as odd to lay claims to a policy of strength and power without having the means to back it up. In this way France exposes herself to a reminder from the British Commons that we are acting as if we had won the war, whereas we were really beaten, and to another from Washington the same day that the little army we have owes its equipment and arms to foreign aid. The facts prick the pretty bubble of French power. They confirm our criticisms and this confirmation is a bitter one."

When these words appeared in the editorial of a Paris newspaper on June 1, 1945 (during the Syrian flare-up), none but two or three Parisian journalists, all on the same paper, could have the courage and lucidity to write them. But Albert Camus in particular was by then so widely known for precisely those two virtues that everyone attributed the unsigned articles in *Combat* to him. Indeed, ever since he and Pascal Pia had founded the clandestine newspaper *Combat* to mock the German and Vichy censors, Albert Camus's editorials have been distinguished for their clairvoyance and directness.

Unknown before the war save in his native Algiers, where he was a ship broker, journalist, and vigorous social reformer in the local press, Camus moved to the mainland of France in 1940 when threatened with tuberculosis. That was the time when many were leaving France for North Africa; it was not the last occasion on which Camus, then only twenty-seven, bucked the popular current.

After the liberation, when his newspaper came out into the open and took its place as the most vigorous in Paris, Albert Camus became the spokesman of the "pure Resistance" group. Far more independent than François Mauriac in the *Figaro* or Maurice Schumann, the voice of London now come to Paris, or any of the Communists, he dared attack the narrow Gaullisme that was then gaining ground; "We have a row to hoe together but do not owe a cult to his person," said *Combat* on June 18, 1945. "Admiration, gratitude, respect, are not to be confused with devotion. . . . The taste and the ambition for personal power have often been attributed to Charles de Gaulle. We have no idea whether or not such imputations are true. Yet dictatorships are never set up without some pretext or a widespread popular consent. It is up to us to provide neither. In the end, anarchy and the weakness of political parties open the door to dictators."

In literature likewise, Camus is an independent, for he early took his stand against existentialism, that mystical current which has spread in the last months from the Café de Flore to the editorial rooms of *Mademoiselle* and *Time* magazines. Though a close friend of Jean-Paul Sartre, who takes every occasion to praise his works, Camus has not climbed on the bandwagon that gentleman is driving with the brio of a Paris taxi driver. Today when intellectuals will go to any lengths—even to reading Kierkegaard—to find out what existentialism means, Camus is that rare man who has actually read Kierkegaard and still is not an existentialist. Yet Camus is recognized as one of the two or three most vivid young writers in France, and his arrival in America this month is awaited by many as one of the cultural events of the season. Sartre has paved the way for him; Vercors has praised his young friend in New York, Chicago, and San Francisco;

our little reviews are beginning to mention his name with something like reverence; Genêt made some swash comments in *The New Yorker* on his popular play now running in Paris.

All of Camus's literary work rests on his philosophical essay, *Le Mythe de Sisyphe* (1942), which, taking its title from the legend of Sisyphus and his eternal rock-pushing, analyzes a contemporary intellectual malady, the recognition of the absurdity of human life. The concept of the absurd is born of the conflict between man's eternal longing for a logical explanation of the universe and the complete irrationality of life. It is the divorce between man and his life, the actor and his setting. Now various philosophers—Heidegger, Jaspers, Chestov, Kierkegaard, and Husserl—have been keenly aware of this divorce, but all have taken refuge in some metaphysical leap to a realm of safety. In other words, they have all recognized and accepted the absurd. Camus recommends, rather, living lucidly within the absurd, enjoying life all the more fully because it has no meaning, taking advantage of the most complete liberty on earth once eternal liberty is suppressed. This attitude is tantamount to a permanent state of revolt against the absurdity of life (but not suicide, which Camus dismisses, with apparent paradox, as a mere acceptance of the state of things; and the existentialist view is merely a philosophical suicide). The "absurd man"—the man intelligent enough to recognize the conflict—lives most freely by refusing nothing and by remaining painfully lucid in the face of life's irrationality. Four examples of the absurd man are the Don Juan, the actor, the adventurer, and the artist.

The problem, which cannot be stated justly in a paragraph, is not far from the one that tormented Dostoevsky and Franz Kafka. Indeed, Camus wrote a fascinating essay on Kafka in 1943 that is now appended to the recent editions of his *Sisyphe*. And the first illustration of his theories, the novel *L'Etranger* (1942), is reminiscent of *The Trial* and *The Castle* by Kafka. Its hero, Meursault, is an alien in a universe whose unreason and illusions he does not share; he is thus the perfect "absurd man" of modern times "with no recollections of a lost home or hope of a promised land." In his sorry life everything is left to chance and he is supremely indifferent to all that happens to him, for he has no scale of values. Everything that occurs—his smoking a cigarette, his making love, his shooting of an Arab, his drinking too much wine at lunch, and his condemnation to death—is treated on the same plane because seen by him in the same light. But, like his creator, Meursault is superlatively lucid despite his resemblance to a somnambulist. Hence every step in his story implies a criticism of life.

If *The Stranger* becomes fully explicit only after a reading of *Sisyphe*, similarly two plays, published in 1944, illustrate variously the same essay. Written in 1938, *Caligula* is disturbing chic audiences in Paris right now; if the paper shortage only permitted, they would do better to stay home and read this youthful dramatization of a few philosophical ideas embodied in a handful of marionettes. The Emperor Caligula enjoys absolute power; when he revolts against the conventions and sets an example of the absurdity of existence, nothing prevents him, therefore, from going the whole hog. "One is always free at the expense of someone else," he comments on his murders and rapes, and, "Since no one understands fate, I have impersonated fate. I have taken on the stupid, incomprehensible face of the gods." *Le Malentendu* recounts, with something like the art of Edgar Poe, another instance of the blind stupidity of chance. Yet this time the spectator occupies a God-like position from which he sees both sides of the wall of misunderstanding. And, as we witness this succession of fortuitous events, we feel as if we were observing the antics of ants.

With a series of letters to a German friend, originally published clandestinely when the Germans were all too close, and an essay on revolt, both issued in 1945, this is all of Camus's work published since the victory. A novel entitled *La Peste* is announced in Paris now. In it the Algerian city of Oran, isolated by a plague, will be described through the diary of a doctor who revolts desperately against the ravages of the disease. Alone he can do nothing, yet he must resist. Camus witnessed the plague that isolated France for more than four years.

To those who ask how the negative attitude of Albert Camus, keenly haunted by the absurdity of life, could have led to the vigorous positive mood of his editorials, *La Peste* should then provide an answer. The Camus of *Combat* has called consistently for a new political purity, a new social justice. The negation, he has said, cannot be ignored because that is what our generation has met on its path. But the honest, just man will struggle anyway, if only to satisfy himself. This is the arch-lucidity of Albert Camus.

On *The Stranger* (*L'Etranger*), by Albert
Camus, translated by Stuart Gilbert (New
York: Alfred A. Knopf, Inc., 1946). *New
York Herald Tribune Book Review,* April
14, 1946.

"THE STRANGER"

Albert Camus is almost completely unknown in America. Born
thirty-three years ago in Algiers, he became known to his French
countrymen only during the dark years of the German Occupation,
when were published in rapid succession his first novel, a philosophical essay on the problem of suicide and the philosophy of existentialism, and his first two plays. The Germans apparently saw nothing
to fear in his pessimistic view of man's position in the universe as an
absurdity. But meanwhile, under a false identity, he was instrumental
in establishing the underground newspaper *Combat,* in which for two
years before the liberation and for some time thereafter his vigorous
editorials rallied the best energies in France. In New York, where he
arrived at the end of March, he has already spoken for the French
youth who survived that anguished epoch, in which from a consummate journalist he became a most provocative French writer.

The Stranger originally appeared in 1942. Written in the first person singular and in a deliberately flat style, it tells the story of a very
ordinary little man who becomes involved in an extraordinary experience, kills a man, is tried and condemned to death. The very flatness
of the recital and of the hero doubtless makes French readers think of
Duhamel's will-less Salavin and of his models in Dostoevsky; it is most
likely to remind us of Steinbeck and Faulkner, two of the idols in
present-day Paris. Most certainly Camus has been influenced by American writing. But when the name of Franz Kafka comes to mind, one
is really getting warm.

"The whole art of Kafka," wrote Albert Camus in 1943, "consists in forcing the reader to reread." This is precisely what Camus does too. Upon reaching the last page, one decides there must be more to the novel than that, and one turns back to the beginning again. Fortunately the book is short. During the first reading the neutral hero has gradually become more and more likable and the reader becomes involved in his story, even though he doesn't seem at all involved himself. One even gets somewhat excited about the injustice that is meted out to him.

Elsewhere in his essay on Kafka, Camus says: "There are works in which the events seem natural to the reader. There are other, rarer ones in which the character himself sees what happens to him as quite natural. By a strange and yet self-evident paradox, the more extraordinary the character's adventures are the more you are aware of the natural quality of the story, which is in direct ratio to the divergence between the oddness of a man's life and the simplicity with which that man accepts it."

In *The Stranger* the events are by no means so peculiar as in *The Trial* or *The Castle,* for instance. The hero takes part in them much as a somnabulist would, and he thinks he understands them, but it would be impossible for him to explain them to anyone as he sees them. He has the relentless lucidity of certain drug addicts, though he acts as in a dream.

"A world that can be explained even with false reasons is a familiar world," Camus writes in his *Myth of Sisyphus*. "But in a universe suddenly deprived of illusions and enlightenment, man feels himself a stranger. This exile is irremediable, since it holds no recollections of a lost home or hope of a promised land. This divorce between man and his life, the actor and his setting, is indeed the feeling of absurdity." Here then, in a philosophical study published a few months after *The Stranger,* is the key to the novel. Meursault, the unintentional murderer, enacts a parable of man's fate. Since there is such a thing as free will, he must have been free to kill or not to kill. But he cannot see it that way: if there was no other coercion there was that of the dazzling sun. He is given a trial in which he enjoys the democratic right to defend himself, but somehow every statement for the defense turns against him. As each act pushes him to another apparently insignificant act, he becomes ever more clearly a microcosm of human destiny. Meanwhile Meursault's wide-eyed lucidity makes him an observer of a role he is really acting out. If he had understood earlier, he might have committed suicide, like the young French poet after the other war who refused to play a game in which everyone was cheating.

The hero is a symbol. He is the lowest common denominator of man caught between his infinite aspirations and his finite possibilities. The Meursault of the novel sees clearly with a hard, steady gaze; his trouble is that he can't talk, for he lacks the faculty to tell what he sees.

It always takes courage to introduce a new foreign writer. What goes in his own country may not appeal here. Just now the French have more reason than ever for prizing pessimism and lucidity. But Albert Camus does not write for the moment. His message will have a universal appeal to some minds, to those who like Kafka and Dostoevsky, who know why they like Gide and Malraux. And like the best writers of his nation, this young man writes with an assurance, a mastery that are apparent in the excellent translation by Stuart Gilbert. It would be unfortunate for him if he did not, for at the outset of his career he has set himself among the moralists who discourse, for our edification, upon our most fundamental problems.

On *La Peste,* by Albert Camus (Paris: Gallimard, 1947). *Partisan Review,* Summer 1947.

"THE PLAGUE"

"When a war breaks out, people say: 'It can't last; it's too stupid.' There is no question about it: war is certainly too stupid, but that does not prevent it from lasting. Stupidity always clings to its point; people would be aware of this if only they weren't constantly thinking of themselves. In this regard our fellow citizens were like everyone else, they thought of themselves, in other words they were humanists, that is to say that they did not believe in scourges. A scourge goes beyond the human scale and consequently people say that it is unreal, that it's a bad dream that will soon be over. But it isn't always over right away and from one bad dream to another men themselves are finished instead, and the humanists to begin with because they didn't take any precautions. Our fellow citizens were not any more guilty than anyone else; they simply forgot to be modest and they thought that scourges were impossible. They kept on doing business as usual, they planned trips and they had opinions. How could they have thought of the plague which suppresses the future, and travel, and discussions? They thought they were free and no one will ever be free so long as there are scourges."

When Albert Camus makes these remarks early in his new novel, *La Peste,* it should be at once apparent, even if it were not earlier, that his subject transcends an imaginary plague isolating the Algerian city of Oran from the rest of the world.

"On the morning of April 16th," the narrative begins after an introductory chapter, "Dr. Bernard Rieux came out of his office and stumbled on a dead rat on the stair landing." We all had such significant warnings in the years preceding 1939, but like the good doctor we kicked the rat aside and went about our serious business. As the number of dead rats began rapidly multiplying within our city we too started worrying, as he did. And when the plague was upon us in all its horror, we sprang into action and did what we could.

To French readers in 1947 this vividly depicted plague in Oran will surely seem a parable for the enemy occupation of France from 1940 to 1944. The same problems are evident here: the common suffering of all, the pain of separation from loved ones, the formation of isolation camps, the restrictive laws and hardships in obtaining the necessities of life, the being cut off from the outside world, the search for a cause to these sufferings, the effort of some to escape and their illegal dealings with a band of outlaws, the tendency of others to consider themselves outside the common lot, the spontaneous organization of all able-bodied men to combat the plague, the black market, the people's faith in prophecies, the exhortations of the radio from outside countries, etc. Camus shows brilliantly by examples how a scourge of this kind undermines all moral and intellectual life, absorbing every activity of the mind and body.

But there is a larger implication here, broader than the allegory of France's momentary fate, more general even than the whole recent war. The basic problem, as in his first novel, *The Stranger,* is a philosophical one which is dear to Albert Camus: that of our common responsibility in this life and our inability to escape the *condition humaine.* No matter how absurd or meaningless that fate may be, we still must accept it and play our role. No one can take refuge in the fact that he doesn't belong here (Rambert), or in a permanent attitude of ironic detachment (the old sufferer from asthma who took to his bed twenty-five years ago and claims that he alone knows how to live), or in the belief that God has planned everything in life with a purpose (the priest Paneloux), or in an attitude of complete moral anarchy (Cottard), or in the refuge of art (Grand), or in a certainty of one's own superiority (the state's attorney Othon). One of the characters, the philosophical Tarrou, reflects that all humanity can be divided into two categories, the scourges and the victims. There must be another category, he adds, formed of the real doctors—but there are not many of them. Putting himself deliberately among the victims, he is striving toward the third category through sympathy. Maybe someday he can become "a saint without God."

Camus's essay *Le Mythe de Sisyphe,* was written directly against philosophical existentialism, but because he had read Heidegger, Husserl, and Kierkegaard and because he knew Sartre he was confused with Sartre. *La Peste* should go a long way toward clearing up this misunderstanding.

A better novel than *The Stranger, The Plague* (as it will doubtless be called in English) benefits from the fact that its narrator, who is no less lucid than the earlier one, is much more articulate. Hence the universality of his struggle should be more immediately apparent.

Camus writes with the same simple directness with which he speaks (he toured America in the spring of 1946 so that we all had a chance to hear him). But his charming informality has no suggestion of the formless. The sobriety of his style somewhat obscures the fact that this is a most expertly written work, for nothing is so confusing as simplicity. There is great variety in this prose: the two sermons by the Jesuit priest are worthy to be compared with the brilliant one in Joyce's *Portrait of the Artist as a Young Man;* at another point we have a passage that is reminiscent of Proust and, again, a satiric description of various types of bureaucrats of which Anatole France would not have been ashamed.

In short, Albert Camus has maintained the high promise of his first works: already he is one of France's major novelists and what the French call a *moraliste* to boot.

The New York Times Book Review, December 8, 1957.

ALBERT CAMUS: NOBEL PRIZE, 1957

In "The Artist at Work," a satirical short story, Albert Camus makes a significant play on the words "solitary" and "solidary" which reminds us of Matthew Arnold's statement that "all men are solidary and co-partners." This is a leitmotif with Camus. In October 1955, when the weekly *Express* with which he had been associated became a daily, he explained his reluctance to set aside even momentarily his creative work for the purpose of descending into the arena of politics. Yet he could not resist the call or evade the responsibility, feeling that "perhaps it is not bad for a writer, both solitary and solidary with his fellow citizens, to make known his considered conviction and to declare that he will fight freely, in his articles, for freedom first of all."

Far from being a pure intellectual circumscribed by the already impressive list of his own works, Albert Camus is one of the few men deeply involved in the problems of his generation who have maintained in their lives the necessary and perilous equilibrium between commitment and aloofness. While other idealists saw salvation in Communism, he had the strength to maintain repeatedly that "none of the evils that totalitarianism claims to remedy is worse than totalitarianism itself." Hence he never allowed his works of imagination to border even remotely on propaganda, as did some of his contemporaries.

This is surely one reason why the Swedish Academy is awarding the

Nobel Prize for Literature to him. An elder who preceded him to Stockholm for the same reason, François Mauriac, praises him for having heard the burning question asked in this tragic moment of history and having answered it in youthful tones echoed by a whole generation.

André Gide, who received the same prize just ten years before Camus, likewise heard and answered the question. I like to think of Gide and Camus together—not only because of the admiration I shared with each for the other but also because chance once allowed me to see them together. It was in the summer of 1946 when we crossed Paris in an open jeep. As Gide, in high-crowned black hat and flapping cape, kept turning around to talk with us perched on the back seat, the mutual respect and fraternal feeling of the two future prize winners was striking. The younger had learned much from the older man, and it occurred to me that my affection for Camus reflected the degree to which he was, with André Malraux, Gide's most authentic heir. As with Gide, his indifference to the demon of personal possessions and his frugal nature kept him younger than his age and enviably free in mind. And, despite his international outlook, it seemed that in his case too he was a true European as a result of being deeply French. Furthermore, both had been dominated by a passion for truth and justice and freedom.

Even as a very young man, Albert Camus wrote with an assurance that belongs to maturity. In his early philosophical essay published before he was thirty, *The Myth of Sisyphus,* from which most of his later work springs, Camus analyzes a contemporary malady, the recognition of the absurdity of human life. Born of the conflict between man's longing for logical explanations of the universe and the complete irrationality of life, the concept of the absurd tormented many nineteenth-century philosophers and led the existentialists to a philosophical suicide. Camus recommends admitting the conflict and remaining painfully lucid in the face of life's irrationality. Nine years later, in *L'Homme révolté* (*The Rebel*), he studied various forms of revolt against man's fate, scrutinized the relation between nihilism and state terrorism, and pointed the way to a new political philosophy based on balance and freedom.

Between those capital essays he had brought out his first two novels, *L'Etranger* (*The Stranger*) and *La Peste* (*The Plague*)—well known and by now amply commented throughout the world. The heroes of both these narratives, although one is a passive agent and the other an active fighter in the cause of good, share their creator's lucidity, and hence every step in the story of each implies a telling criticism of life. And the second novel clearly shows how Camus himself, haunted by the negative absurd, could still effortlessly adopt a positive mood in his newspaper editorials, calling consistently for a new political purity, a new social justice in a world now dominated by merchants and police-men. Someday we shall be able to read in English that very superior journalism, of which two volumes have so far appeared under the title *Actuelles,* which might be rendered by "Prevailing Currents."

Along with the novels, Camus has continued to indulge his early love for the theater by writing and producing four plays and adapting as many others from Spanish, English, and early French drama. His *Caligula* illustrates, through an Emperor who can freely impersonate blind fate, that one is always free at the expense of someone else, whereas *Le Malentendu* (*The Misunderstanding*) recounts, with an admirable creation of suspense, another instance of the stupidity of chance. *L'Etat de siège* (*State of Siege*) in 1948 dramatizes the allegory of *The Plague* through personifications of beneficent and malevolent forces at war. Two years later, *Les Justes* (*The Just Assassins*) soberly isolates a dramatic incident lived by anarchistic nihilists prior to the Russian Revolution.

Then *La Chute* (*The Fall*) (Camus's first novel since *The Plague*) aroused wild enthusiasm in Paris and stayed on the "best seller" list here for twelve weeks. A brilliantly constructed fable for our times, it ironically probes modern man's guilt complex and sniveling hypocrisy. Like a prophet crying in the wilderness, its curiously repulsive narrator (significantly named Jean-Baptiste Clamence) analyzes himself and indirectly his readers in a way that forces rereading. The six stories of *L'Exil et le royaume* (*Exile and the Kingdom*), which appeared just a few months ago in Paris, throw light on, and receive light from, *The Fall*. Despite their varieties of tone and mood, they all depict a state of spiritual exile from an indefinable kingdom that is within man. As Roger Martin du Gard (another elder whose Nobel Prize dates from twenty years ago, on whom Camus has written most pertinently) recently said, each new work by Camus "carries him one step further on a solitary way, laid out long in advance, which leads somewhere."

Several of those recent stories are laid in Algeria, as were the first two novels. Indeed, the importance of North Africa in the author's background can hardly be overemphasized. His humble birth and early poverty in the suburbs of Algiers led directly to his cult of the Mediterranean and its benign sun. A hearty adolescence spent largely on the beaches and in the stadium as goalkeeper on the local rugby team developed his muscles and taught the value of teamwork. At the age of twenty-two, he applied that lesson to the small theatrical company of university students and factory workers he was then directing in his own adaptations of Dostoevsky, Malraux, and Gide. Later he put it to practice in his newspaper work both in the clandestine and in the legal periods. And today that experience helps him in directing his own plays and his adaptations (such as the recent one of Faulkner's *Requiem for a Nun*) for audiences at the Angers Festival and in Paris. As a result, many would rank him with Jean-Louis Barrault and Jean Vilar as an inspired man of the theater. In fact, he not only directs his plays but even occasionally acts in them. Last winter when one of the actors in *Requiem* suddenly fell ill, Camus took his place on the stage.

As a native of Algeria, he has also observed the colonial problem and race conflict at close hand. On October 21, 1955, he warned in a stirring editorial that "Great, signal amends must be made the Arabs. But by France as a whole and not with the blood of the French in Algeria." Unlike most of his countrymen, he feels solidarity with both the French and the Arabs in the present painful conflict. He has already done what he can to further understanding and promises to play a part again as soon as there is hope of building a unified Algeria.

Frequently Albert Camus has affirmed the dignity of the artist in the modern state, which too often considers him a useless parasite. Generally our governments recognize and try to utilize the artist only after his death, when it is easy to make him say what they want. "Then it is," writes Camus, "that a defeated Germany shouts the name of Goethe rather than of Bismarck to excuse its slaughter. Then it is that Tolstoy and not Catherine the Great serves to camouflage modern Russia's strangling of liberty."

Camus is not dead, thank God, and no one can use him for purposes other than his own. His writing, whether it takes the form of novels, plays, essays, or day-to-day polemics, consistently proclaims the dignity of the individual, the necessity of justice, and the primacy of freedom. Open to all the prevailing currents, Albert Camus can properly be called the conscience of our era. The novel he is presently writing and the stage adaptation he has long been making of Dostoevsky's *The Possessed* will in no way be influenced by the harsh spotlight under which my friend is now sweating. No writer of today has his feet more solidly on the ground than he, nor stands better balanced upon them, ready to meet the future with a disarming smile. It is immensely encouraging that, instead of waiting until his work is finished, the Nobel Committee already recognizes its essential unity by bestowing upon the forty-four-year-old Albert Camus the highest honor of international letters.

PARIS WITHOUT CAMUS

Literary and theatrical circles here in Paris have been stunned by the sudden death last Monday of Albert Camus at the age of forty-six.

Choked with emotion, people speak of the beloved spokesman of his generation who gave a new value to such simple words as justice, freedom, lucidity, humanity.

As one of his friends said, no one knows whether to spell them with capitals, because they were so important and pure to him, or in small letters, because in his personal humility he handled them so simply.

The common people, who know that a Nobel Prize-winner has been brutally snuffed out by an accident and who sense that one of France's chief moral values has suddenly disappeared, are more struck by the horror of it.

They see the powerful car driven at ninety miles an hour by his friend and publisher Michel Gallimard, blowing a tire on a straight, slippery road near Sens and crushing the writer against a plane tree in an exploding mass of iron.

Among friends of Camus, consternation is closely followed by anger at the sudden and absurd way his amazing career ended. They know that he had his ticket for returning to Paris by train as he usually did and that only a last-minute decision to get here a few hours earlier led to the catastrophe. Their only possible consolation lies in the reflection that Camus, who had such an invincible horror of old age and death, was spared one and had no time to face the other.

Albert Camus

The staggering news reached most people here at theater time Monday night. By chance, no play of Camus's is running in Paris at the moment, although his powerful adaptation of Dostoevsky's *The Possessed* is now touring the provinces after a long Paris run.

Jean-Louis Barrault, who greatly admired Camus as dramatist and director, quickly closed the doors of his Théâtre de France and reimbursed the audience that had come for a Claudel play. Other theaters observed an impressive minute of silence. I, who had come to Paris a few days ago chiefly to discuss with Camus details for Sidney Lumet's direction of *Caligula,* learned the tragic news in an orchestra seat of a very off-Broadway type of theater.

Still I cannot accept the fact that *Caligula* will open next month at New York's Fifty-fourth Street Theatre without Albert Camus in the wings, as I have so often seen him here.

For Camus had been, since the age of twenty, a complete man of the theater—dramatist, director, and actor. Barrault, crushed by grief over the tragic loss of the man he considered his brother, has just revealed that when he was recently assigned the management of the Théâtre de France (Odéon), he asked Camus to share it with him.

"I would have taken care of the material side of things and he would have provided the genius," says Barrault.

It is known that even before that, Camus had refused the direction of the Comédie-Française in order to finish the novel he was writing.

But, as the actor Pierre Blanchar says, we shall all continue to see his serious or smiling face behind every line of his plays, *Caligula, The Misunderstanding, The Just Assassins, State of Siege,* and those brilliant adaptations of Calderón, Faulkner and Dostoevsky. Every production of a play by Camus, such as the one now going into rehearsal on Broadway, will henceforth be a homage to that great poetic spirit who in a few short years became the ideal witness and conscience of our epoch.

As his immediate family and closest friends are sadly burying Albert Camus at Lourmarin in the south of France, all the great names in the world of the arts here are paying their respects to him in the press.

But the best things are being said by some of the humbler writers unknown outside of France, who have read him fervently and even in some cases worked closely with him. Every attentive reader of Camus, after all, has felt a human contact, recognized a fraternal personality, and sensed an ennobling hope. Thus one critic writes:

"We are not just weeping over the premature disappearance of one of the greatest talents of our time; with the death of Camus, the very value of man seems diminished. Thanks to him, we were less hesitant, less uncertain in the confusion that always surrounds us."

Another, who helped to edit the newspaper *Combat* with Camus, curses his profession of journalist for forcing him to write through his tears and then blesses it because such a man as Albert Camus devoted to it so many years of too short a life.

Introduction to *Resistance, Rebellion and Death* (*Actuelles*), by Albert Camus, translated and with an introduction by Justin O'Brien (New York: Alfred A. Knopf, Inc., 1960).

SUBJECT TO HISTORY

It was as much for the positive stand Albert Camus took on the issues of the day as for his creative writing—or rather it was for the combination of the two—that he was awarded the Nobel Prize in 1957 at the early age of forty-four. Because, in everything he wrote, he spoke to us of our problems and in our language, without raising his voice or indulging in oratory, he illuminated, as the Nobel citation stated, "the problems of the human conscience in our time." Over and above intellectual or political leadership, he provided the moral guidance the postwar generation needed. By remaining flagrantly independent, he could speak out both against the Russian slave-labor camps and against United States support of Franco's Spain. By overcoming the immature nihilism and despair that he saw as poisoning our century, he emerged as the staunch defender of our positive moral values and of "those silent men who, throughout the world, endure the life that has been made for them."

Indeed, one of the things that endeared Camus to all of us is that he spoke for all. As he said in the brilliant credo he voiced in the Stockholm town hall upon accepting the most universally distinguished award, ". . . the writer's function is not without arduous duties. By definition, he cannot serve today those who make history; he must serve those who are subject to it." Whether we fight in the regular army or wage war as civilians in the shadows of some *maquis,* whether we succumb to famine or slink into exile, whether we are crushed by dictators or put to death by due process of law, are we not all "subject to history"?

In the last year of his life, Albert Camus chose from the three volumes of *Actuelles* the twenty-three essays he considered most worthy of preservation in English. They deal with the perennially current issues that periodically tore him from his creative writing to speak out, as he said, "in the service of truth and the service of freedom": war and resistance in a Europe dominated by prisons, executions, and exile; the tragedies of Algeria and of Hungary; the horror of the death penalty; and the writer's commitment.

The very title *Actuelles,* which unfortunately could not be carried over into English, is typical of the man—concise without being precise, allusive without being descriptive, and modest. Indeed, this mere adjective in the feminine plural meaning "current," "prevailing," or "of present interest" almost requires a gloss in the original. What noun did Camus suppress for greater ambiguity—*pensées, réflexions, vues?*

To some readers these essays will introduce an utterly new Camus— what one might be tempted to call the *Camus actuel.* But he wrote them concurrently with his novels and plays and in them explored the same themes he touched upon in his creative work. An essential part of the man and the writer, these occasional articles and speeches reveal more clearly the position of one of the most lucid spirits of our time— one who was both committed and aloof, or, as he himself implied in his moral tale "The Artist at Work," at once solidary and solitary.

And Camus would never have allowed anyone to consider these essays as incidental to, or less important than, his plays and novels, for he recognized them as a significant part of that *opera omnia* with which he now—too soon, alas—must face posterity.

Columbia University Forum, Winter 1961.

ALBERT CAMUS, MILITANT

Perhaps the rapid, sweeping fame of Albert Camus was a compensation granted him by fate, which had decreed in advance that he was to have but forty-six years of life. If his career was to be complete and his renown universal, everything had to move swiftly, and the world had to accept him at once. His tragic death in an automobile accident on 4 January 1960 at the height of his creative life fits the growing legend of the man who once said: "I have too much youth in me to be able to speak of death." And yet, throughout his work he constantly returned to the contemplation of death; he was a death-haunted man.

The agents of fate who speeded Camus's world-wide reputation were legion: friends and publishers, translators from Norway and Finland to Yugoslavia and Portugal, from Poland to Japan. Most likely, he couldn't even have pronounced most of their names properly. Now that Camus is dead and his second posthumous work is to be published in America, in my translation, I am urged to look upon myself as one of those myriad agents—a minor one because I didn't begin to translate his work until four of his books were available in English. But having frequented Albert Camus in all sorts of circumstances—on a lecture platform during his first visit to this country; in Paris with André Gide; at a lunch table in Paris where the late American novelist Richard Wright was his other guest; in his office as an editor of the Gallimard publishing house; on a Parisian stage where he was rehearsing a cast of actors in *Caligula*—I early succumbed to the warmth, simplicity, and straightforward charm of the man who has been snatched from us. In his person as in his writings, he established at once a fraternal relationship with those he was addressing and no one could remain impervious to his boyish smile.

That smile is uppermost in my memory, which now sees Camus most frequently as a young visitor to our shores, quite simple and un-affected, leaning on the mantelpiece at Columbia's Maison Française, or in my apartment in Greenwich Village with a cigarette in his hand, answering questions thrown at him by a group of eager-eyed students sitting at his feet. Like an astute politician, he was ever particularly interested in youth, for he knew that the future lay in them. Besides— despite the weight of his experience, so different from any we had known—he seemed so young himself.

But my first personal contact with Albert Camus, even before seeing him in such intimate surroundings, took place in March 1946, very shortly before Knopf published the first Camus book here. I say "per-sonal contact" because as an American officer in Paris in October 1944, I had first heard of the young novelist-dramatist-philosopher of whom all Paris was talking. His books were already *épuisés* and *introuvables* but, knowing that the Gallimard firm always kept a certain stock in the cellar, I managed to come home with copies. Then, in early 1946, almost simultaneous announcements spoke of *The Stranger* to appear here and of Camus's first visit to America.

No American Francophile could remember any lecture in French that had ever drawn an audience of more than three hundred in New York. Yet, on the evening of 28 March 1946, we were to be at least four times that many in the huge auditorium at Columbia University known as McMillin Theater. To be sure, it was the first such manifesta-tion, as the French say, since the war, and the three lecturers were named Vercors, Thimerais, Albert Camus.

The Silence of the Sea, published here by Pantheon in French and in English, and variously attributed to all the great French writers from whom we had felt so dreadfully cut off for four years, had established overnight the reputation of the pseudonym "Vercors." "Thimerais" re-

mained unknown, for his moving essay entitled *La Pensée patiente,*
which the Editions de Minuit had clandestinely published and circulated in 1943, had not yet reached us.

But many already knew that Albert Camus, at the age of thirty, had
brought out a novel (*The Stranger*) that was greatly admired in France,
an essay with a very strange title, and two plays. A few Americans
in uniform had come back with copies of the newspaper *Combat,* of
which Camus was said to be one of the founders.

This was about all that New Yorkers knew about the three young
Frenchmen who were to speak on the 28th of March. But everyone was
eager to hear French spoken again and to see in flesh and blood some
survivors of the black years of the Occupation. M. Claude Lévi-Strauss,
Cultural Counsellor of the French Embassy at the time, had the idea
of holding the meeting under the patronage of an interuniversity
committee, and, inasmuch as I had just shed my uniform to resume
duties as an associate professor of French at Columbia, he named me
chairman of the committee.

Consequently, Vercors, Thimerais (whose real name, Léon Mot-
chane, is better known among physicists and mathematicians than
among literary people), and I picked up Albert Camus in midtown to
arrange for the symposium. It was already announced as "The Crisis of
Mankind" and the title must certainly have been Camus's. The day before the big show at Columbia, the four of us went up to Camus's room
in one of those mothy hotels on upper Broadway. I shall never forget the
utter simplicity and the smile, reminiscent of a Paris street urchin, that
distinguished the youngest among us, nor the admiring glance cast at
him by an attractive girl in the elevator. The moment we were in his
room and the athletic young man had stretched out on the bed with
a few notes in front of him, he easily dominated the group.

And the following evening, however eloquently the two others spoke,
Camus easily dominated the debate. Making no distinctions between
victors and the vanquished in the war, he rapidly sketched a horridly
debased conception of man that was, he said, the legacy of World War
II. Had not *all* of mankind, forgetting ancient ideals, descended to the
very vilest means in its intramural strife? But with his conviction,

and with his unassuming, youthful manner, the moment he launched into his unflattering subject—which permitted examples drawn from Algiers, Auschwitz, the streets of Paris and Madrid—it became apparent that he was in fact defending human dignity and asking justice for all. When he told us that, as human beings of the twentieth century, we were all of us responsible for the war, and even for the horrors we had just been fighting (the concentration camps, extermination by gas), all of us in the huge hall were convinced, I think, of our common culpability. Then Camus—who was never one to castigate without embodying an affirmative suggestion in his sermon—told us how we could contribute, even in the humblest way, to re-establishing the honesty and dignity of men.

Just then, one of our students passed up to the stage a note saying that thieves had stolen the receipts, intended for war orphans in France. After Camus's moving remarks, I could do nothing but announce that the "Crisis of Mankind" was at the door and that our charitable endeavor would be of no benefit to French orphans. Fortunately, a man of good will rose in the middle of the audience and proposed that on the way out everyone pay his entrance fee a second time. At once the two girls from whom the little black box had been stolen rushed out to the lobby and set up their box office again.

No one was surprised to learn the next day that the second "take," the only one left, amounted to far more than the first one. After all, Camus had spoken meanwhile and everyone had left under the spell of his persuasive words. One of the other speakers, back in Paris, told the story to the *Figaro,* which published a half-column about it—all to the glory of America, the land of gangsters and of generous hearts.

And it is quite appropriate that Albert Camus should have first addressed his American public, or what was to become his American public, on such a subject. He was at the time still editor-in-chief of *Combat,* which had introduced a new purity and vigor into French journalism. In one of his early editorials he had opposed humanity to mediocrity as if it were quite natural to define mankind by what is not mediocre. And in all of his editorials he had militantly defended the dignity of man and man's aptitude for greatness. "The Camus of

Combat," writes Etiemble, "showed that a journalist can distinguish himself by character while distinguishing the language, making of an editorial or of the humblest article a work of art."

One of the best photographs of Camus shows him standing at the imposing stone in the printing plant of a newspaper. With a pencil in his right hand and the ever-present cigarette in his left, he is correcting one of his editorials while an attentive printer stands beside him ready to run off another proof. Camus looks confident and happy, although working under pressure. Did he not say in the last year of his life that there were two places where he had been supremely happy? One was on stage either acting or directing a company of actors and the other was a newspaper composing room. In both places he belonged to a team working in harmonious effort toward the realization of a specific aim. And in both situations he was likely to be the moving spirit.

Unfortunately, Camus the journalist and polemicist is still inadequately known in America. And yet, throughout his too-short and most active life, he never abandoned the journalism that had been his introduction to writing. In Algiers in 1938, at the age of twenty-five, he had joined the staff of *Alger-Républicain,* and the following year his forthright reportage on the misery of the Kabyle tribes of Algeria had caused a sensation and incurred the wrath of the government. He was even then working on his play *Caligula* and already planning his first novel, *L'Etranger.* Unable to find work in Algiers because of the official distrust of him, he had gone to Paris, early in the Occupation years, to work for *Paris-Soir,* one of the biggest dailies. Now beyond doubt a professional journalist, he may even then have dreamt of one day having his own newspaper marked with his personal stamp. The opportunity came after he joined the powerful resistance movement known as *Combat* in 1942 and helped found the clandestine newspaper of the same name, of which he became editor-in-chief. Despite his postwar position as an editor in the Gallimard publishing house, despite his growing fame from the publication of *L'Etranger* and *Le Mythe de Sisyphe* and the staging of his plays, *Le Malentendu* and *Caligula,* he continued to edit *Combat* until 1947. There it was that he could exert his most direct influence. As one of his young associates, Roger

Grenier, wrote of that period: "The whole administrative staff of the newspaper, the whole team of printers, all those who approached him, even if they had not read his books and were far removed from the world of books, realized fully who Camus was and were comforted and enriched by contact with him."

For several years after 1947, Camus held no regular position in journalism—partly because of uncertain health and partly because his income was then assured by his position with Gallimard and by the royalties from his growing shelf of books and plays. Yet he continued, through occasional articles and speeches, to take a stand in those causes that were dear to him. Then in the autumn of 1955, when the weekly *Express,* for which he had frequently written, became a daily with the impressive collaboration of such as François Mauriac, Pierre Mendès-France, and François Mitterand, he returned to regular journalism, contributing to *L'Express* at least two articles a week. It was then that his statements on the North African problem reached the widest possible public. After *L'Express* again became a weekly, Camus tended to avoid journalistic commitments that would tie him down to frequent deadlines. Still, his name continued to appear irregularly among the by-lines of numerous Parisian weeklies. Until his death in January 1960, Camus was never completely divorced from the career he had begun in Algiers as a youth.

By setting an example of lucidity and courage in facing and answering the questions that torment us, Albert Camus did leave behind a model of superior journalism. Whether read in the newspapers for which he wrote them or in the three volumes in which he collected them under the modest title of *Actuelles* (1950, 1953, and 1958), his articles gave the postwar generation the moral guidance it seemed to need. The very independence of mind that put him on the government black list in 1939 allowed him to attack simultaneously Russian labor camps and American support of Franco. In facing squarely the anguishing problem of Algeria from 1938 to 1958 (one whole volume of *Actuelles* is properly devoted to this) he saw steadily, as only an Algerian Frenchman could, both the point of view of the Arabs and that of the more than a million French in Algeria. And his stirring series of articles on the Hungarian revolt of 1956, the most forthright to appear in France, allowed him to repeat and to document his memorable statement that "None of the evils that totalitarianism claims to remedy is worse than totalitarianism itself." The longest essay in the entire collection is the now famous "Reflections on the Guillotine," in which he vividly and convincingly marshals all the arguments for abolition of the death penalty. But even those pages, with their balanced appeals to reason, to sentiment, and to the senses, are no more moving than the brief evocation of his co-worker in the Resistance, the young poet René Leynaud, executed by the Germans for his patriotic activity.

"The era of chairbound artists is over," Camus once wrote. And, although he did not invent the now-popular term *engagé,* he personified for our time the committed writer. He achieved in his personality as in his work a delicate equilibrium between commitment and aloofness, between the state of solidarity and the state of solitude. As he said in "The Artist and His Time": "Even if, militants in our lives, we speak in our work of deserts and of selfish love, the mere fact that our lives are militant causes a special tone of voice to people with men that desert and that love. I shall certainly not choose the moment when we are beginning to leave nihilism behind to stupidly deny the values of creation in favor of the values of humanity, or vice versa. In my mind neither one is ever separated from the other and I measure the greatness of an artist (Molière, Tolstoy, Melville) by the balance he managed to maintain between the two. Today, under the pressure of events, we are obliged to transport that tension into our lives likewise. This is why so many artists, bending under the burden, take refuge in the ivory tower or, conversely, in the social church. But as for me, I see in both choices a like act of resignation. We must simultaneously serve suffering and beauty."

Obviously Camus's polemical and journalistic articles helped him maintain that personal equilibrium, without which his novels and plays would not be the consummate works of art they are. And yet, as he implies, the same tone of voice is in everything he wrote.

Indeed, the journalistic writings show once again, as does the first novel, that, from the start of his career, Albert Camus wrote with the assurance that belongs to maturity. And the Camus of *Actuelles* (for, despite having translated these pieces under the title of *Resistance, Rebellion and Death,* I can see them and their title only in French) will always make me think of that evening in March 1946 when the young Pascal, or La Bruyère, or Voltaire stood up on the platform and told us off in our smugness and righteousness. It matters little by which of these names we call Camus, because he so obviously belongs among the moralists, with whom the French tradition abounds.

FOCAL CENTERS

Introduction to *From the N.R.F.*, an image of the twentieth century from the pages of the *Nouvelle Revue Française,* edited with an introduction by Justin O'Brien; translated by Angelo P. Bertocci and others (New York: Farrar, Straus and Cudahy, Inc., 1958).

THE "N.R.F."

"Paris was where the twentieth century was," said Gertrude Stein as a justification for her moving there. To be sure, ever egocentric and increasingly provincial, she saw that capital of art and intellect chiefly as the ideal setting for herself and her friends. Yet her awareness, surprising only because of its early date, was based on facts. Years later, Denis de Rougemont, that Swiss-born champion of European unity who is as remote from her Left-Bank parochialism as anyone could be, corroborated her feeling when he stated that during the last half-century "Paris was the geometric locus of the modern adventure." As examples, he cited cubism, Apollinaire, the School of Paris, the Diaghilev ballets, surrealism, the group of "Les Six" in music, Proust, Gide, and Valéry, and their commentators, and their adversaries of every stamp.

Surely it is significant that all the writers he mentions were regular contributors to the *Nouvelle Revue Française,* for no periodical so uniformly symbolized the twentieth century in Europe as it did. Of course, for someone living in Paris and reading all the books as they appeared, attending all the theater openings and concerts and art exhibits, skimming through a score of *avant-garde* publications which expounded as many experimental movements, participating in theoretical discussions and political congresses, perhaps the *N.R.F.* was not absolutely essential. But he who was in Madrid, or Berlin, or New York—anywhere far from the heart of the ferment—could get all this in each issue of that monthly review. Indeed, it reached him edited and classified, for in those pages the intellectual activity of Paris was displayed as in a prismatic spectrum.

This might imply that the *Nouvelle Revue Française* merely reported on that activity, as so many journals are content to do. On the contrary, it was from the beginning both a center of literary creation and a critical review. Beside its essays and shorter reviews in which the keenest and most disciplined minds in France commented on the artistic manifestations of the age, appeared novels, poems, plays, stories, and manifestoes by the new writers whom the periodical was constantly discovering. And the eclecticism evident in the make-up of each number, in which quality provided the only uniformity, kept it from ever becoming the organ of a school or clique. Thus even the Parisian who kept up with everything but did not read the *N.R.F.* missed something that his friend in Calcutta or Boston enjoyed. Having visited the new Picasso show, read Céline's novel, seen the latest play by Giraudoux, and attended the riotous demonstration put on by the surrealists, he may have felt that he could forego the *N.R.F.*'s critical comments. At the same time, however, he would have missed Gide's "Open Letter" to Cocteau that was to shape the latter's future, a play by Claudel that would not be staged for a decade, new poems by Paul Valéry or Henri Michaux which might wait years before appearing in book form, and the revelation of a new novelist named André Malraux or Jean-Paul Sartre.

But an informed Parisian who did not read the *Nouvelle Revue Française* is altogether hypothetical. On the contrary, he probably tore open his copy each month with feverish impatience, for the *N.R.F.* regularly offered him literature at its very source—a laboratory in which he could see tomorrow's literature "in the making." Advanced without being sectarian or dogmatic, it soon distinguished itself as the most alert periodical of the age. Its nice balance between creation and criticism and the intimate relationship between each author and his subject made it a model for such reviews in all countries. In London Eliot's *Criterion* and later Connolly's *Horizon,* Unamuno's *Revista de Occidente* in Madrid, and in Berlin the *Neue Deutsche Rundschau* would not have been quite what they were had the *N.R.F.* never existed.

Success was, as always, cumulative. What started with a handful of writers rapidly became the review that set the literary tone in Europe. And, inasmuch as its contributors wanted their books to appear under the same imprint, it gave birth to a publishing house that has since become the most powerful in France. Today there *are* other publishers besides the Gallimard-N.R.F. firm, but Sartre and Camus quite naturally turned to the house that published Malraux and Saint-Exupéry and Montherlant, just as Malraux's generation desired to be included in the same list as Claudel and Gide and Proust. And in mid-century the young writer knocks first of all at the door through which Sartre and Camus have entered. The same is true of English and American writers in translation. They feel really launched in Europe when accepted by the same firm that first issued Conrad, Hardy, D. H. Lawrence, James Joyce, Meredith, and Orwell in France, that introduced Sherwood Anderson, Caldwell, Dos Passos, Faulkner, and Hemingway.

The beginnings were modest enough. In February 1909 a small group gathered around André Gide founded the *Nouvelle Revue Française* for the purpose of re-examining French and European values without the prejudices of any school or party. The title was intentionally noncommittal. The early years were spent largely in the struggle to substitute its new criteria for those of the surviving symbolist periodicals. *L'Ermitage,* for which many of its contributors had written, had recently died, and Paul Fort's *Vers et Prose,* filled with second-generation symbolists, had allied itself with a moribund tradition. On its symbolist left, as Thibaudet said much later, it had *La Phalange* and on its classical right, *La Revue Critique des Idées et des Livres.* The powerful *Mercure de France,* founded in 1890 as an organ of the new poetry and by then dominated by the critic Remy de Gourmont, had already become the prosperous fortnightly of documentation and information that it is today.

Jean Schlumberger, the only survivor among the founders of the N.R.F., has written in *Eveils:* Our understanding did not grow up around a program; rather, our program was the expression of our understanding. We did not boast of a new formula, being beyond the age when genius is thought to reside in magic words. But we had in common a few great admirations, balanced by energetic rejections, and a few principles that must be characterized as both aesthetic and moral. Our bond lay in a way of being, in an ethic, rather than in a way of writing; consequently our unity never partook of the uniform. It did not hamper our individual self-affirmation and brought together new recruits without hampering them either. So that—and this is a rare phenomenon—the impetus given by one generation, instead of stopping with it, was picked up by the following generation." The six or seven writers, sharing a common desire to handle all the problems concerning literature and its relationships to life, felt that their contributions when taken together would assume a weight they could not have had in isolation.

For the first two years, Jean Schlumberger—who in his eighties is proud of having designed the swash monogram that has now been used for a half-century—grouped the manuscripts, balanced the contents of each issue, got the numbers out approximately on time—in short, made a regular periodical out of the rich and fragmentary material at hand.

The one among the founders who was to become the most famous never permitted his name on the masthead, yet André Gide was indisputably, then and after the war, the chief mover and *éminence grise* of the venture. "Of all of us," writes Schlumberger, "Gide was the one who took our undertaking most to heart, or rather who had the greatest ambition for it. His letters, notes, telegrams, of that period are full of recommendations, plans, outbursts of impatience, complaints. The gap between what he imagined and what material circumstances made of our issues caused him sleepless nights. He was ready to write addresses, to lick stamps, he would even have delivered the issues to subscribers; but he fell ill over misprints, bad alignments, omissions, unpleasant mistakes." Elsewhere, the poet St.-John Perse, describing the Gide of 1909 in the *N.R.F.* homage to Gide of November 1951, particularly extols "a sense of values that has never failed; an innate sense of the mainsprings and, as it were, the very essence of French genius; a predilection for the human in the written word and of the universal in the individual work; the perception, in everything, of its quality, urgency, and veracity." This is what Gide was for men twenty years younger who, without knowing him personally, "were happy to know that he was there, reference and guarantor of a French literary authenticity."

The new periodical aimed, as it stated in an early advertisement, to group writers of the most diverse nature "but all equally concerned with a discipline." Indeed, discipline and an inseparable austerity soon became characteristic of the *Nouvelle Revue Française*, as can be seen in the three books that best preserve the critical attitudes of those early years: Gide's *Nouveaux Prétextes*, Henri Ghéon's *Nos Directions*, and Jacques Rivière's initial volume of *Etudes*. To avoid the slightest suspicion of mutual indulgence, for instance, the group established the unwritten rule never to review books published by its members. Such scruples were so unthinkable that no one noticed them, yet that rigor explained much of the specific character of the *N.R.F.*, which early earned for it (despite the fact that most of its writers were Catholics) the epithet of "Calvinistic." Of course, as time went by and review and publishing house produced an ever greater share of the literary production, that rule was of necessity forgotten.

By February 1912—that is, after its first three years—the periodical had but 528 subscribers and distributed 244 complimentary copies. No wonder that Gide, Schlumberger, and Gaston Gallimard (who served both as business manager and head of the new firm under the *N.R.F.* imprint) had to contribute a third each to meet the deficit. Yet by September 1913 the editor could claim 3,000 subscribers.

But circulation statistics tell very little as to a journal's standing and influence. Much more important is the fact that in early 1914 Marcel Proust, who never doubted his genius, wrote a friend that the only periodical in which he was eager to see fragments of his work appear was the *N.R.F.* Obviously he could feel that way simply because he wanted to be associated with the writers who would dominate the future. And he was not wrong. During the days before 1914, Jacques Copeau as editor, ably seconded by the very young Jacques Rivière as managing editor, published the early work of a whole generation of new writers. The names of François Mauriac, Jules Romains, Jean Giraudoux, Georges Duhamel, St.-John Perse, and Valery Larbaud stood beside those of their still inadequately known elders in the monthly table of contents. The ability to attract the best among the young, together with the stimulating ideals expressed in Schlumberger's initial editorial, did more than anything else to introduce fresh air into the stuffy Parisian literary circles and to effect what might be called the revolution of the years 1909 to 1914. Incidentally, it also identified the *N.R.F.* as the extreme promontory of French letters. For example, Jean Cocteau—although his own early poetry was severely criticized by the review for its lack of discipline—now looks back on that period of his youth when he "dreamed of someday entering the noble, often sinuous, dance led by the *Nouvelle Revue Française.*"

Like most other serious periodicals in France, the *N.R.F.* ceased functioning during the World War. When it resumed in June 1919, its unique place in modern literature was already assured by the far-sightedness it had shown in the early years of struggle. Many of its discoveries had become, or were well on the way to becoming, major figures of modern letters. Four of the founding group had dropped out: Henri Ghéon because of his conversion to Catholicism and almost exclusive interest in hagiography, Michel Arnauld (Marcel Drouin by his real name) through devotion to his profession as a teacher and a kind of atrophy of his creative talent, André Ruyters for business considerations that took him to Abyssinia and China, and Jacques Copeau through complete absorption in his revolutionary Théâtre du Vieux-Colombier. But Jacques Rivière, fresh from four years of meditation in a German prison camp, assured an inner continuity by taking over the editorship. At his shoulder stood two of those mature and consummate artists who had labored with him before 1914, to whom must be added the most fervent of the early recruits.

Never was a man more ordained by nature to direct such a periodical. Rivière's keen and subtle mind, in which the rationalism of his elders was tempered with emotion and sensitivity, and his catholicity of taste combined to make of him the ideal guide and counsellor. During the six years of his editorship—for he died in 1925 at the age of thirty-nine—he recruited from his own generation more than a score of writers who were to remain with the review. At the same time, he never failed to discern the special new qualities of the younger men. For instance, just during the first half-year from June through December 1919, he published a new play by Claudel, fragments of Proust's work in progress, Gide's *Symphonie pastorale*, and poems by Paul Valéry, while reserving a large place for those his own age and younger, such as Giraudoux, Martin du Gard, Montherlant, and Romains. In 1921 he brought out some of the first poems by Raymond Radiguet, then eighteen years old. He never spared his advice, his encouragement, or his time; and his innumerable long-hand letters to contributors, when they turn up now in autograph-collections, amaze by their perspicacity and tact. As Valery Larbaud wrote in the special volume of *Hommage* that the *N.R.F.* issued after his death, "We always wrote partly for him, who remained our critic and judge. We were concerned, eager to know his opinion, and overjoyed when that opinion was favorable, for it was the judgment of a subtle, reflective mind untouched by fashions, which never let itself be misled or taken by surprise."

The younger writers he discovered saw him pick up their manuscripts as if duty-bound toward them. "Even the young he rejected," wrote the young Jean Prévost, "he enriched with advice. He improved those he accepted almost without their knowing it. His system was to urge each in the direction of his own personality, to bring out and praise the best of what was offered him." Indeed, his published correspondence with Proust shows that he managed to advise even that supreme individualist.

In April 1925, Jean Paulhan, one of those whose talent Rivière had discerned, succeeded Rivière. An even greater eclecticism and a marked preference for the exceptional (or *goût du monstre* as one of his admirers put it) led him to broaden further the review's interests and keep it in the vanguard. To be sure, the times worked obscurely to help him in this regard, for the insidious spread of the totalitarian ideal and the headlong rush toward a second World War beset the writer with new dangers and fresh problems that he could not ignore.

While maintaining the allegiance of those brought to the *N.R.F.* by Rivière, Paulhan attracted an equal number of still younger writers. In 1926, for example, he published the first writing of the twenty-five-year-old André Malraux, and after that each of Malraux's powerful novels originally came out serially in the review. Many poets who won general appreciation only after the last war were likewise available to *N.R.F.* readers at the outset of their careers: Francis Ponge in 1926, Henri Michaux in 1927, and Georges Schehadé in 1933. Paulhan revealed the young novelist Marcel Aymé as early as 1927 and in 1936 Raymond Queneau, now a prolific writer and editor of the Gallimard firm. During those years Paulhan's exigence earned him the nickname of "the writer's conscience." One youthful critic tells how at a weekly reception in the editor's office Paulhan drew his new contributor out onto the terrace overlooking the rue de Beaune to tell him, "I've read your manuscript. It's quite good. But it's not just right. In other words, it's not *you*. You'll have to rewrite the whole thing." Under such scrupulous guidance, the *N.R.F.* rapidly consolidated its position as the literary organ of a whole generation.

In June 1940 Jean Paulhan brought out his last issue at the moment when France was falling before the Nazi onslaught, and the old *N.R.F.* expired simultaneously with the civilization it had faithfully reflected. Later that year, the Vichy government and the German authorities attempted to annex the periodical by placing at its head the Fascist-minded Pierre Drieu La Rochelle, who remained as editor until his suicide in 1944 as he was about to be judged by his countrymen.

Because of that final tawdry chapter, the National Council of Writers outlawed the *N.R.F.* even to its title. However, once the excesses of the *épuration* were past, the Gallimard firm was able to revive on its publications the glamorous three letters, still in the original monogram designed by Jean Schlumberger. During that time a postwar multiplication of literary reviews resulted from a comprehensible desire to divide up the former empire of the *N.R.F.*, in which there had been enough substance to nourish several periodicals. Finally, in 1953 the monthly was resurrected as the *Nouvelle Nouvelle Revue Française* (with the first *Nouvelle* in smaller type) under the joint editorship of Marcel Arland and Jean Paulhan. Today, though it does not enjoy quite the exceptional position of its predecessor, the *N.N.R.F.* remains decidedly one of the most stimulating monthlies in Europe. Naturally its table of contents, like its format with the wide-spaced printing in black and red on an ivory cover, is faithful to the pattern established by Gide, Copeau, and Rivière.

The great years of the *N.R.F.*'s full maturity and widest influence, then, coincide with the two decades between the wars. In all domains of thought and activity those were decades of crisis. Unrest characterized the twenties, during which the relief of the war's end and the elation of victory gave way to uncertainty and disquiet as the European search for new criteria to take the place of lost prewar values often assumed the form of frantic improvisation and varied experimentation. International uncertainty only increased while the League of Nations sought to maintain newly established boundaries and statesmen of every country made concessions in favor of fresh alliances. And as economists juggled with the problems of reparations and war debts, inflation spread with devaluation following devaluation. Eventually the financial crash of the early thirties destroyed even the newly made fortunes. Simultaneously, labor continued seething after the successful general strike of 1920 until it was able to dictate to the Popular Front government in 1936 through a series of sit-down strikes.

To the restlessness that marked the twenties and continued into the thirties was added a new anxiety as premonitions of war multiplied. Gradually a pervasive *malaise* inspired by the past found its justification in the grim vision of the future. Caught between Fascism on the south and Nazism to the north, France saw Mussolini attack Abyssinia at about the same time that the Saar plebiscite voted for annexation to Hitler's Germany. In another year, the Nazi occupation of the demilitarized Rhineland coincided with the outbreak of civil war in Spain. Finally, in 1938 when Hitler seized Austria and the British and French governments abandoned Republican Spain to Mussolini, every Frenchman must have seen war as inevitable. Even at the time, the Munich agreement later that year seemed merely to postpone the clash, and the actual declaration of war in September 1939 surprised no one.

During those two decades, Europe passed almost imperceptibly from a general state of physical and moral restlessness to a predominantly political and social anguish. If a single word had to characterize the whole span of twenty years, "unrest" would be more comprehensively appropriate than "anxiety."

Literature and the arts quite naturally reflected the attitudes of the age. Goaded by insecurity, artists and critics produced varied riches and lively intellectual controversy, while tending ever toward deeper involvment in political and social problems. Because of their geographical position and their traditionally analytical minds, the French were the closest and most cogent witnesses to the significance of the twentieth century. But fortunately they were not satisfied to witness; their entire heredity led them also to interpret—and hence to guide. Already in June 1919, Rivière could write in his initial essay after the first war: "We intend to be a critical review: to discern, to choose, to recommend. . . . We think we perceive that direction which the creative instinct of our race . . . is about to take."

Many of the functions of discernment and choice that the editor claimed for his publication early became apparent chiefly in the selection of creative works it published. And, however eclectic that choice was, an impressive majority of the *N.R.F.* writers have joined the ranks of the great. Just as it once could be said that the conservative *Revue des Deux Mondes* was the antechamber of the French Academy, so publication in the *Nouvelle Revue Française* brevetted many a young author. Critics of the review used to accuse if of recognizing real ability only in its friends, though it might more easily have been pointed out that it accepted as friends only those who had real ability. During the extensive demolitions carried on immediately after the armistice—in which the dadaists were but the most violent of the wrecking crews— most of the solid prewar reputations were destroyed. To the young of the twenties, Barrès, Bourget, Anatole France, all the symbolist poets, and all the dramatists might as well never have lived and written. To replace them, four writers, previously unknown or appreciated by but a small group, suddenly appeared. To the advantage of not being associated in the public mind with the prewar period, they added that of nevertheless being old enough to serve as masters for the young. And all four of them were closely identified with the *N.R.F.*—Claudel and

Gide from the very beginning, Proust and Valéry since 1917. With such authors both on the Gallimard "list" and in the periodical's table of contents, the *N.R.F.* could have afforded to leave the exceptional manifestations to the "little magazines." Still, as a critical review, the *N.R.F.*, while frequently taking a general inventory of new values and attempting to define the period, showed an interest even in the most eccentric movements and sincerely encouraged those among them that promised the most positive contribution.

Both Rivière and Paulhan, in fact, were singularly open to the new and hence disinclined to rely on their capital resources. For instance, an advertisement for the periodical published in a Gallimard book catalogue in 1936 read: "Just stop to think what contemporary review would accept, if they had just been written, *Gargantua* and *Candide*, *Une Saison en enfer* and Saint-Simon's *Mémoires*, *Le Rêve de D'Alembert* and *Les Fleurs du mal?* And how naturally they would fit into the *N.R.F.* But the *N.R.F.* is not merely an anthology, however interesting and lively. Criticism occupies a major place in it; none of its choices is devoid of commentary and justification. Going out to meet the future with the greatest possible freedom and the most possible reflection, the *N.R.F.* agrees with André Gide that 'French genius is constantly being newly vitalized, and the sap naturally rises to the tip of the twig.' "

As time went on, the contributors to the review—like the rest of the world—lost some of their dispassionate attitude and tended to become involved or, as their admirers might say today, "engaged." In his initial essay of 1919, Jacques Rivière predicated a total separation between literature and politics, hoping that the group of thinkers he was beginning to guide would manage to remain "both writers without a political bias, and citizens without literary prejudices." But here he failed to foresee the evolution of the times; in the socially conscious thirties it became virtually impossible for the articulate intellectual not to voice his opinions. Yet even then he did not become so involved as to lose his critical sense, if it is possible to generalize from one of the most amusing pages of André Gide's *Journals*. In 1933 a young Communist brought the older writer, who had by then declared himself on the side of Soviet Russia, an article that had been refused by Paulhan. Despite the young

Comrade's invoking the interest of the party and threatening Gide with unspecified reprisals, the founder of the *N.R.F.* categorically refused to force the editor's hand. But the pages of the *Nouvelle Revue Française* itself provide many a more subtle example of the functioning of the French *esprit critique*.

For, no matter how much prestige and popularity it gained through regularly publishing the best imaginative literature, the periodical was first of all a critical review. Rivière and Paulhan were themselves primarily essayists and critics and must have devoted the greater part of their attention to that section of each issue, counting for at least a third of the total number of pages, devoted to essays and critical comment. In addition, the main group of five or six major contributions to each number almost invariably included two longer essays. After all, most of the imaginative writing came in without being specifically solicited, whereas the book reviews and general articles of literary, theatrical, and artistic intelligence had to be commissioned. Through such assignments, the editor was able to form his own corps of critics, and it is only human for an editor to have a warmer feeling for the writing that he himself evokes. It is obviously easier to suggest subjects even to the most independent essayist than it is to give a plot to a novelist or a theme to a poet.

Jean Schlumberger tells in *Eveils* how jealously the group of founders in the early years protected the review section—their fortress whose positions only they could defend adequately. "We were most circumspect," he says, "about introducing among our reviews those of a few invited guests. They never assumed the tone that struck us as just right: too adulatory or too diffuse or too lyrical. And, besides, we had to handle them with gloves to get them to change a sentence." That was true in the beginning, but after 1919 many newcomers from Thibaudet to Crémieux, from Arland and Malraux to Sartre and Grenier caught the proper tone at once and even helped to pass it on to the best critics of today. In this sense as much as in any other, the *Nouvelle Revue Française* may be said to have formed several generations of writers.

A primarily critical review aiming "to discern, to choose, to recommend" must reserve space for the works of imagination it has chosen—

if only for exemplary purposes. But the guiding principle of the periodical can be seen more explicitly in its exposition and commentary, to which the editors of the *N.R.F.* consistently devoted at least half of each issue. And that expository prose, in all its diversity, shows the French mind at its best: judging men and events, trends and movements, parties and credos, books and paintings and symphonies. It illustrates how the Parisian intellectual first responded to Freud, to Proust, to the young Malraux, to Picasso; how Catholic and existentialist viewed Bergson, and a Thomistic philosopher viewed Franco's war; how the Fascist, the conservative, and the Communist envisaged the invasion of literature by politics. In other words, it provides a new perspective on the troubled twenties and thirties as seen by a group of eminent witnesses, many of whom served also, by those very essays, as catalytic agents in the restless ferment that produced the present.

Letter to Sylvia Beach on the publication
of *Shakespeare and Company* (New York:
Harcourt, Brace and Company, 1959). *The
Reporter,* October 1, 1959.

SHAKESPEARE AND COMPANY

Dear Sylvia,

Your book is a delight. It will be widely read by all those interested
in Joyce, Hemingway, Scott Fitzgerald, etc. And by those who par-
ticipated, even in a small way, in the mad twenties. Besides, how could
anyone concerned with Franco-American relations possibly ignore it?
You know that we are legion; just think of the excitement recently
caused by your exhibit of the "Années Vingt" so handsomely staged
by the United States Embassy in Paris. I should certainly review it if
I could only think of a way of handling so personal a volume of
memoirs.

For the tone of voice throughout your book—and this is what makes
it so attractive—is inalienably yours. While reading it I felt that you
were simply talking there across the table. In telling of your first meeting with Joyce in the summer of 1920, for instance, you throw in this
paragraph:

"There, indeed, was Ezra, stretched out in a big armchair. According
to an article of mine in the *Mercure de France,* Pound was wearing
a becoming blue shirt matching his eyes, but he wrote to me immediately to say that he had never had blue eyes at all. So I take back the
blue eyes."

That is precisely your modest, charming self that your friends have
long admired. But how you manage to get it down on paper without
spoiling it remains a mystery. The same quality is apparent in the de-

licious story of how you succeeded in passing off on Frank Harris a copy of Louisa May Alcott's *Little Women* as exciting "hot stuff" for train reading. It is also present in your account of the dinner with Arthur Symons and Havelock Ellis, the one regaling himself as a *fin gourmet* and the other limited to mere vegetables and plain water. As it is in the story of the distinguished-looking lady in black bowing like royalty to everybody at the opening of George Antheil's *Ballet-Mécanique* in 1925—who turned out to be your own concierge and naturally knew everyone.

This is about where I came in, Sylvia. Our first encounter took place just after my freshman year when, like most alert Americans in Paris, I dropped in at 12 rue de l'Odéon, under the hanging metal sign representing a Frenchified Shakespeare, to buy a copy of *Ulysses*. That was a reprint of the original *Ulysses* in 732 pages with several misprints per page, which you had labored so to bring out in Paris after it had been banned in all English-speaking countries. Quite an adventure to smuggle it through our customs, but no self-respecting traveler dared return without one. No wonder that Lawrence sent emissaries as imposing as Richard Aldington and Aldous Huxley and finally came himself to urge you to publish *Lady Chatterley's Lover!* Your paragraph explaining why you couldn't take on that assignment would be more convincing if you had stressed that Lawrence's novel, already published in Florence in the same circumstances that had governed your issuing of *Ulysses,* did not really need your services.

As you doubtless recognized even then, I really belonged on the other side of the rue de l'Odéon because of Adrienne Monnier's Maison des Amis des Livres at No. 7, which specialized in the best of French literature. Both you and Adrienne maintained circulating libraries—a very new idea in France at the time—and neither of you ever compromised as to the quality of the books you lent and sold. The photographs of writers cluttering the walls of your two shops clearly indicated in advance who were your private gods. And many of us suspected that occasionally photographs and gods crossed the street.

But your gods were not always mine. (I wish I had been there when Jack Kahane arrived and asked about Joyce: "How's God?") Naturally your memoirs center about Joyce—after all, you were his closest friend and only publisher for many years, during which anyone could see him sitting by your desk and conferring with you—but your readers will be grateful to you for providing such a general picture of the twenties and thirties in Paris. We didn't always get from you the Contact Editions, the limited publications of Harry and Caresse Crosby, the *Transatlantic Review, This Quarter,* or *transition* (of which you tell the stories here), simply for their fragments of *Work in Progress.*

I, for one, am grateful for every word you say about André Gide, Valery Larbaud, and Jean Schlumberger, ever ready to spring to the defense of your idealistic endeavor with subscriptions, funds, and private readings.

By the way, you know as well as anyone that Gide's *Geneviève* was not a play (p. 211), that Léon-Paul Fargue was not one of the official founders of the *Nouvelle Revue Française* (p. 150), and that Musset's famous line, which Valéry claimed not to understand, does not read as you give it (p. 159).

But such slight inaccuracies would naturally pop up in your conversation, as in anyone else's. Especially in yours, Sylvia, since you talk of so many disparate things here. What is much more important, you have preserved in your writing the best of your conversation—the gentle, precise tone of voice you inherited from that long line of Presbyterian ministers and took over to Paris during the First World War. No one with such sharp features as yours has ever spoken with such uniform kindness of his friends and enemies.

What a shame that so many are gone who contributed to the exciting literary life of those days! Adrienne Monnier would particularly have reveled in your account and, inviting a group of writers to her apartment, would have celebrated its appearance with one of her incomparable roast chickens preceded by the familiar *quiche lorraine* that you have forgotten to mention.

Your recent honorary doctorate from the University of Buffalo, while it can't altogether substitute for such intimate ceremonies, has the advantage of telling a larger public how you served, during those twenty years until your friendly shop was closed by Nazi intervention, as an ideal cultural ambassadress for things American and British. Even though "comparisons are odorous," as your partner's Dogberry says, it is hard to imagine a British Council or a USIS doing so effectively what you did in our beloved Sixth Arrondissement. I wish I could think of a way of reviewing your fascinating book.

Cordially,
Justin O'Brien

THE THIRTIES

The Symposium (New York University),
July 1932.

VALERY LARBAUD:
COMPLETE MAN OF LETTERS

Of the few living French writers who deserve to receive some recognition outside of France only about half have met with any appreciation in America. Though Valery Larbaud most certainly belongs in this group, it is no exaggeration to say that he remains utterly unknown in this country. And this is all the stranger when one reflects that he has more claims to our attention than almost any of his countrymen: besides being a great creative writer, he is one of the most significant *anglicistes* of this generation and in this capacity he was the first to introduce Francis Thompson, James Joyce, Conrad, Thoreau, Edith Sitwell, Ernest Henley, and Chesterton to the French, and he has written one of the best studies of Walt Whitman in any language. He also enjoys the distinction of being the most successful exponent of a style of writing which, originating in France, has since the publication of *Ulysses* become the monopoly of English and American writers: the interior monologue.

Most well-informed Parisians would be surprised to learn that Valery Larbaud is not so familiar to readers on this side of the Atlantic as Marcel Proust, Paul Valéry, and André Gide. For of these four men, unquestionably the outstanding figures of the last twenty years in France, Larbaud is the most eminently translatable, the one who would seem least Gallic to an Anglo-Saxon audience. [Although they cannot be considered as of the same generation (Larbaud was born in 1881, Gide in 1869, Proust and Valéry in 1871; and this difference of ten years is most significant when one considers the literary importance of the 'nineties), they must be grouped together as spiritual peers.]

Though his fame has not spread to the United States, Larbaud's works have been translated into almost every European language including the Czech, and in South America, where he has for years contributed a weekly article in Spanish to *La Nación* of Buenos Aires, he is the arbiter of literary taste. And yet, free from the necessity of earning his living and as devoid as a literary man can be of vanity, he has never lent himself to publicity. He set out in the very beginning to write for "the happy few"; and unlike most of his contemporaries, he has consistently avoided the innocuous social advantages that usually accrue to a name distinguished in the world of letters. In *Ce vice impuni, la lecture* he gives an admirable description of the spiritual brothers to whom he addresses his works:

"Poor *élite* of the incommunicable secret, *élite* without temporal authority, insignificant in number, divided into very small groups scattered among the various linguistic domains. And yet it continues to exist from century to century, and eventually its critical judgments always force themselves upon the masses. The truth is that it is one and indivisible in spite of national boundaries and that literary, pictorial, and musical beauty is to it as true as Euclidian geometry is to the common run of minds. One and indivisible because in each country it represents at one and the same time what is most national and what is most international: what is most national, since it incarnates the culture that formed the nation; and what is most international, since it cannot find its equals, its intellectual level or its spiritual atmosphere except among the *élites* of other nations: birds of a feather flock together."

Although the frequent reprinting of Larbaud's early works proves that he has not altogether succeeded in escaping popularity in his own country, he has been most successful in creating for himself a cosmopolitan group of admirers. If the Larbaud Club, whose foundation Paul Morand has suggested to take place fifty or a hundred years hence, were to be formed today, it would enscribe Edmund Gosse, H. G.

Wells, and Arnold Bennett as the founders of the English group, the critic Ernst Robert Curtius as the president of the German chapter, the novelist Ramón Gómez de la Serna and the critic Enrique Díez-Canedo to represent Spain, James Joyce and James Stephens for Dublin, and the Italian group would be so large that it would include the whole *mondo letterario* and consequently would be immediately disbanded by Mussolini. The direction of the Parisian headquarters would probably be disputed by Gide, Valéry, Morand, and Giraudoux, with Crémieux, Charles Du Bos, and Frédéric Lefèvre occupying the executive positions.

The very thought of a club devoted to the admiration of Larbaud is an indication that, as Crémieux has said, what interests us most in Larbaud's work is Larbaud himself. This statement is slightly misleading, for it is not the author's superficial, social personality that interests us, but rather his profound, human personality. The same consideration prompted the formation of what is perhaps the most famous of such *chapelles:* the Stendhal Club. Nor is it purely fortuitous that the reader's reaction to these two writers should be very much the same. At a hundred years' distance, both Stendhal and Larbaud approach their work in the same state of mind, their attention directed almost exclusively to the interior rather than to the exterior world. Though the manner in which each utilizes his observations often differs from that of the other, they are both primarily psychological analysts. This preoccupation invariably begins in introspection and develops into an interest in the mental processes of others and finally, when it is expressed in literature, into a method of characterization. It will always remain impossible to determine just how much of Stendhal, or Proust or Larbaud there is in Julien Sorel, the Baron de Charlus or Barnabooth, but this will never prevent us from feeling quite certain that each has modeled his characters largely in his own image—that is, in the image of his essential personality divested of its accidental peculiarities.

To do this one must be extraordinarily familiar with one's own image: hence the desire to be a bit more intimate with oneself than the ordinary man is with himself, the need of knowing oneself *en profondeur*. Montaigne and Rousseau portrayed themselves in order that others might know them precisely as they were; but Stendhal was the first man to write his autobiography for the purpose of getting to know himself. At the age of forty-nine, between the writing of *Le Rouge et le noir* and *La Chartreuse de Parme,* he began *La Vie d'Henri Brulard* with the following reflection: "I ought to write my life: then perhaps I shall know, in two or three years when this is all over, just what I have been, gay or sad, a great intellect or a fool, a courageous man or a coward, and in short, happy or unhappy."

Larbaud, to whom the keeping of a notebook is as important as it was to Stendhal, has similarly always sought to achieve what he calls *self-sapience.* This egocentric point of view with its accompanying analytical method, permitting the author, and in turn the reader, to become more intimate with his characters, is precisely what gives every reader an opportunity to recognize himself in Larbaud's works. Accustomed to considering fictional characters as the reflection, more or less distorted, of living human beings, one suddenly comes upon characters who are reflected in a triple mirror, so that, seeing them in the round, one can better observe them and know them more intimately than one can know anyone in life except oneself. It is moreover due to this quality that Stendhal's protagonists seem to us men and women of our own epoch.

With great penetration Paul Bourget in his earliest essay on the subject discovered the link between this phase of Beyle's nature and his cosmopolitanism: "When carried very far, the analytical attitude almost always ends in dilettantism. The same laws govern our intellectual life and our physical life. We are subject to the needs of our faculties, just as we are to the needs of our organs. He who has the gift of analyzing seeks and provokes occasions for analyzing, multiplies his experiences, abandons himself to his emotions, complicates his pleasures, refines his sorrows—emotional manoeuvre which little by little transforms the analyzer into a dilettante. This dilettantism assumes different forms according to the character of the individual and of the epoch. One form which, if not new, is at least often renewed is that which results in the habitual frequentation of foreign countries." And the psychological analyst's manner of traveling "presupposes that rare faculty of creating one's pleasures for oneself and the even rarer faculty of interpreting those pleasures. It consists in submitting one's person to the pressure of a new country, just as the chemist submits a body to the pressure of a new temperature, while observing with a complete absence of prejudice the little pleasures and sufferings which that novelty entails."

Thus Stendhal and Larbaud indulge in a form of dilettantism far more vigorous and saner than that of the *fin-de-siècle* decadents. More fortunate than Henri Beyle, Larbaud did not have to join the army or wait for a diplomatic appointment to see Russia or Italy; his travels began in childhood, and even today he never stays long in his Parisian apartment or his house in the Bourbonnais. He has lived in, and mastered the language of, almost every country in Europe. This is somewhat of an overstatement: Larbaud has *visited* all the countries of Europe, but he has actually lived for a long time in but three countries outside of France: England, Italy, and Spain. He speaks and writes the languages of these three countries and in addition reads Portuguese, Catalan, Rumanian, and German. Consequently his cosmopolitanism is broader than Stendhal's and his example proves even more conclusively the truth of Valéry's remark that the cosmopolitan thinks in all languages and that his linguistic caprices represent the effort of a very strong personality to create for himself a quite personal idiom. Both of these great travelers write their notebooks in a sort of international *coterie-Sprache* invented for the purpose of better conversing with oneself—which, in a modified form, is sometimes carried over to their works of fiction.

It is not odd then that Valery Larbaud, who started the trend toward cosmopolitanism in contemporary French literature with which we are perhaps most familiar in the works of Paul Morand, should have made his literary debut (1908) with a thin volume of poems purporting to be written by a South American millionaire who "sings Europe, its railways and its theaters and its constellations of cities." These vivid images of continental capitals and small towns untouched by tourists are like a series of delicate etchings remarkable for their economy of line and the evocative power of a few significant and well-chosen details. Caviar to the general, these exercises in free verse nevertheless profoundly influenced the poets of Larbaud's generation: Paul Morand, Jules Romains, etc.

Five years later, in 1913, the *Poèmes d'un riche amateur* were reprinted together with the *Journal d'A. O. Barnabooth,* their imaginary author, which was begun in 1902. Writing under a pseudonym and in the first person as Henri Beyle had done, Larbaud presents a keen analysis of his own emotional states. Indeed, the parallel between this work and *La Vie d'Henri Brulard* becomes even more striking when one recalls that Stendhal outlined his autobiography, somewhat humorously, in these terms: "Le plan est: un exalté dans tous les genres qui, dégoûté et éclairé peu à peu, finit par se consacrer au culte des hôtels," for *A. O. Barnabooth* is nothing more nor less than a picture of a twenty-three-year-old millionaire suffering a progressive loss of illusions in an effort to find himself (unlike Brulard, however, he begins with "the cult of hotels" and ends by settling down in domesticity). This is why the younger generation saw in Barnabooth the prototype of the modern man: endowed with an ardent idealism, a solid cultural background, and a fabulous income, he tears himself free from all social obligations and wanders alone throughout Europe striving to solve his spiritual problems. And every time he approaches a decision or a judgment he interrupts himself to dissect his thought and determine just what percentage of vanity, of self-deceit, or of affectation has entered into it:

"The danger, with us men, is that when we think we are analyzing our personality we are in reality creating out of whole cloth a fictional character to whom we do not even attribute our true inclinations. We christen him with the pronoun of the first person singular and believe in his existence as profoundly as in our own. Thus it is that Richardson's so-called novels are disguised confessions, whereas Rousseau's *Confessions* are a novel in disguise. Women, I daresay, do not deceive themselves in this way.

"The image each of us creates of himself: how readily it can be seen at a glance in older men! With me it's simply not yet formed—and that's what makes me believe in the sincerity of my self-analysis. But with the coming of years my character will doubtless crystallize; then

I shall write I without hesitating, in the belief that I know who it is. That is fatal, like death. . . ."

Like the traveling dilettante Bourget characterizes, Barnabooth constantly uproots himself physically and morally, experiencing every possible change of milieu, of habits, and of outlook in a vain effort to dissociate his true personality from fortuitous influences. Love, friendship, wealth, poverty, the various countries he lives in and the adventures he plunges into, constitute a series of laboratory experiments from which he emerges without having been able to isolate the one element that remains constant throughout them all, without having been able to determine, in fact, that such an element exists.

"And while I discuss myself in this manner my life flows on like a story that I am listening to, and my fate impels me at every moment (these ups and downs were foreseen from time immemorial), and without knowing it, I am creating the disease that will some day kill me." Accepting his defeat, he gets married in London and says farewell to Europe as he sets out for the South American ranch where he was born and which he has never seen since.

Just before the war then, Larbaud, with Proust, whose *Swann's Way* appeared in the same year, sounded the keynote of a new literature that was to dominate the postwar period in France. At about the same time Pirandello was doing likewise in Italy. Since everything in the world of physical phenomena is in a state of flux and exists only in relation to something else, these writers directed their attention to the intangible world of the spirit to find certainty and stability. Withdrawing into themselves, they sought reality through a dissociation of the personality; introspection became their tool, and utter sincerity toward oneself, the chief postulate of their art. As we now know, their search resulted only in greater uncertainty and the carrying over into literature of the relativistic attitude prevalent in scientific circles, but their example became the most conspicuous force in the ten years of intellectual restlessness following the cataclysm of the war.

Another very important manifestation of recent growth is simply an offshoot of the same tendency. For this creation of a new literary method based on introspection and glorifying sincerity inevitably led to a desire to trace one's memories back to childhood and to record the spontaneous impressions and desires of a virgin mind: hence the overwhelming popularity of the novel of adolescence.

In this respect too Valery Larbaud was a precursor. His *Fermina Márquez,* first printed in 1910, served as an inspiration, if not a model, for Jacques de Lacretelle, Jean Cocteau, Roger Martin du Gard, Raymond Radiguet, and others who have distinguished themselves in the recapturing of the first fine careless rapture. An extremely delicate portrayal of life in a *lycée,* this novel concentrates upon reproducing the tenuous atmosphere of those years between fifteen and nineteen spent within the shelter of an aristocratic institution just outside of Paris. The frequent visits of the two beautiful sisters of one of the South American boys upsets the whole student body, and the different reactions of the various students to this situation offer an opportunity for profound characterization and psychological notations. There is Santos Iturria, the dashing, sophisticated boy whom all the others imitate and who shrouds himself in mystery by making midnight excursions to Montmartre; there is Joanny Léniot, who "had entered Saint Augustin at nine, hardly knowing how to read. At first he had felt so utterly alone—surrounded by these fellow students who spoke a language he couldn't understand—so like a prisoner, so forsaken that, in order not to feel the horror of his existence, he had begun to work furiously. He turned to study as a man turns to drink: to forget. He was one of those characters on whom boarding school stamps an ineradicable stigma; he sensed this and struggled as best he could against these influences." Then there is little Camille Moûtier, who was so tortured by his classmates that, unable to restrain his desire to cry, he often had to amuse the refectory by making faces that helped him to hold back his tears.

Besides its original subject, *Fermina Márquez* introduced an innovation into the form of the novel, for it is written in a series of episodes whose common denominator is the heroine herself. But the factor that really binds this novel into a whole is far less tangible than this; it is to be found in an extremely subtle unity of atmosphere, a device, if device it be, particularly dear to Larbaud. Because of its novelty *Fermina Márquez* produced a great impression when it appeared; it is doubtful, however, whether anyone would now consider it as successful as Larbaud's subsequent works.

The stories collected in *Enfantines,* for the most part written between 1908 and 1912 but not printed in book form until 1918, clearly indicated the path Larbaud was to follow to his greatest advantage. As the title suggests, he is still dealing with children but this time instead of writing an episodic novel he has given each episode its full value and left it as a short story. Besides, *Enfantines* suffers from no overdelicacy of touch: here the portraitist has abandoned pastels for oils and developed a vigorous, confident handling of the brush so that he never fails to achieve his effect. More than anyone else, Larbaud has penetrated that other world in which children live and been able to evoke its ingenuously fanciful charm. The characters are traced with the same psychological method and the same truth to detail as those in *Barnabooth:* a taciturn, unhappy little girl has a violent "crush" on one of her schoolmates and years later tries to analyze her emotions at that time; a boy, in love with a young shepherdess whose finger happens to be badly cut, spontaneously cuts himself in the same way and is shocked when another of his playmates guesses his motive; three children create a dream world and people it with fantastic creatures; another little boy while waiting for his music lesson discovers a face in the veined marble of the fireplace and endows it with a personality and an existence; and above all that faultless "Portrait of Eliane at Fourteen" in which the author traces step by step the painful awakening of adolescence.

In four of these eight stories Larbaud most vividly recreates that dreamworld that imaginative children elaborately construct as an escape from the adult world surrounding them: the complicated games they play with imaginary companions, the fictitious confidants more real than the parents in whom the child cannot confide, and formed, as it were, by a projection of the child's personality, and finally the inanimate objects that suddenly assume a life of their own. Just as Cocteau did a year ago in his *Enfants terribles,* Larbaud recognized that no picture of childhood could be true which did not begin with glimpses into this mysteriously supernatural realm.

If the reader is ever justified in reading an author into his characters, one can see in these stories a reflection of Valery Larbaud's childhood. Misunderstood, even more than is the usual lot of children, by those about him, he was forced to withdraw into himself and there to cultivate the company of his own thoughts and the scrutiny of his own emotions. Just this unforgettable page on the parent-children relationship:

"School life gave us so many memories which have nothing in common with those of our parents; you would think *they* had forgotten everything about their childhood. . . . And gradually we came to realize that that already old part of our existence which we lived right before them, on their very knees, was almost as foreign to them as our school life: they have a version of it that differs from ours. You would think they had never known us. They tell strangers anecdotes about our early childhood that contain none of the things preserved by our memory. They slander us. You might even think at times that they had appropriated, to apply them to us, children's sayings they had read in books. That makes us ashamed in front of people; but since we are cowardly we laugh at ourselves with the grown-ups." In fact Larbaud *has* put much of his childhood into *Enfantines,* just as he has put his years at the Collège Sainte-Barbe-des-Champs into *Fermina Márquez* and his adolescence and maturity into *Barnabooth* and *Amants, heureux amants.*

Surely this last-named work is Larbaud's masterpiece. Though they are less ambitious than *Barnabooth,* these three long stories, or short novels, have yet to be surpassed for compactness of composition, lyric beauty, and vivid characterization. Here for the first time Larbaud uses the interior monologue form exclusively in two of the stories, "Amants, heureux amants" and "Mon plus secret conseil," written in 1921–22.

This date is significant, for in 1919 he had met James Joyce and immediately afterward he began to read *Ulysses* as it appeared in *The Little Review;* two months before Sylvia Beach's publication of that work in book form, Larbaud delivered a critical lecture on it that was later published in the *Nouvelle Revue Française* and in part in *The Criterion.* This marked the first intelligent criticism *Ulysses* had received. Upon coming into contact with the "stream of consciousness" method that the world then thought Joyce had invented, Larbaud immediately recognized what he had been seeking for years. His success in handling that difficult medium in "Amants, heureux amants" and "Mon plus secret conseil" showed how congenial it was to his nature; to anyone looking back over his earlier works it is evident that Joyce's example merely accelerated his evolution toward complete maturity by providing him with a solution to his problem of expression sooner than he would have found it by himself. In *Fermina Márquez* (1910) there are whole chapters of only occasionally interrupted interior monologue, while *A. O. Barnabooth* (1913) is written largely in the same form (which is there made more natural because it appears in a diary) and three or four of the stories in *Enfantines* (1918) likewise. Consequently Larbaud felt a debt of gratitude to Joyce for having clearly indicated the outcome of his own experiments, a debt he expressed in his dedication to "Amants, heureux amants":

> To
> James Joyce
> my friend, and the only begetter
> of the form I have adopted
> in this piece of writing.

Shortly after this, Joyce revealed that he himself owed the discovery of the interior monologue to Edouard Dujardin, whose *Les Lauriers sont coupés,* published in 1887 and completely overlooked by literary critics and historians, was the first work entirely composed in that form. Having come across the book twenty years before, he had drawn from it the formal inspiration for certain episodes of *Ulysses*. Immediately Joyce and Larbaud set about to see that Dujardin be given credit for his invention; in 1924 *Les Lauriers sont coupés* appeared in a new edition with a preface by Larbaud and it is at present being translated into English by Stuart Gilbert under the title of *We'll to the Woods No More.*

In "Amants, heureux amants" Larbaud dares to ignore conventions and tell a story *altogether* from the inside by suppressing the hand of the author and letting everything be expressed through the mind of the character himself. The interior monologue is an unspoken, unheard flow of thought caught on the threshold of consciousness and *supposedly* set down before it has passed from the crude state to that of organized speech. It is nothing more than a literary form, according to Larbaud's definition, by means of which the reader penetrates the thoughts of a given character and thus learns, from within, the series of circumstances and the atmosphere in which that character is living. But since art implies selection and composition, some organization of this amorphous stream of consciousness must take place before the resulting document can have anything more than a scientific interest. It is in this most subtle composition that Larbaud shows his skill, for while keeping always literally *in character,* he gives life not only to the one who speaks in the first person but also to the other characters and the world in which they live as seen through the eyes of the involuntary narrator. One such "narrator," Felice Francia of the title story, half senses this relation himself:

"In a few years, next year perhaps, I shall see all that as if it had happened to another, whose impulses and errors in judgment amaze and amuse; and my present train of thought, if I can remember it exactly, will give me the impression of a poor, far-off thing, weak, barely funny and pathetic. Then neither she, who so absorbed me, nor the others will count any longer. And even now, if I take the trouble of unraveling what is taking place in me, even now neither one nor the others are trumps in my game. In that sort of game of cards that I play every day with myself and whose stake is my personal satisfaction, that vague self-approbation, that contentment one feels at the end of a well-filled day, they are not trumps; at most face-cards which count for a few points, but which won't make me win. I can play them. And by staying here alone, I do play them. And it will be a curious and rather pleasant feeling when, taking up the cards again some day or other, I turn them over—to play them again immediately. Perhaps especially because of the memories they will call up: the country where that took place, the weather at that time, what I was busy with, what I was doing, the poetry or music that went singing through my head, all the movement of my life in which they were concerned, being the only persons at that time whom I liked to watch live, the only ones sufficiently indifferent in a pleasant way, after all (yes, that's all it is), to share my solitude, the only thin bond attaching me to people."

The manner in which Larbaud evokes the scene of his action in each of these stories is very characteristic; he had already developed the technique in *Barnabooth:* the setting gradually forms itself as its details, for one reason or another, rise to the surface of the stream of consciousness; the device is similar to Browning's in his dramatic monologues, but less artificial. Moreover the setting, together with the theme, determines the atmosphere of the story much as in a poem, so that these stories, laid in Montpellier and Naples, are vastly different in the total impression each produces.

A few of those who have appreciated the advantages offered by this new form of writing *from the inside out* have wisely insisted upon the fact that it is by no means suitable to all subjects. Larbaud has always limited its use to stories or passages whose subject called for such a treatment: the portrayal of a child's mind (and occasionally of an adult but childlike mind) in which dream and reality are inextricably confused; or the realization of the complex and contradictory aspirations of a sensitive young man in whom several natures are constantly struggling for supremacy.

Since *Amants, heureux amants* Larbaud has published but one story, *Deux Artistes lyriques* (1929), in which he employs a more conventional style of exposition. The slightness of its theme and the rich development he has given it, together with its brilliantly sketched south Italian setting, incline one to link it with the essays of *Jaune, bleu, blanc* (1927) rather than with the earlier stories. The latter volume presents, as it were, a group of samples of Valery Larbaud, so many facets of his personality does it reflect. A traveler's notes and letters from Italy, England, Spain, and Portugal interspersed with essays on Paris and what it means to be a true Parisian, philological digressions, humorous *divertissements,* and a delightful dramatic monologue in prose. Many of these literary *hors d'oeuvres* are taken almost directly from his notebook, which always travels with him, but all, no matter what the value of their subject, are finished, polished products. Nevertheless these sketches give us an intimate picture of the author at work and reveal his varied interests. We see here the literary craftsman applying himself to linguistic problems and questions of style, the modern cosmopolitan and his voluptuous manner of identifying himself with the life of a foreign country while still maintaining enough perspective from which to judge it, the discriminating critic and discoverer of talent, and finally the sincere and self-effacing scholar.

A reading of this one volume (though it is by no means advisable as the best way to approach his work) would convince anyone that Valery Larbaud is a worthy counterpart of the Renaissance humanists. Since childhood he has "instinctively sought that supreme delight which consists in the pure and disinterested activity of the mind." And like his predecessors of the fifteenth and sixteenth centuries, he has consistently pursued his passion with a double ardor, so that the scholar in him has always kept pace with the creative writer. As one might suspect from the classical allusions in his works, he is as steeped in the culture of ancient Greece and Rome as he is in that of modern Europe. His vast erudition is matched only by his faculty of nice appreciation. Usually he passes his discoveries on to his friends and occasionally his enthusiasm finds an outlet in a more general form of proselytizing; hence he has come to be known as the great divulger of unrecognized talent. Whether it be a question of a forgotten French poet of the Renaissance or of an Argentine writer of today, he knows just how to launch his favorite—and always with modest dignity, without assuming the pose of an impresario. Besides all the English and American writers he has introduced to France, the Spaniards Ramón Gómez de la Serna and Gabriel Miró and the Italian novelist Italo Svevo owe their French reputation to him. In his articles for *The New Weekly* of London, on the other hand, which he wrote directly in English, he was the first to speak in England of Gide, Claudel, Valéry (four years before *La Jeune Parque*), and Giraudoux.*

---

* Besides his contributions to foreign periodicals he has actively collaborated in the following literary reviews: *La Plume, La Phalange, La Nouvelle Revue Française, Les Cahiers d'Aujourd'hui, L'Effort Libre, La Revue de France, Littérature, Les Ecrits Nouveaux, Intentions, La Revue de Paris,* etc. In 1924, together with Paul Valéry and Léon-Paul Fargue, he founded that superb quarterly *Commerce,* which prints a great part of the writings of its three editors and of Paul Claudel before they appear in book form.

In this capacity of disinterested literary explorer, Larbaud (and in this he again parallels the humanists) is greatly aided by his extraordinary ability as a translator. To him translation at once offers both a means of concretely presenting his compatriots with his discoveries in other linguistic domains and a valuable exercise. Writing is to him a profession which presupposes a long apprenticeship and for the practice of which one must keep in training; the discipline of translating makes a writer more sensitive to the resources and nuances of his own language. As early as 1901 his first translation appeared, a rendering of Coleridge's *Rime of the Ancient Mariner* in unrimed verse. Since then he has translated some of Walter Savage Landor and Walt Whitman and almost all of Samuel Butler, *Erewhon, The Way of All Flesh, Erewhon Revisited, Life and Habit,* and *The Notebooks.* Besides this, he has often published fragments from other English and several Spanish and Italian writers. His authority on matters pertaining to foreign literatures is so widely accepted that no matter who makes a French translation the highest official consecration it can hope for is a preface or a revision by Valery Larbaud. In this way he has sponsored Logan Pearsall Smith's *Trivia,* Coventry Patmore (Paul Claudel's translation), and the recent French version of *Ulysses.* Not long ago, in an attempt to establish "the eminent dignity of translators in the Republic of Letters" and as a preface to a work on the art of translating which he is now preparing, he wrote a beautiful essay on St. Jerome, "The Patron of Translators," in which he put these words into the mouth of the blessed author of the Vulgate: ". . . and in your hours of discouragement and doubt, or of remorse, to recover your self-confidence or to expiate some sin against your exigent Muse, humbly submit again to the yoke, and humbly translate; in a spirit of charity and justice, and for the glory of one of your brothers, translate. . . ."

To a nation unfamiliar with a centuries-old tradition of great creative writers who have found recreation in exercising their hand at translations it may seem incredible that a mature artist should divide his precious time between his own works and those of others. But in seeking a deeper interpretation of his entire scholarly activity—his excellent translations, his patient explorations, and his profound critical studies—one cannot but discern that Larbaud is striving to bring into closer communication the intellectual aristocracies of the various races that inhabit Europe. Whether one considers it from the point of view of this attempt to create an enlightened cosmopolitanism by unifying that scattered spiritual *élite* to which he has always addressed his works or from the point of view of his manifold enrichment of French literature, Valery Larbaud's career follows a single direct course. Though he already belongs to the great French tradition, he will also live as the internationally recognized founder of a new intellectual commerce.

On *Pity for Women* and *Costals and the Hippogriff* (*Les Jeunes Filles: Les Jeunes Filles, Pitié pour les femmes, Le Démon du bien, Les Lépreuses*), by Henry de Montherlant, translated by John Rodker and Thomas McGreevy (2 vols.; New York: Alfred A. Knopf, Inc., 1938 and 1940). *The Nation*, April 23, 1938, and *The New York Times Book Review*, October 20, 1940.

MONTHERLANT: "PITY FOR WOMEN"

French critics have always been kind to Henry de Montherlant. Under the patronage of Maurice Barrès, he returned from the war of 1914 to 1918 to become one of the spokesmen of the young generation. More articulately than the other twenty-year-olds, he expressed the cult of adolescence and the new gospel of sports. Before Sydney Franklin and Hemingway, he distinguished himself in the Spanish bull ring and wrote of it; simultaneously with Giraudoux he sang the praises of the *footballeur*.

Pity for Women is a translation of the first half of a multivolume novel, *Les Jeunes Filles*, which, as anything which deals with the sentimental relations between men and women is bound to do, nourished a great amount of French conversation. Hardly less controversy was elicited by the second half, published in English as *Costals and the Hippogriff*.

Superficially the story of a lusty he-man who takes his pleasure where he finds it and narrowly escapes a twofold punishment—marriage at the hands of one girl and leprosy at the hands of another—this is an infuriating and profound novel. At first it is merely infuriating and there are moments when the patient reader feels like wrapping a wet towel around his head—a feeling which Montherlant, who knows his reader almost as well as he knows his very real characters, has foreseen. But by the time the same reader has finished the first half, he cannot but recognize the author's gift for characterization and his deep insight into human problems.

The book will be called an indictment of woman, of marriage, of charity. It is none of these things, but it is an ultra-stimulating study of relations between the sexes. In France this novel had a tremendous *succès de scandale;* it deserves the same reception here. An ironist, an egotist, a Byronic *poseur,* Montherlant aims to shock. And he succeeds in shocking with his ideas, his situations, and his vocabulary. But the directness, the biting quality, the assurance in analysis, and the rich style suffice to prove him a born writer, *un écrivain de race,* one can say without any hidden reference to his title of Count or to the antiquity of his Catalan-French family, who writes racily. A French critic once described him as a dandy with a grain of jovial brutality and another of systematic insolence.

At seventeen Henry de Montherlant became a rather accomplished bullfighter during his vacations in Spain. With the romanticism of a schoolboy who had learned his lessons well, he saw himself as an ancient worshiper of Mithra, slaughtering bulls and offering them to the sun god. Since then he has come to identify himself rather with the bull—but not with the sacrificial bull. The turning point was marked by his dramatic poem on Pasiphaë. For some time, Montherlant has looked to the casual observer like a fabulous Minotaur demanding his annual tribute of virgins. Now, however, that he has finished his long misogynistic novel, his hunger should be satisfied. It is safe to assume that the Minotaur will not call for a virgin for a long time—at least not for literary purposes.

In the earlier volume we meet Pierre Costals, a young writer full of vanity, cynicism, and insolence, at times supremely caddish, at others oversensitive. To him cling three young girls: a mystic little peasant named Thérèse Pantevin, whose passion for the hero she has never seen eventually turns to madness; the provincial intellectual Andrée Hacquebaut, calling first for a brotherly affection and later for a demon lover whom she unsuccessfully pursues in Paris; and Solange Dandillot, whose cold beauty captivates the seducer. Individual pages attain a lofty level indeed. The interior of the bureau for veterans' pensions, the dismal walk in the rain with Andrée, Solange seen in the bosom of her family, and Andrée's vehement letter accusing Costals of being a Charlus are all brilliant passages.

Costals and the Hippogriff, containing the concluding sections entitled originally *Le Démon du bien* and *Les Lépreuses,* record Costals' struggle with the fearsome hippogriff of marriage. As soon as Solange has become his mistress, she wants something more and, to get it, mobilizes her mother. She marshals her forces cleverly, and just as Costals' pity for women had led him to encourage even his least attractive and most hysterical admirers, the same misdirected charity causes him to toy with Solange's matrimonial inclinations. The subject is obviously farcical: a confirmed bachelor and Don Juan plays with a mistress bent on trapping him into marriage, confers gravely with her mother, consults his lawyer as to the means of breaking the contract later if he should ever come to make it, even writes a letter she could sign before the ceremony which he could later use against her to regain his cherished liberty. At one moment he goes so far as to plan her murder after the wedding, if nothing else avails.

When the cards are most heavily stacked against him, Costals flees— first to Genoa and the opulent arms of Signora Bevilacqua, later to Africa and the animal frenzy of sixteen-year-old Rhadidja. But to Genoa he calls Solange, prolongs the dangerous skirmish far from Mme Dandillot, then sends her home so that he can feverishly write a book about her; from Africa he returns convinced that Rhadidja has made a leper of him and offers to marry Solange if she will take him, disease and all. The game must start all over again. The real lepers, as he lives to discover, are women—*all* women. This is a situation that would have pleased Plautus and Molière. Certain scenes—like that in which he gives Solange a non-engagement ring, when she promises not to talk of marriage, and takes her back as mistress—are high comedy.

But this novel is either more or less than farce. For one thing, the character of Costals keeps it from having a universal application. Possibly Montherlant thinks of Andrée Hacquebaut and Solange Dandillot as summing up all womankind. He admits that Solange may come to bore the reader, but only because she is naturally a boring type. On the other hand, her awakening to womanhood (ugh! says the Minotaur) is most feelingly described; she will bore the reader much less than she did Costals. The unhappy conclusion to be drawn from Costals' experience is that even the most naïve, untrammeled, and voluptuous young girls become Andrée Hacquebauts in time. The hero is really the controversial character: sly and brash, bold yet cowardly, selfish yet often sacrificing himself momentarily, lecherous, brilliant, and childish, he is an individual. As an artist, Costals is convincing: though we cannot judge his work, we know he has the temperament. If you stop to consider how difficult it is for a novelist to make his hero a creator himself, as all novelists sooner or later want to do, and to convince us that he is a bona fide artist, you will recognize at once part of Montherlant's achievement. Living for three things—his literary work, his sexual pleasure, and his illegitimate son—Costals is incapable of real love for a woman.

On the other hand, it is not hard to see Costals as a rather pathetic creature. Despite his successes and his arrogance, he suffers because he is not brutal enough; his pity for the women who cling to him continually makes him transgress against his principles. Happiest when making love to the simple African girl who has no claims upon him, or when hunting his random prey along the Paris boulevards, he is always getting involved in the complications that women artfully weave about him.

Instead of a farce, is this a thesis novel? The unfortunate Appendix (Montherlant has a weakness for such post-mortems), in which the author lays all the ills of society—unrealism, "dolorism," the wanting-to-please, gregariousness, sentimentalism—at woman's door and explains all of woman's sins as resulting from her sense of inferiority, leads one to look through the novel for a thesis. Certainly this is not an anti-marriage tract. As Montherlant himself said in an interview with the novelist Jean Fayard, he would not in that case have chosen "someone so unlikable and out of the ordinary as Costals" for a mouthpiece. No, the only thesis one can disengage from this novel is that an artist of the type of Costals should not marry; and that is not worth disengaging.

Everything comes back to the strange hero, the center of the novel. It is because of his ugly but oddly fascinating character that the novel is first infuriating, then entertaining, and finally profound. When the book appeared in France everyone read Henry de Montherlant for Pierre Costals; that is the danger of making one's hero a novelist. The truth of the matter is that Costals doubtless represents one facet of his creator's personality carried to the extreme. About thirty years ago—when Montherlant was just a child—a very keen French critic, Albert Thibaudet, made this remark: "It rarely happens that a writer who puts himself into a novel makes of himself a living creature. . . . The authentic novelist creates his characters out of the infinite directions of his possible life; the artificial novelist creates them out of the single line of his real life. The genius of the novel makes the possible come to life; it does not resuscitate the real." Costals probably represents Montherlant as he is glad not to be, and in this sense the creation of that hero meant for the author a kind of personal catharsis. This explains why Costals is so real.

On *Selected Essays,* by Henry de Montherlant, edited and with an introduction by Peter Quennell, translated by John Weightman (New York: Macmillan Company, 1961). *The Reporter,* September 14, 1961.

MONTHERLANT: BULLFIGHTER IN THE ACADEMY

When Henry de Montherlant was elected to the French Academy last year, he was, as a special favor and at his own request, excused from the usual formality of announcing his candidature. Many of his immediate elders—Jean Cocteau, André Maurois, Jules Romains—already wore the embroidered green uniform, but they had gone through the formalities, including the deadly visits to the living members. Of the more remote generation of giants, only Paul Valéry had been admitted the first time he knocked; Claudel had lost out to a nonentity and then returned years later; Proust had died too young; and Gide had refrained from knocking. Alone of his age group, which includes Louis Aragon, Jean Giono, Marcel Jouhandeau, and André Malraux, Montherlant was spontaneously *invited* to sit among the Immortals. But, even before reaching the age of sixty, he had seemed eminently eligible for the Academy: as novelist, essayist, and dramatist, he had lived for his writing and produced more than forty published volumes.

Many articulate Frenchmen had seen him as the greatest living writer of France. Gide had spoken of his "undeniable authenticity," and Camus had been stirred by his essays. Romain Rolland and Louis Aragon, both Marxists, declared him to be as thoroughly French as one could possibly be; and Malraux saw him as reflecting the same heroic tradition that he himself embodied. Such unanimity is rare enough

215

in France to warrant special handling, particularly for an intellectual whose title of nobility goes back at least to Louis XIV.

Henry de Montherlant was born in Paris in 1896 of a family of remote Catalan origin established in France in the eleventh century. In 1914, he went almost directly from his Catholic school to the front. Seriously wounded by shrapnel, he began writing, even before the war was over, of his youth and the excitement of battle. Under various Romantic influences, he aimed to develop his personality to the utmost; turning his back on the unrest of his generation, he asserted himself as the champion of vigor, sport, and health.

His first book, *La Relève du matin* (1920), with its glorification of adolescence (the one period when man really possesses a soul, according to him, is between the ages of thirteen and eighteen), was followed by *Le Songe* (1922), a semiautobiographical novel of heroism at the front, and a series of lyric stories and poems singing the beauty of sport, virile energy, and teamwork. In 1925 he fled Paris to seek heroism in cruder countries and crueler climates, spending most of the next ten years in Spain, Italy, and North Africa. There are many advantages, he claims, in cutting yourself off from the world and "placing yourself in a posthumous condition":

"You find out who your real friends are. You find out to what extent your work can stand on its own feet. You see other people doing things and you yourself—although able to do as much—doing nothing: this is a satisfying spectacle. You feel, and know yourself to be, forgotten and this fills you with a mysterious joy; the flattering tongues have ceased to wag and the encircling silence already foretokens the symphonies of eternity. You learn to accept insults from those who know you are too far away to retaliate and, in any case, devoid of social power; soon you approve of such insults, because they are part of the natural order of things; the day comes when you even like them, and perhaps even provoke them. When you come up again after plumbing these depths, you are proof against many things. It is not possible to gain much hold over a man whose ideal is death in life—or at least to be dead to the world, since such a death is, in fact, the true life."

When he did "come up again," he was the author of *Les Bestiaires* (1926, the same year as *The Sun Also Rises*), a vivid novel of bull-fighting and sentiment set in Spain, *La Petite Infante de Castille* (1929), and the essays of *Mors et Vita* (1932)—all revealing the youthful, egocentric romantic, proud of being a member of the exclusive Catalan religious brotherhood of Monserrat, just as he was proud of being, though a Frenchman, a genuine bullfighter.

But in his novel *Les Célibataires* (1934), written after the prolonged crisis of the "hunted traveler," he abandoned his aggressively subjective attitude to handle ironically a theme remote from himself. The ironic mood also dominated his major series of four novels dealing with love and marriage, from *Les Jeunes Filles* of 1936 through *Les Lépreuses* of 1939 (entitled *Pity for Women* and *Costals and the Hippogriff* when they appeared here two decades ago in a two-volume translation). In France the novels caused a scandal. Was this long epistolary account of a young novelist's dabbling in sentiment and sex intended as a tract against women or against marriage? Montherlant had already written in the foreword to a volume of essays:

"Before 1925, I accepted the idea of getting married for reasons of social propriety or even social interest, and I had been on the verge of this kind of action. Now it seemed hateful to me . . . if, as a bachelor, I already found the humbler preoccupations of life a constant nuisance, what would it be like were I a married man? There is a serious way of being philosophically minded, of being religiously minded, and of approaching artistic creation which is incompatible with marriage, at least for certain kinds of men: either my wife would be neglected and would suffer, or the deepest part of myself—my soul—would be ruined, or, more probably still, both would be damaged. Lastly, I wished to remain free to accept any of the possibilities hanging over me: either war, or (if I became a believer) the total form of the religious life, or (in the absence of religious belief) still greater austerity—or again, other, new adventures. In short, I realized in time the madness of forging new bonds for myself, when I had set out to achieve detachment."

Yet, despite the clamor caused by each of Montherlant's books in turn and their attendant success, despite his rather late and dazzling fame in the French theater, beginning with *La Reine Morte* at the Comédie-Française in 1942 and continuing with at least ten plays since then, Henry de Montherlant remains but little read and little known in England and America.

Is he "too French" for our taste? Hardly, for the French themselves don't know what to think of him, except that they agree as to his eminence, saying that, unlike some others, he *deserves* to be in the French Academy. Rather, the paradoxes of his complex personality upset our criteria of judgment. What can we make of an avowed unbeliever who remains a Catholic obsessed with problems of faith (and describes his attitude toward Catholicism as "that of the Mediterranean towards its beaches, now caressing and now retreating. Or, like a cat biting and licking at the same time"); of an ascetic who glorifies the life of the senses, claiming that "the act of carnal possession gives the strongest possible conception of what is called the Absolute"; of a Frenchman who fights in the Spanish bull ring; of an aristocrat who often ridicules nobility and hereditary privilege; of a solitary who consistently extols human brotherhood; of the chief spokesman for the modern cult of early youth who nevertheless "spits on" the self he was between seventeen and twenty-seven; of an intense patriot whose severity toward his country has occasionally made his fellow Frenchmen suspect his loyalty; of a victim of the First World War who permanently maintained himself ready for the next war and rushed to the front in 1939; of a highly successful dramatist who claims to despise the theater as a sort of Punch and Judy show or "the tumbling of clowns"? To these, as to other apparent contradictions in his ideas and behavior, Henry de Montherlant gives an answer in one of his early essays:

"The good life always depends on a balancing of contrary forces, such as the ancients symbolized in Mercury's wand, which consists of two hostile serpents rocking together in love and between them supporting the winged branch. The reason for this is simple; Nature sets us the example. Nature, within herself, makes night alternate with day, heat with cold, rain with drought, calm with tempests; and, within bodies, fasting and food, activity and sleep; but no one argues from this that Nature is incoherent or that her variety leads to confusion. Like her, I refuse to make a choice. I wish to enter ever more completely into the universal law of alternating rhythms and the divine interplay of compensation; to put it in the language of my times, I wish to be effective in all directions. It is a pedantic conception to see the yea and the nay in opposite camps and wearing different coloured jerseys, like football teams."

It might be argued that the French should be as upset by the paradoxes of Montherlant as we are. But they have all his work readily at hand, to recall or consult, whereas we have been offered but samplings and at infrequent intervals. Weidenfeld & Nicolson in London and Macmillan in New York have now embarked upon a uniform edition of his works, and for the first time we have his *Selected Essays,* a collection of his aggressively independent, occasionally maddening essays written between 1918 and 1955 as "an introduction to their many-sided author's point of view." Skillfully selected by Peter Quennell and admirably translated by John Weightman, they preserve in English that haughty, astringent, almost frightening insolence that makes French critics constantly refer to his *ton royal* and his *grandeur.* What he says of Saint-Simon's style in one of his few purely literary essays applies directly to his own:

"But he had the instinct, the antennae of a master-writer, and that is why his style is not dated, like that of authors who adopt a fake peasant or a fake popular speech. It is characterized by a staying power, a verve, a venomousness, a hypersensitivity and a sheer pleasure in the writing which in themselves would be enough to give it life, that is to ensure its success."

On *Verdun* (*Prélude à Verdun, Verdun*),
by Jules Romains, translated by Gerard
Hopkins (Volume VIII of *Men of Good
Will;* New York: Alfred A. Knopf, Inc.,
1940). *The New York Times Book Review,* March 8, 1942.

ROMAINS: "MEN OF GOOD WILL"

There are two classes of readers today: those who have kept up
with *Les Hommes de bonne volonté,* and those unfortunates who have
fallen by the wayside. *Verdun*—the eighth volume in the translated
series—will be read with enthusiasm by both classes and will cause
many of the unfaithful to turn back to the volumes they have missed.
After the present installment no one can fail to await eagerly the appearance of the remaining volumes (the author says there will be eleven
more in French, amounting to five or six more in English), which will
bring this broad chronicle of our time down to the present. Here for
the first time in this series Jules Romains hits his stride.

One bright morning in 1903 a young student at the Ecole Normale
Supérieure, named Louis Farigoule, had a revelation as he was walking
up the slope of Montmartre. There suddenly seemed to be a collective
consciousness in the street filled with horse-drawn cabs, shop displays,
and pedestrians, and he felt mysteriously one with the people and
things around him. Meditating on this mystical experience, he recognized its affinity with the new sociology of Emile Durkheim and Lucien
Lévy-Bruhl, the theories of group-psychology, and the brotherhood-of-
man poetry of Walt Whitman, for this young man was extremely well
read. When a year later he published his first volume of poems, under
the pen name of Jules Romains, he gave it the significant title of *L'Ame
des hommes. Manuel de Déification* in 1910, following closely on the
novel *Le Bourg régéneré* (which showed a collective consciousness being

formed spontaneously through an electric phrase idly scribbled on a public wall), states the metaphysics of his system, since the new social group is to him a kind of god.

In rapid succession poems, novels, plays, and even one movie scenario preached and illustrated the doctrine of the irresistible force of unanimous emotions: love, hatred, wrath, enthusiasm, curiosity—of the extraordinary expansion of one man's idea or emotion when it is shared by a group, and of the progress that the group's thought or emotion, on the other hand, makes in the individual member of the community.

Two of the prose works, one profoundly serious (*Mort de Quelqu'un*) and the other boisterously farcical (*Les Copains*), are accessible in translation and deserve more attention than they have had in America. The former is perhaps the most explicit embodiment of the unanimist theory. In a Paris tenement a nobody dies and the whole novel recounts his posthumous life. For the first time his neighbors become aware of his existence, inquire about him, take up a collection for a funeral wreath. The janitor enjoys an unaccustomed importance since he was the only one to have known the dead man and the first to learn of his death. The old father, summoned by telegram, talks to strangers in the train to Paris, telling them all about his son, creating new groups in which the thought of the all but anonymous Jacques Godard will be prolonged. Finally, a year after he had seen the hearse go by, a young man, ignorant of the identity of the dead man but vaguely recalling that funeral, reflects on death and immortality. Thus a most ordinary death gives birth to a new consciousness in others and creates a group absorbed by a single thought.

By means of a very different technique, *Les Copains* illustrates the same thesis. The seven gay companions decide, over an excess of red wine, that two small French towns, Ambert and Issoire, are not to their liking and must be punished. Arriving then at Ambert in the middle of the night, the pals go to the barracks dressed in top hats, Prince Alberts, and rosettes of the Legion of Honor. The most impressive-looking one introduces himself as the Minister of War and commands the colonel, as a surprise maneuver, to simulate the crushing of a sudden revolution that very night between three and four. Eager to comply, the colonel fills the town with his troops who shoot innumerable blank cartridges; all the inhabitants awake; the streets fill with people; and the excitement knows no bounds. For the first time sleepy little Ambert exists in all its unanimity. After a most unconventional sermon by another of the companions in the Ambert church the following Sunday, which has the same electric effect, and in Issoire the unveiling of a nude statue of Vercingetorix which comes to life and pelts the populace with rotten apples, the seven friends feel that they have avenged themselves on the two harmless communities.

The war of 1914 to 1918 was a terrific shock to young Farigoule-Romains, then professor of philosophy in a *lycée* and chief exponent of the unanimist school of writing. Not that he had failed to see it coming. But when the catastrophe was upon us, he suddenly saw his little group-souls swallowed up in a vast herd movement that trampled on his theories. The theater audience to which he had addressed his stirring "Ode à la foule qui est ici" suddenly forgot its beautiful unanimous thought and joined the general panic in the street. His long poem *Europe*—published in 1916—reveals his bewildered attempt to arouse such dead groups to revolt against the large mob spirit. But the war definitively shattered his faith in the beneficent effect of group emotion and action.

When Romains does introduce unanimism into his postwar works, he uses unanimous thought as a humorous device (that already classic modern comedy *Knock* with its hearty satire of scientific theorizing and of the public's gullibility) or else rather bitterly pictures the individual in revolt against the group, as in the plays *Musse, Boën,* and *Le Dictateur.* In one trilogy, *Psyché,* the group is treated sympathetically, but this time it is a very special group formed of but two individuals, Lucienne and her husband Pierre. Through these three novels Jules Romains traces the growth of a couple's love. From the dim glow of a live coal in a very drab heap of ashes it spurts out bright tongues of flame which finally transform themselves into blue phantoms fluttering above reality. After the intense physical rapture, at once so delicately and so vividly described, Pierre and Lucienne, separated by several oceans, transcend their bodies to join in a psychic union more thrilling than any physical communion. Here the collective soul does possess something godlike, and illustrates, instead of a limitation of the original unanimism to the classic couple, rather an extension of the theory to the realm of psychic probability beyond the confines of demonstrable knowledge. Before this trilogy love played no part in Romains's work, but when he did turn to that subject—which had always seemed to him somewhat shopworn—he produced a startlingly original work. During the early twenties—also the years of his most rollicking comedies which charmed Paris until Giraudoux began writing for the same stage of the Comédie des Champs-Elysées—Romains made a practice, in fact, of periodically adding to our belief in the possibilities of human evolution. It was then, for instance, that he announced and attempted to prove with numerous experiments (which have subsequently served as a basis for Dr. Viaur's tests on the human heart in *The Depths and the Heights*) his contention that we can be trained to see with our pores and thus possess an undeveloped paroptic sense.

Now that he could no longer believe in his original unanimism, Jules Romains's versatile mind, which even in undergraduate days showed a like aptitude in science and in letters, was seeking justifications for his persistent faith in mankind. If human beings could read with the pores of their shoulders (what a boon for the busy critic!) and overcome distance to produce a physical presence by an act of the will, then man was worth educating and struggling for. Little by little his confidence returned and with it an interest in humanity as a whole— that humanity which he has lately sung in his epic poem on the white race, *L'Homme blanc*. Today Romains accepts the human race whether or not it can do tricks with its faculties.

This explains how in *Men of Good Will* he can return to a more mature and more sober version of unanimism. Throughout this hero-less cycle we see and feel the multitudinous life of a great city as no novel has ever made us see and feel it before. The very number of individual characters creates an impression of almost limitless scope, and behind and around those individuals surges the continuous, anonymous crowd. The earlier volumes are punctuated with brilliant chapters devoted to that crowd and its city seen from a godlike point of view between plunges into its amorphous mass to examine representative specimens picked at random. It is not easy to forget the epic descriptions of Paris going to work in the morning, of the express trains approaching through the suburbs, of France staggering under the blow of August 4, 1914.

The first half of the section entitled *Fin d'un monde* concerns Abbé Mionnet's secret mission to Rome on behalf of the French government to discover what the papacy's foreign policy is, and the high point of the Roman chapters is certainly the brilliant portrait of Merry del Val, papal Secretary of State. The second half traces Europe's precipitate course toward war, chiefly as seen by that astute and mysterious observer Maykosen, and reaches its peak in the portrait of Lenin as an exile in Cracow. Playing around these main themes—because Romains deliberately forbids himself to pursue a direct course—are numerous minor themes to remind us of some of the hundreds of characters introduced in earlier volumes. The sex life of Champcenais, of Sammécaud, of the dog Macaire, of the old maid Bernardine, Marie de Champcenais's colorless mysticism (one of the poorer realizations), Quinette's obsession with murder, Jallez's and Jerphanion's reaction to "Agathon's" tendentious summary of the attitude of youth in 1913, and Germaine Baader's superstition provide further documents on the variegated life of the great capital which is the center of *Men of Good Will*.

Unlike Martin du Gard, Romains makes free use of historical figures, putting into their mouths conversations they might have had; the reader thus enters Poincaré's study, sits at the café with Jaurès, and steps aboard the Kaiser's yacht. This liberty became a necessity the moment Romains decided to cover all of life, all types and all activities, and Maykosen's interviews with the great are no more important to the work as a whole than the chapter on little Louis Bastide, who thinks of suicide because he cannot understand mathematics.

But *Verdun,* more than any other section of the series, employs the unanimist technique throughout. The final chapter of *Death of a World* re-created the outbreak of the war; the opening fifty pages of *Verdun* form an essay on the first eighteen months of the war: the initial hopes and disillusions, the eventual settling-in for a long game of patience opposite an apparently unbreakable German wall. Then Romains turns on a searchlight and flashes it up and down the front, at times moving rapidly, at others letting it rest on an individual man or a certain sector. In a trench in Champagne it picks out Lieutenant Jerphanion and on the heights of Vauquois—that horrible slaughterhouse whose description is a masterpiece of objective writing—the schoolteacher Clanricard, now a Lieutenant too. It lights up General Duroure leading a group of deputies on a tour of inspection, and, in a rapid circular movement away from the battlefields, it shows us the Kaiser being interviewed again by Maykosen, the Deputy Gurau and General Galiéni worrying in advance about Verdun, and Joffre in his headquarters assuring Paris that Verdun is safe. The spot to which Romains's searchlight returns most often, until it focusses permanently on it, is Verdun, the most dangerous point on the whole front.

Finally the terrible German bombardment begins and we share the anguish of the French soldiers in the trenches wondering why their artillery does not answer. From this point forward, while the greatest battle of the war continues to rage around Verdun, the only momentary relief comes from the episodes at the rear. Haverkamp, become a munitions-maker and profiteer, lunches with government officials; Jerphanion, in one of the best but least novelistic passages in the whole volume, analyzes with his former classmate Jallez his impressions of the front; Mareil makes love to Germaine Baader. All our old friends among the characters remain remarkably consistent despite the events. Jallez and Jerphanion continue to discuss everything in their often ponderous *Normalien* manner; Quinette is still riding on the subway, meditating new murders behind a dignified full beard; Clanricard is still grappling with moral problems, though in a trench where men are dying like flies; Gurau is still struggling against corruption and ignorance to save his country. The only familiar character who succumbs in the war so far is Wazemmes, whom we saw start life as an apprentice in a painting establishment of the rue Montmartre; Romains is obviously reluctant to kill his characters in the war, although verisimilitude will not permit them all to survive. He knows as well as anyone the terrible toll which the first years of the war took among young intellectuals who had the rank of officers, and in the next volume he will doubtless have to sacrifice Clanricard in order to spare Jallez and Jerphanion, his chief mouthpieces.

Despite the mass of detailed documentation that lies behind this re-creation of the first world war (French military experts have been unable to find any serious inaccuracies in the novel), Romains's point of view is rather that of a civilian than that of a military man. Instead of yielding to the brutal influences of life in the trenches and slipping back into the infectious uncritical attitude of the barracks to which they were presumably all subjected during their military training, his young intellectuals at the front retain their lucidity and analyze their emotions with an admirable if often unconvincing aloofness. Discussing this work with its author last spring, I told him that I could not read it without wondering constantly if my reactions to the horror of war, somewhere in the trenches of the future, would resemble those of Clanricard and Jerphanion. Jules Romains replied: "That's just it! The more young men feel like that on reading my book, the fewer chances there will be of another world war."

That Romains is implicitly opposed to war here, one can see in the irony of his frequent contrasts between the men in the front lines and the officers of the General Staff or of division headquarters. General Duroure's meteoric rise from obscure retirement as a colonel to the command of several divisions in the Vosges, a brilliant and satiric construction based on the study of numerous documents, finds a parallel in Haverkamp's opportune transformation from a real-estate agent to an unscrupulous manufacturer of army shoes and hand grenades. Romains pictures the war not as a tremendous mass movement but rather as a turmoil of individuals and groups spiritually out of contact with each other. Men are little more than passive agents and the war has got completely out of hand. Despite his heroic organization of the defense of Verdun, Pétain is not the master of events; nor is Joffre, in his headquarters at Chantilly. And there is a pitiful significance in the Kaiser's question to the mysterious journalist Maykosen: "How long do you think this war is going to last?"

Jules Romains

On some readers *Verdun,* published in French over a year ago, will make a somewhat painful impression today as France settles in for another long war. But this should not be a deterrent, since the novel pictures in advance what may soon take place on the western front and does so more vividly than the war correspondents will be able to do. *Verdun,* the most faithful and most nearly complete account of the first world war in any novel, proves more conclusively than ever that even if he does lack certain qualities of a Gide, a Mauriac, or a Martin du Gard, Jules Romains is the most *vigorous* novelist in France today.

Men of Good Will is not only better reading than the tabloids; it is superior to all but the very best literary output of our day. The English translation is good without being brilliant. Often too free, or even careless, it should have been done with the sober fidelity with which Scott Moncrieff rendered Proust. Occasionally it lapses so far as completely to falsify a sentence. When will translators learn, moreover, that "luxury," "trouble," and "honest" are deceptive cognates for the French words they resemble?

Aftermath, the sequel to *Verdun,* pictures the adjustment to peace in the years 1919 and 1920. Although it is of the same high quality as the seven volumes leading up to *Verdun,* it cannot fail to disappoint some of those readers who discovered Romains only last year. To many his *Aftermath* will seem an anticlimax. But after all, even Dante and Milton—Romains likes the noblest comparisons—found hell easier to depict than heaven.

In reality *Aftermath,* like all the other installments in the American edition, comprises two volumes, separately entitled *Vorge contre Quinette* and *La Douceur de la vie.* The first of these, laid in Paris, enlivens the post-Armistice world by bringing back to the center of the stage Quinette, the multiple murderer, the cultured bookbinder of the Rue Dailloud for whom life really began back in 1908 when a stranger entered his shop with blood on his hands. Since the night when Quinette left that man's body in the Bagnollet quarries with an acid-soaked sponge on his face, he had almost completely dropped out of the picture. Once he had been seen on the subway meditating a new

228

killing behind his distinguished black beard; at that time the corpses to his credit numbered four or five, and he seemed to be developing a technique. By then you should have recognized Quinette as Landru, the infamous modern Bluebeard whose suburban garden revealed a necropolis.

Now Quinette's life threatens to undergo another violent change when a well-dressed young man enters his shop and says in tones of polite indifference: "The purpose of my visit is to have a chat about the murder of Virginie Paternal, née Virginie Bourron." This new stranger is Claude Vorge, a pre-surrealist poet, who, far from wishing to give Quinette over to the police, is seeking in him a spiritual guide, or, as he says, the dark angel of Rimbaud's apocalypse.

All of this is child's play for Jules Romains, who would have made a superb writer of mysteries. But the best chapter of *Vorge against Quinette* comes when Romains, who has finally succeeded in making even his dullest readers recall Landru, shows Quinette opening a newspaper and learning of the arrest of the real Landru. This is no longer on the plane of detective fiction; rather it is Pirandello standing in a cold sweat before a mirror and asking: "Am I really I or am I not I?" In a few pages the novelist achieves the effect of a maddening hallucination.

So far this sounds very little like heaven, however; but the comparison with Dante still holds. Heaven comes in *The Sweets of Life,* and the first part of *Aftermath* serves as a purgatory after the hell of *Verdun.* If Vorge is a man obscurely seeking grace, our old friend Jallez, the hero of the second part, has definitely found grace. There is some injustice in thus granting all the rewards to a man who did not go through the war, who suffered hardly at all; but it is worth noting in passing that when Romains ascribes some of his own youthful poetry to one of his young characters, he chooses Jerphanion. Perhaps the scales are even. At any rate, Jallez finds heaven in the Nice of 1920 and particularly in an idyllic liaison with the adolescent Antonia, a child of the Old Town. His flirtation with Mme Valavert, who lives on the other side of the Casino, contributes to his sentiment of a quasi-divine euphorium.

Between the two volumes which compose *Aftermath* the contrast is almost brutally sharp. Unquestionably Romains aimed to reproduce here two typical postwar attitudes: on the one hand, the morbid unrest, the cheap sophistication, and the search for sensations; on the other the longing for peace and quiet in which to meditate and take stock, the quest for solid values. Such a vivid antithesis is very Hugonian, and like Hugo, Jules Romains knows his public extremely well—except when he makes a *gaffe* like that of the pseudo-revelations of his recent extracurricular *Seven Mysteries of Europe*. Just as Hugo deliberately put into his plays, according to his own confession, ideas for the thinkers, emotions for the women, and action for the crowd, Romains skillfully doses his cycle, and even each installment, with a little of something for everyone. The addicts of each kind of fiction will find some pages here to delight them. Thriller, love story, philosophical tale, novel of analysis, essay on social problems, historical sketches—all these and many other types are to be found rolled into one. Because of the vast scope of this work, Romains has been hailed as the modern Balzac. The variety of his technical skill recalls even more Victor Hugo. No other living French writer, in any case, so much resembles the great virtuosos of the past.

Unlike *Verdun,* the present installment of *Men of Good Will* can hardly be enjoyed without some knowledge of the eight preceding volumes. This is doubtless because Romains here returns to the tracing of individual lives, neglecting the vast crowd and its unanimous movements. Although he has presumably passed the middle mark of his cycle, he is still, in keeping with his original plan, introducing new characters; no fewer than eleven appear for the first time in *Vorge against Quinette* alone. The greatest responsibility, however, for carrying the story onward falls on the experienced shoulders of our old friends. Furthermore—and this seems to contradict the preface to the whole work—those old characters are beginning to meet each other. Jallez makes the acquaintance of both Quinette and the Abbé Mionnet and tells us that he has known Vorge in the past. It would appear as if Romains's world were getting smaller; maybe it will end by looking somewhat like Landernau after all. Unlike earlier installments, besides, no historical characters figure here; we only read about Landru in the papers. But the author maintains the same omniscient attitude to which his method condemns him. He knows everything about his many creatures; he is within them all, and if he does not bring the Kaiser or Lenin or Jaurès back to the stage it is because he also knows that they are not pertinent to this phase of his story. If only Romains had meditated Gide's remark that a character who is going away can be seen only from the back, his work would have gained in verisimilitude.

It would be too much to expect *Aftermath* to maintain the pitch reached in *Verdun*. Nor does it strike either the depths or the heights of its author's talent that were sampled in the installment entitled *The Depths and the Heights*. Almost every volume so far has contained its anthology-piece—in this case it is surely the Sunday that Antonia and Jallez spend at Falicon—and doubtless when the entire cycle is completed, *Verdun* will take its place as the volume-size anthology piece of the whole work. At present one can judge only the parts and be grateful to Jules Romains for having undertaken and in great measure realized so ambitious a portrait of our time.

The French volumes 19 and 20, combined in English as *The New Day,* begin to rise to another "threshold of an epoch," as the original preface said. Postwar France has acquired a new social consciousness and all eyes are turned toward Russia, where a great experiment is taking place. The time is 1922; on all sides people are wondering, as Jerphanion says: "This great light lighting the east; is it dawn or conflagration?" The former socialists Sampeyre, Laulerque, and Clanricard are intrigued to the point of wanting to see for themselves. Workmen and artisans like Edmond Maillecottin, Roquin, and Miraud are enthusiastic and a bit jealous. Jerphanion is actively preparing an informal reconnaissance trip for himself and his chief, ex-Minister Bouitton. In Rome Jallez is pulling wires to get the League of Nations to send him to inspect the famine in the Ukraine. There he joins forces with the English journalist Bartlett and together they make a pact with the mysterious Russian Poliapof.

In the next French volume, called here *The World Is Your Adventure,* the most enterprising of these characters have actually reached

Russia. Jallez and Bartlett pass through a phantom Odessa, glimpse the starving regions and travel down the Volga by boat until the Cheka catches up with them to provide Jallez with a taste of jail life. Jerphanion and Bouitton receive all the honors of Moscow and Nizhni-Novgorod and meet our old friends Haverkamp and Champcenais, the unscrupulous wolves of high finance.

If such a bare summary sounds dull, this is because this tenth installment of *Men of Good Will* is pedestrian. To be sure, Jules Romains as usual has periodic recourse to the sex life of his characters to brighten up the journey for us readers. But in this volume the mechanics are more than usually obvious. The banal adultery of Laulerque and Mathilde is too neatly balanced by Jallez's idyl with Elisabeth Valavert, just as the piquant conversation between Nania and Clanricard on the importance of the sexual act in the new society finds its counterpart in that between Bartlett and Jallez on "the sexual life of the ever-wandering unmarried man."

This is not to say that such conversations have lost any of their *brio;* Romains's protagonists still analyze as keenly as ever. And certain pages—such as that in which the one-armed Clanricard embraces his former pupil who is going to find his niche in Morocco or that in which Elisabeth and Jallez sit in the little bar and silently muse over their first afternoon as lovers—will probably always remain deeply moving. But in between, the reader has to wade through much that he could come by more easily in Walter Duranty or Louis Fischer.

By the end of the present installment faithful readers will have followed Jules Romains through no fewer than 5,876 pages (counted in the original text), and some of them may even remember the distinctive characteristics of Hector Trampagut, Ernest Torchecoul, Eusèbe Frottemouillard, Michele di Lammermont, and the other eight hundred different characters. At this point one cannot help envying whoever first said that the men of good will in question were the readers.

On *Seven Mysteries of Europe* (*Sept Mystères du destin de l'Europe*), by Jules Romains, translated by Germaine Brée (New York: Alfred A. Knopf, Inc., 1940). *The Nation*, December 7, 1940.

ROMAINS: A LETTER FROM JALLEZ TO JERPHANION *

I 'll send you the book. You won't have to worry, *mon vieux*, about the censor's letting it pass, since there is not a thing in it to which he could take exception. If you were still in Paris, the book might risk falling into the hands of Otto Abetz, the High Commissar for occupied France. He would chuckle over it royally and you'd never get it, for he is one of M. Romains's new protagonists!

No, calm yourself at once. The *Seven Mysteries of Europe* remain mysteries after a reading of this volume. To them, in fact, is added an eighth: how could we, who grew up with Romains and have never lost contact with him, have been ignorant all this time of what a great man he has become? A vigorous novelist, *tant que vous voudrez*, international president of the P.E.N. Clubs, and all that that implies. I am even willing to take on good faith his spurning of the Academy— though, on the side, I'd be grateful to you for verifying certain current rumors of at least a temporary weakening on that score. I'll accept Romains's statements that all the French generals had read his *Verdun* and found it good and that almost all the statesmen of Europe had read his *Men of Good Will*—that ought to set *us* both on a pedestal, too. But I, for one, never suspected what great political power he

* The two young intellectuals who figure prominently in *Men of Good Will*. In portraying them Romains drew largely upon his own youth.

233

wielded. Did you know that it was he who put Delbos into the Ministry of Foreign Affairs in 1936, who by a radio speech in November 1938 kept Daladier's ministry from being overthrown and the general strike of November 30 from being a success? Talk of two birds with one stone! But there's something better yet. Maybe my acidulous friend was right when he used to declare that Romains was a dangerous man because his unanimism foreshadowed fascism. You may remember Romains's "July 9 Plan"? I never read the pamphlet, but I recall Jean Thomas's interest in it. Well, it appears that the Nazis knew it well and received him so pompously in Berlin in 1934 because they thought he was going to become the French dictator. Where were *we*, Jerph, where *were* we?

I'll tell you how it happened. Just after the first armistice, when you were trying to settle back into civil life and forget the horrors of Verdun and I was writing you from Nice about my idyl with Antonia, Jules Romains vowed that he would prevent the next world war. In more recent years, finding himself occupying "an absolutely unique position in Europe, and even in the world," and profoundly dissatisfied with what the professional politicians and diplomats were doing, he undertook by himself direct "personal action on vital points." The description he gives of the Belgian Henri de Man fits Romains admirably in this most recent avatar: "He had a certain mistrust of democratic methods, a belief in action, personal, direct, and even secret, and a taste for authority." Meanwhile, other such free lances in other capitals were beginning to undertake the same defense of peace. Together they formed a kind of mysterious, unregimented "order of chivalry."

Here is an example of how they worked. Henri de Man came to Paris with a secret message from King Leopold to Daladier in 1938, his idea being to act directly on Daladier, Chamberlain, Hitler, and Mussolini without the intermediary of the chancelleries. Naturally he went first to Romains, who welcomed the plan enthusiastically and took him direct to—Bonnet, then Foreign Minister. A year later, with the war already on, Romains goes to Belgium to see the king and no one but the king. Henri de Man will surely arrange the interview, but alas, he sends Romains to Foreign Minister Spaak, and Leopold never comes into the picture. The members of this chivalric order Romains calls Men of Good Will; some of them are Henri de Man, who became head of the Belgian government of capitulation, Otto Abetz, now military governor of a conquered Paris, and von Ribbentrop. Isn't this a libel against us, the original men of good will? Shall we resign together?

In dealing with such men Romains seems to have been the dupe, but don't judge him until you get to the eloquent apology for well-wishing dupes in the last chapter. By his own testimony he seems also to have been generally unsuccessful in his "quite unofficial missions," when he set out to patch up some situation or other. Besides the two Belgian failures, it is noteworthy that his report to Gamelin on the Maginot Line was ignored, that his plan for the Saar plebiscite—inspired by Ribbentrop, Rosenberg, and Goebbels—was shelved by the French government, and that when he got a promise from Spaak he could not move Daladier. All is summed up in the incident of February 6, 1934. At the height of the riots he sent Daladier a card urging him to hold on firmly; within a few hours Daladier resigned. But what if Romains was right each time? It is impossible to believe today that the Saar plebiscite would have resulted differently or that Henri de Man's scheme for wringing the hearts of Hitler and Mussolini would have availed anything or that the letter Romains wanted Daladier to write to Leopold would have saved Giraud's army and obviated the necessity of Dunkirk.

No, our friend has not even approached a solution of the European mysteries, and I can't help wondering how deeply he even penetrated them. He never met Hitler or Mussolini, and the only English statesman he quotes directly is Harold Nicolson. He appears never to have had contact with the southern end of the Axis, and his German relations were limited to the years 1934 and 1935, plus two formal dinners in Paris in 1938. He confesses his English chapter to be "drab and blurred" because England is that way, just generally anonymous.

I hate to think what this book may do, Jerph, to Romains's reputation as a writer—and hence, incidentally, to ours as fictional characters. Yet, let's not be unfair: in this book Romains is still the novelist. Reading it rapidly, one can't but be intrigued by the atmosphere of underground secrecy, the mystery-men shuttling across the Continent, the constant evasion of possible spies. In fact, there are direct comparisons here with the fictional work: Abetz's use of Romains reminds me of M. Karl and Laulerque; the unofficial missions correspond on a larger scale to Quinette's spying on secret societies; one of the Daladier interviews Romains himself likens to that between Maykosen and the Kaiser. Reading the book more attentively, one notices the creative writer's technique—imaginary conversations when real ones are lacking, the fact that the most important things "said" by Romains's interlocutors are most often his interpretation of a glance or a gesture. And then just think of how much he has made here of how little! The novelist appears on almost every page, and I prefer to see this book as a confession of how Jules Romains has attempted to live some of the episodes of his novels. Let's put it, then, on the shelf reserved for documents contributing to the literary history of our time. And as fictional characters shan't we climb down right away?

On *Les Hommes de bonne volonté* (*Men of Good Will*), by Jules Romains (Paris: Flammarion, 1932–1952). *Decision*, June 1941.

ROMAINS: PLEASE PASS THE ILL WILL

I

"The man after whom this street was named had a word for it," said Bigoudoxe as he and Salepion walked briskly up the Rue Cambronne on the odd-numbered side of the street. Both of them knew instinctively that the wholesale firms and warehouses they were passing were on the Ségur telephone exchange. In the same way they also knew the height of each ceiling.

"No, that's manifestly unfair to the cyclic novel," Salepion replied meditatively. Since it was Thursday, they would not have to return to the *lycée* for hours. "It has long been my contention that the cycle answers a need of our epoch for escape. The brief weekend excursions offered by the art of our fathers no longer satisfy us; we need an escape which is at once intense in the pleasure it offers and also capable of being prolonged indefinitely. But I shall develop those ideas in a letter to you when I really have time. Let us limit our attention here to Jules Romains and his *Men of Good Will*. For years I have been wanting to discuss that work with you, but until now I have feared being unfair to its author, who in his preface, you may remember, asked us to suspend judgment. . . ."

"And now?" Bigoudoxe's question was swallowed up in the roar of a Citroën motor which a mechanic was racing in the garage at number 57.

237

"Well, I have just finished the nineteenth volume. Think of it, old man—5,553 pages! I've counted them. And in those pages I have met no fewer than seven hundred and thirty-eight new characters, labeled, may I add, with such monickers as Cornabœuf, Mouillevin, Torchecoul, Chiquette, Desboulmiers, Eliphas, Empuis. . . ." Bigoudoxe interrupted enthusiastically:

"I have met them too, and I made a collection of the L's: Lambron de Crauze, Lammermont, Laouteron, Leheudry, Lechapelu, Lejars, Lhermitain, Liguevin, Luymarie. . . . But we're fine ones, you and I, to criticize him on that score." Their pace slowed as they mingled with the crowds sauntering by the grocery and hardware stores on the Rue Lecourbe.

"We have as good a right as anyone," said Salepion exhibiting a superior smile. "Don't forget that I descend from a long line of school teachers; my patronymic was originally a professional taunt with a descriptive value. But the important thing is not so much the absurdity of the names as the vacuity they cover. Do you actually remember any of those Miaulards, Nanthiats, Parampuyres, Quingeys? Or, for that matter, do you recognize any signs of real life in such prominent characters as the murderer Quinette, the academician Allory, or Germaine Baader the kept woman? To me they are all intellectual creations testifying to Romains's conscientious documentation and lively imagination, but no blood flows in their veins. . . ."

Bigoudoxe was inclined to agree. As they attacked the slope of the Rue du Général-Beuret, still in the fifteenth arrondissement, his eyes caressed the thinly clad buttocks of the girl in front of them. He wondered if Yvonne would be waiting for him outside her aunt's shop at ten o'clock.

II

The room was rapidly growing dark. What little light filtered in from the quiet Rue Servandoni fell on the polished bald head of Mgr. Forniconches. The secret mission on which the Bishop of Toulouse had sent him had been singularly successful. In the person of Father Tramboule, almost completely hidden in the darkness on the other side of the room, he had found just the man to inform him of the Parisian literary world's attitude toward the Church.

"In short, if I understand you aright, my dear friend"—he had met the young priest only the day before, but Mgr. Forniconches was a diplomat—"the horrors that Jules Romains attributes to the Church: breaking of vows, financial malpractices, espionage, political intrigue, and even pederasty in the Curia are rather the result of ignorance than of malevolence on his part. I had thought that he might be instigated by the Lodges. Isn't he a Mason?"

Father Tramboule replied before the question was asked and in the crisp, lightning-like speech affected by graduates of the Ecole des Sciences Politiques. "I don't know, but doubt that he is. You have only to look at other volumes in which he handles other subjects. The one which deals with the world of debauch, for instance. . . . Of course we are not in a position. . . ." His smile, compounded of unction and slyness, something of which communicated itself to his voice, made it unnecessary for him to finish his sentence. "Former classmates have assured me that life in the fleshpots is not at all like that. Proust's descriptions are probably closer to the truth, that is to the truth of twenty-five or thirty years ago, but Romains could have derived all his information about flagellation, gambling dens, the delinquency of minors, and the aberrations of old men from the trashy books on sale under the arcades of the Palais-Royal. For his descriptions of the Church he has doubtless had recourse to equally trashy sources."

"This is most unfortunate. As you know, my friend, we can deal much more easily with malice than we can with good honest ignorance." There was an intentional touch of the Midi in his accent as he pronounced the last word.

As the bells of Saint-Sulpice chimed the hour, Father Tramboule rose to take his leave, declined Mgr. Forniconches's invitation to dinner at his pension, and picked his way down the stairs worn by generations of provincial ecclesiastics.

III

In his little flat on the Rue Piat, the old locksmith Fernand Lharve set down the book he had just finished and raised his eyes to the ceiling. It was two meters ten from the floor, as they all were in this part of Ménilmontant. Now that he had no more family living with him he had taken to spending two evenings a week at home reading. This habit offered a welcome contrast to the evenings spent in the café with his old friends Groudes and Buval. On the shelf beside him, which he had installed himself on its wrought-iron supports, stood all the works of Hugo that he had been able to buy in the Nelson edition. After a union organizer had spoken of them enthusiastically, he had also bought the ninth and tenth volumes of *Men of Good Will*. His first excursion into contemporary literature was a revelation to him, for here he found the same neat antitheses to which his beloved Hugo had accustomed him: on the one hand the people like himself in the north end of the city; on the other the rich manufacturers and middlemen in their private houses of the Faubourg Saint-Germain or hobnobbing with German capitalists in their castles on the Rhine. They had prepared the war, which had taken his two sons. If only he and his friends in Belleville, La Villette, and Les Batignolles had known all this then. But what could they have done? He remembered as vividly as if it were yesterday the general strike of October, 1910, when he and Groudes had cheered for the tram employees and gone to see the excitement at the Gare du Nord. Why didn't the people realize better then what they were fighting for? Despite all that had happened since, he recalled the anguish caused by the Agadir affair. And to think that at that very moment men like Champcenais were in Germany selling out to the *alboches* and flirting with Christine Zülpicher! Romains made you see it all so clearly. He had known a family just like the Maillecottins. He would have to ask Delhrobide about Gurau; he did not remember him as foreign minister under Caillaux. Delhrobide would be able to set him right.

IV

"Simply an embittered *avant-garde* poet," thought André Plucquart, looking across the brilliantly lighted table at young Cazerme, who had just spoken so disparagingly of Jules Romains. The dinner table of the Marquis Adhémar Baillalencque de Chichecotte, in the new house he had recently bought on the Avenue Charles Floquet, was hardly the place for a literary discussion, and he—whom the other guests knew only as the king of the cosmetics industry—was surely not the person to nourish such a discussion. Nevertheless he could not agree with the upstart opposite him that Romains's novel was an "aimless composition of preposterous dimensions laboriously built up out of a patient and often heavy-handed documentation." He was about to formulate a reply and brave the youth's sarcasm when his foot, which had been moving about under the table to ease a slight strain on his thigh muscles, encountered something soft which seemed at once to exert pressure on the side of his shoe. Stealthily he reappraised Mme Cluquedeau, who was sitting on his right. Her plump arms and the wisps of hair below her chignon (she had turned to talk to the General) were decidedly appetizing. Plucquart returned the pressure under the table and maneuvered for a better position. He tried to recall whether he had ever heard her first name. Just then General Presterat began to make himself heard:

"Documentation or no documentation, I can assure you, young man, that his *Verdun* is a brilliant creation—yes, brilliant." He lingered on the word as if he had just invented it. "All of us at G.H.Q. read it with the deepest interest and found not a single inaccuracy in it. I tell you, it is as if he had studied at the Ecole de Guerre."

"I have nothing against *Verdun*," replied the courageous poet, "save that it has no relation to the rest of the work. Or perhaps you would say that the fourteen volumes leading up to it are merely introductory." He felt reasonably sure that the General had read only one section of the novel. And indeed, employing a familiar defensive tactic, the General had become absorbed again in the conversation of Mme Cluquedeau.

"What I object to especially," Cazerme was saying, "is the evident intention throughout the novel to thrill by any means. Murders, spy rings, secret societies, sexual perversion, rape, revolution, historic moments, and famous personages—Romains uses them all to hold the reader's attention. Whenever he is in danger of losing that attention, he introduces an unexpected sexual experience, even if he has to have recourse to the old maid Bernardine or the dog Macaire. By a skillful vulgarization of the multiple-plot technique used by Gide in *The Counterfeiters* and by Huxley in *Point Counter Point,* he plans. . . ."

"Ah," thought Plucquart as he raised to his lips a delicate Lalique glass filled with Pommard 1923, "so that's her name! Charming, and so appropriate!" He had just heard M. Cluquedeau address his wife as Reinette.

V

When later that evening, Father Tramboule left the wet cobbles of the narrow and foul Rue de la Bûcherie and stepped into the acrid-smelling corridor of the Hôtel de l'Egypte, he was no longer wearing his cassock and clerical hat. But for his handsome profile and prominent cheekbones, he would have been indistinguishable from the hundreds of petty clerks then roaming the nearby Boulevard Saint-Michel in the hope of being taken for students. He knew that Tatia Douliastrelsky, whom he was to meet in the fourth room from the landing on the third floor, was an agent of Free Masonry and he had sensed in their earlier encounters that she had even more significant international affiliations. Ostensibly he was coming to report on his conversation with Mgr. Forniconches. Actually he was drawn to this squalid room more by the memory of Tatia, the woman, the satin-skinned as he called her in his mind. *"Ce n'est pas pour rien que j'ai quitté la soutane ce soir pour prendre l'épée,"* he muttered as he began to mount the stairs. He wondered if Forniconches kept his vows.

VI

Eve Vuichorgues stepped gingerly into her bath. That very morning the *Temps* had carried a story about a woman who had slipped in her tub and broken her wrist. Once safely seated, she proceeded to scrutinize closely the almost imperceptible lump on the side of her left breast, just where the swelling surface meets the line of the ribs. This was a ritual with Eve, not because she feared that this little blemish might mar the beauty of her plump body, but rather because she entertained a vague feeling that "that was the way cancer always began."

Fortunately the lump had neither grown nor become harder since her last inspection. Resolutely she put out of her mind the thought of painful operations, often repeated, and of disfiguring scars. Sliding down in the tub, she rested her head against the porcelain slope. If only she were expecting that writer whose book she had just been reading rather than the too-faithful Antory, who had phoned from his club to say he would come to the Rue de Presbourg apartment in an hour. Now *there* was a man who understood women! He knew everything that passed through their heads. And so many other things besides. The only trouble was that he seemed to have sex on his mind a good deal—every bit as much as Antory. Eve had to admit that his book contained some long passages that did not interest her—and even, occasionally, a page or two that upset her for days after, like the would-be rape of the dead woman. But all that was amply made up for by the delicate feeling he showed in the two women in Nice: the bored society woman and the naïve little newsgirl. She could see herself in either role. After mature reflection, however, her preference inclined toward the little girl of the Old Town. Yes, she *had* been like that; even at that age she had known what she wanted. She imagined the writer as tall, broad-shouldered, and with a leonine mane of blue-black hair. Young, of course. And impulsive in his movements. What was his name now? Paris . . . Londres. . . . Could it be Parisien? Funny how names escaped her.

VII

After following a devious course that had taken them to the Parc Montsouris and then to a little restaurant on the Avenue du Maine, where they had dined, Salepion and Bigoudoxe were walking down the Rue de la Gaîté in the direction of the Montparnasse station. Blind to the bright lights of the cinemas and deaf to the automobile horns, they were still talking of *Men of Good Will*.

"I can't endure his omniscience," said Bigoudoxe. "He knows everything taking place in every character's mind, and he never loses sight of any of the seven hundred and thirty-eight little puppets. I see what you mean when you say they don't lead a life of their own."

"Do you remember," asked Salepion, "the author's little note to us at the end of the fourth volume? There he as much as said that the first four volumes were simply introductory. From then on he would follow a different rhythm in his narrative, he promised, keeping abreast of certain major events and characters for a longer period of time, not abandoning them until they had reached a common level, as it were, the 'threshold of an epoch.' He also alludes to a plan he was following, a plan that would deform reality as little as possible. I think I see some of that plan. The first four volumes are stationary, limited as they are to events of the last three months of 1908. Volumes five through sixteen rise in a crescendo to the chief crisis of the war, the battle of Verdun. In them he shows the various classes of society and chief fields of human activity either preparing for war or hopelessly unconscious of its approach. This is where his Hugonian anthitheses come in handy. The rich and the poor, the newly rich and the landed gentry, the military officers and the parliamentarians, the intellectuals and the artists, the clergy and the secret societies, the conservatives and the socialists, etc. Volumes seventeen through nineteen were bound to be a let-down since Romains had to return to the technique of individual plots that he had used at the beginning of his work. His falling back on Quinette is a confession of this weakness in construction. Nineteen again shows an effort to rise to another threshold. . . ."

"Don't you think also," interrupted Bigoudoxe, "that there is significance in his continual suggestion of an opposition between the creators and the wasters or, better, the independent individuals and the joiners? In the first class belong Viaur, Strigelius, Ortégal, Gurau, Jallez, Vorge, and yes, even Quinette. The other group is made up of all those who are forever seeking to join up with some movement or other, or who seek protection behind the façade of an institution: Laulerque, Clanricard, Wazemmes, Mionnet, etc. Maybe this is just Romains's way of turning against his youthful unanimism?"

"Oh, unanimism. . . ." But a Montparnasse prostitute, overhearing as they passed her, laughed suddenly and flung back at them:

"Tchk! tchk! such a word for boys to be shouting on the street!"

On *The World of the Thibaults* (*Les Thibault*), by Roger Martin du Gard, translated by Stuart Gilbert (2 vols.; New York: The Viking Press, Inc., 1941). *Saturday Review*, March 4, 1939; *The Nation*, March 1, 1941.

MARTIN DU GARD: "THE WORLD OF THE THIBAULTS"

R arely has a winner of the Nobel Prize for literature so richly deserved that honor as Roger Martin du Gard. The French Academy can be excused for neglecting him, as for ignoring André Gide, because to don its green livery and sit under its dome a writer must present his own candidature, and neither of those two old friends has sought that official consecration. But the Swedish Academy, which moves on its own impulse, can reward in the divine manner.

Even now, after a career of thirty years, Martin du Gard remains faithful to the attitude of his first hero, who said: "As for literature, write if you wish; but for God's sake don't talk about it." In great part because of this dislike for personal publicity, his work has not achieved a wide recognition outside of France. Like Marcel Proust, he first revealed his talent on the eve of the World War with a substantial novel, *Jean Barois*. Popular acclaim did not come, however, until the publication, stretching over the years from 1922 to 1940, of the ten or eleven volumes of *Les Thibault*, the first of which appeared in this country in a translation by Madeleine Boyd that for some reason was not continued. The present new and very satisfactory translation by Stuart Gilbert contains the whole work, which counts nearly 1,900 pages. This work, great in both quantity and quality, marks the height of its author's achievement. The first and best of the many cyclic novels

245

popular in France since 1920, *The World of the Thibaults* is superior also to that earlier model, Romain Rolland's *Jean-Christophe.*

It is one thing to call a book a masterpiece of irony or its author's masterpiece and quite another to call it a masterpiece. The qualifying phrase reduces the value of that fearful and magic word by at least one-half. A scrupulous reviewer is inclined to sterilize the word thus every time he uses it, but twice or thrice in a lifetime he meets a book about which he feels no hesitation. This is such a case, for this book is a masterpiece.

Perhaps the work's chief distinction lies in the fact that it is a pure novel—in other words, one which aims to represent life rather than to reflect upon it. The ascetic régime Martin du Gard followed for so many years at Bellême, writing a regular number of hours every day in a room lined with reference works and filing cases, recalls the arduous life of Flaubert, the hermit of Croisset, whom he resembles moreover in his willingness to destroy completed manuscripts and re-write the same volume four or five times. In his early paleographical and archeological study at the Ecole des Chartes he acquired a scholarly method which makes of his work the result of a unique collaboration between the historian and the novelist. Yet for all that, he possesses the true artist's faculty for synthesis, which protects him from being blinded by the individual as Jules Romains often is, in whose work documentation too frequently substitutes for creation. Roger Martin du Gard differs from all his contemporaries, besides, in that his style marks an absence of style. In an age of literary affectation, he has written with such directness and limpidity that not even the slightest film, as Gide commented, interposes itself between the reader and the life whose unfolding he follows with passionate interest.

The reality of that life, throbbing and multiform, strikes one from the very first page with its sudden projection of the reader into the drama of Jacques's and Daniel's flight from home. The gradual reve-lation of the various personalities within the Thibault and Fontanin families becomes so absorbing that not until a second reading does one notice the author's skillful use of the multiple plot that Gide and Huxley were to borrow in *The Counterfeiters* and *Point Counter Point.* Jérôme de Fontanin's many infidelities, his daughter Jenny's illness and the Christian Science healer's intervention, Antoine Thibault's reactions to his father's pomposity, all in the first chapters, seize the reader's attention. The rest of the novel contains no disappointment: Antoine's improvised operation on a little girl (already included in French anthologies) and his passionate love affair with Rachel, Daniel's philanderings in the manner of his father, Jacques's tender love for Jenny and his sufferings in the reformatory, Antoine's daring effort to shorten his father's death agony, are passages which show the author's mastery of situations and emotions. At once the reader establishes direct contact with the characters.

For over fifteen years Martin du Gard has lived in seclusion with the same characters, whose number, in view of the extent of the novel, is remarkably small—only ten or a dozen of major importance. As Daniel, now a young painter, says in the second half of the novel: "Everything I have learned I have drawn from the tenacious study of a single model. Why change? You do much better work when you force yourself to return constantly to the same starting point, when each time you have to start all over again and go farther in the same direction. If I had been a novelist, I think that instead of changing my characters with each book I should have clung indefinitely to the same ones, in order to dig deeper." This passage, the only one in which a character seems to speak for the author, reveals Martin du Gard's method. Combining a taste for vast constructions and a lively sense of individual qualities, he still does not claim to reconstruct all of contemporary life in the manner of Balzac or Zola. Rather he gives, under the name of one of them, the history of two families during about a dozen prewar years. Though these families, one Catholic and the other Protestant, represent a large section of the Parisian *bourgeoisie,* the author in no way uses them as symbols. In *The Counterfeiters,* André Gide likewise depicts the dissolution of two families of the same class, one Catholic and the other Protestant, and the dedication of that novel to Roger Martin du Gard implies a recognition of his debt, fully acknowledged elsewhere.

The debt is, however, mutual, as is evident from the unforgettable description (Part Three, chapter 1) of Daniel de Fontanin's discovery of Gide's *Nourritures terrestres*. That breviary of revolt and self-expression gave Daniel the courage to be himself. It may well have furnished also the starting point for *The World of the Thibaults,* for the novel's major theme is that of evasion with the idea of revolt either expressed or implied. Jacques Thibault constantly burns with a peculiarly Gidian gemlike flame. After his first unsuccessful flight with Daniel at fourteen, followed by a period of calm smouldering, he makes another break for freedom, this time fully successful, years later; and his last act, after the outbreak of war, is to attempt to soar above the horrible reality into the ideological. Rachel's mysterious departure for Africa to join a man she fears provides another example of evasion. Gide himself has hardly more often illustrated his doctrine of fervor and unrest leading to a salutary uprooting of body and mind. Nor has he, in *his* chronicle of the liquidation of two families, more vigorously translated into action his early statement: "Families, I hate you! Closed circles around the hearth! Fast shut doors. . ." Gide has unquestionably influenced, and in turn been influenced by, Martin du Gard, thus proving the truth of his contention that literary influence does not create but rather awakens. Even if Gide had never existed, Roger Martin du Gard would still be one of the few truly great modern writers of French prose.

In French the entire novel is simply called *Les Thibault.* But the English title is quite justified since around old Oscar Thibault and his sons Jacques and Antoine, there move other characters and there exists a palpable world made up of objects and places that are as real to us as their analogues in our own lives. Often they are so real as to usurp a place in the reader's life: for whoever has been enthralled by the novel —and I doubt if anyone who has begun has not been—certain squares and corners of Paris and Geneva belong now to Jacques or Antoine. Upon meeting a flesh-and-blood Dr. Thibault in Paris not long ago, I told him that I already knew someone with the same name and title; "Yes," he replied, "through Martin du Gard, but my first name is not Antoine."

In the second volume the canvas broadens perceptibly and the Thibault microcosm reflects more fully the European macrocosm of 1914 and its headlong rush toward war. Jacques, by then a militant socialist, does his part in Geneva, Paris, and Brussels to warn of the impending catastrophe and to organize resistance to a passive acceptance of it. Before the summer of 1939, those chapters might have seemed to some readers too faithful a reproduction of the anguish felt only by the most alert in 1914; today they have an added poignancy and truth because we have all lived through such emotions. Actually, the approach of war, seen from the vantage point of the Second International and contrasted in its last stage with the successful outcome of Jacques's and Jenny's love, forms a stirring narrative. Here more than anywhere else one wishes that the American edition had preserved the chapter headings of the original, since the dates given there help in following the rapid succession of events.

Until his tragic and futile, yet wholly appropriate, death soon after the outbreak of hostilities, Jacques holds the reader's attention most insistently. In a sense the whole novel could have ended there, for its most obvious subject is the story of an adolescent who never grew up, who refused indeed to grow up. A youth marked by "an innate revulsion from injustice" finds himself at fourteen in a world full of injustice. Quite naturally he revolts, first by fleeing home and school, a second time by fleeing his recent past and a brilliant future career, and finally by spurning the whole war-torn world and dying for an ideal. The Epilogue, however, is essential not only to round out the world of the Thibaults, but also to provide a very human and very real apotheosis of Jacques. For by 1918, when his and Jenny's son is four years old and Antoine, fatally gassed, is slowly dying in a hospital, Jacques's spirit has communicated itself to all the other principal characters. Not only Jenny, who now idolizes his memory, but also Antoine and Daniel and even the diplomat Rumelles have seen the futility of the war and come to share the ideas with which Jacques shocked them in 1914. Antoine's diary, at the end of the whole novel, shows him resembling his brother more and more as he approaches death; in him a maturer Jacques dies a second time. More acutely than ever, the reader recognizes that these characters, with whom he has lived in close communion, remain faithful to themselves through all the changes brought by time, accidents, disease, and world catastrophe.

Although the action of the novel covers only the period from about 1905 to the end of 1918, it also reflects very strongly the last twenty years during which Martin du Gard composed it. As a result, it brings out by implication more strongly than any other novel the close affinity between what we called until lately the prewar and the postwar. Chronicling an era that died during the First World War, the author constantly has a thought for death—despite the general robustness and health of his work. Part six deals with the father's agony, part seven ends with Jacques's death, and part eight with Antoine's. Even making allowances for the technical utility and brilliance of some of the death scenes, one must admit that this is a pessimistic novel written by an idealist who nevertheless sees life as it is and deliberately remains objective. Upon receiving the Nobel Prize in 1937—one of the very few times that he has consented to speak of himself publicly— Roger Martin du Gard defined himself as "an independent writer who has escaped the fascination of partisan ideologies, an investigator as objective as is humanly possible, as well as a novelist striving to express the tragic quality of human lives." That quality is here in abundance. Yet the disappearance of Jacques and Antoine is also symbolic. And as he wrote the last lines of his novel, the author already knew that he was witnessing the death of another epoch. But he has wisely left these implications for the reader to make.

Though he is anything but reactionary in politics and his general view of life, Roger Martin du Gard remains a conservative in his literary method and habits of mind. His patient system of documentation that filled his house in the French countryside with reference cards for his great work, his love of the exact sciences that caused him to give medicine such an important role, and his general distrust of religion and metaphysics came to him doubtless during his early studies as a paleographer and archeologist. But they also belong to the nineteenth century. In addition to his faithful and whole reproduction of life, this is another reason why one is so often led to compare him with the giants of the past—Flaubert, Zola, and Tolstoy.

On *Jean Barois,* by Roger Martin du Gard, translated by Stuart Gilbert (New York: The Viking Press, Inc., 1949). *The Book Find News,* No. 80, March 1949.

MARTIN DU GARD: "JEAN BAROIS"

Very few novels deserve republication—and even less translation into a foreign language—thirty-five years after their original appearance. But *Jean Barois* is an exception. Considered a classic almost at once, it has never ceased to be read in France, although the year after its publication saw the birth of such other classics as Anatole France's *Révolte des anges, Du côte de chez Swann* by Proust, and *Les Caves du Vatican* by Gide. Those works have long been well known in English, yet for some reason *Jean Barois* has awaited translation until now.

Throughout his work, Martin du Gard has concerned himself with the most basic problem: the significance of the individual life within this universe. The ethical issue, represented by the question his characters are always anxiously raising: "For what purpose?" is his chief preoccupation. This is the question facing modern man in a godless universe; it is the question that torments Dostoevsky's characters, Gide's and Malraux's, and that forms the leitmotif of the present work of Sartre and Camus.

One may expect *Jean Barois,* then, to be a novel of ideas. But the example of *The World of the Thibaults* should reassure by suggesting that those ideas are embodied in living human beings. Jean Barois, the tragic hero caught in the conflict between faith and science, undergoes a series of painful crises which are vivid precisely because we can identify ourselves with him. Through his struggle for religious emanci-

251

pation, dominated by a burning need for truth, we relive the torment of any intellectual in the modern world. As the novel grows more intense and the hero, like the decade of the thirties, hurls himself into political action and the intellectual debates surrounding that action, we feel recent history coming alive and can appreciate the remark of a French critic that nowhere else can one better study the generation that flourished from 1880 to 1910. Finally the last section, again concentrating the interest on the hero's spiritual evolution, reflects the rebirth of mysticism in French intellectual life just prior to the First World War.

Knowing that Roger Martin du Gard began life by undergoing the most rigorous historical and archeological training helps us to understand his novels. As a graduate student in Paris, he acquired the rigid objectivity and respect for facts which make of *Jean Barois* the most trustworthy portrayal of the Dreyfus case as the crisis of modern France. But he was born with the ability to transcend his documentation and to give his characters a permanent authenticity. His objectivity, indeed, is essentially warm human understanding, and the essence of his art is a studied composition achieving mastery through economy and choice of materials. He may be a survivor of realism, but if so he has an even greater impartiality than his predecessors and a greater gift of creation.

Upon first seeing this novel, a Paris publisher is reported to have exclaimed: "But this is not a novel; it's a case-history file!" And such, to be sure, is its appearance. Letters, telegrams, speeches, newspaper clippings, telephone monologues, appear in it verbatim. The rest of the novel is made up entirely of dialogues as on the stage, with mere notations as to the setting. Neither narration nor detailed descriptions mar the impression of life lived directly before our eyes. The characters describe themselves by what they say and how they say it. Though the skilled craftsmanship is more apparent here than in the later work, it serves the same purpose of suppressing the author and permitting us to enter into direct contact with the real world he has created.

On *Man's Hope* (*L'Espoir*), by André
Malraux, translated by Stuart Gilbert and
Alastair MacDonald (New York: Random
House, Inc., 1938). *The New York Times
Book Review*, November 6, 1938.

MALRAUX: "MAN'S HOPE"

Ever since his first novel, André Malraux has been working toward
L'Espoir (*Man's Hope*). Like all French intellectuals for the past
fifty years or more—like Bourget and Barrès and his master, André
Gide—this brilliant young archeologist turned revolutionary has been
haunted by the antithesis of thought and action. As his spokesman
expresses it in his most recent book, "The path that leads from moral
standards to political activity is strewn with our dead selves." In *Les
Conquérants* (*The Conquerors*), *La Condition humaine* (*Man's Fate*),
and *Le Temps du mépris* (*Days of Wrath*) Malraux conducted a
series of autopsies on some of those dead selves. The result, whatever
the quality of the novels, was negative. *Man's Hope* gives rather a
positive conclusion. In answer to the question as to how one can make
the best use of one's life, Garcia replies: "By converting as wide a range
of experience as possible into conscious thought, my friend."

The theme is revolution and the scene is the government front in
the Spanish war, where the author holds a responsible position in the
air force. In no other modern novel has the revolutionary attitude been
so well expressed. Malraux is inevitably partisan. His Fascists are too
ignoble; the Communists, too pure; but without this outspoken partiality
any account of a revolution would lack relief. It might be argued,
moreover, that the author is too close to the events he records and that
his personal revolution—away from anarchism and toward a common
action—sometimes obscures the revolution.

But what is more important is that this powerful book presents a sort of dramatic analysis of revolutionary action and of the enrichment of the individual resulting from the sharing of such action with his comrades. At the moment of death, Puig, the Catalan anarchist, relinquishes his nihilism, which led only to useless personal sacrifice, and actually grants the possibility of victory. Colonel Ximenes of the Civil Guard, who had spent his life in repressing uprisings, refuses to join Franco and becomes a commander in the government forces, where his mature experience, his Catholicism and his large humanity enrich the young militants, though ideologically they hate everything he stands for. Manuel, the young Communist, grows like a weed in significance, power, and personality as he rushes from battlefield to battlefield and one difficult assignment to another. The Italian exile, Scali, while never wholly losing his individuality as an intellectual, gradually organizes his spiritual forces just as the government does its army. One has only to study these characters and many others to see what has become of the author's "dead selves" in the composition of *Man's Hope*. If Manuel strikes us as the ideal Communist and hence something of a propaganda poster, we must be grateful to André Malraux for presenting so sympathetically a human type like Ximenes, to whom he certainly cannot feel very cordial. Throughout the novel, in fact, he wishes us to be aware of universal values, to recognize that the revolution must be seen as a sort of collective soul.

Opening with a cinematographic series of rapid scenes in Madrid, Barcelona, the Madrid airport, and the Sierras which reveal the government's frantic attempts to quell the Franco uprising, *Man's Hope* covers the first phase of the Spanish war, up to the battle of Guadalajara. After the "careless rapture" of the first days of fighting with sticks of dynamite, patched-up planes, old trucks and insufficient guns —days in which personal heroism and mad sacrifices were the rule— the book settles down, as the war did, to the slow organizing of the government army with its disparate forces made up of volunteers and mercenaries, members of all the parties of the Left, international brigades and Spanish peasants. Of a gathering of officers of the Fifth Corps Malraux says:

"None of the latter had been a soldier six months earlier; among them were a fashion designer, a contractor, a pilot, a factory manager, two members of joint committees of the various parties, steel factory hands, a composer, an engineer, and a garage keeper."

Yet there is no let-down. The crackle of the machine guns is supplanted by the regular reports from the firing squad during mass executions or by the hiss of the flame throwers and the irregular explosions of bombs from the air. At once a panoramic and detailed view of the revolution, this book has nothing abstract about it. But despite its succession of lurid scenes this is no second *Voyage au bout de la nuit* (*Journey to the End of the Night*) either. For there are always joy and hope in fraternity, in struggle, even in sacrifice. André Malraux has found his subject *par excellence*. And the violence of his style, nervous, staccato, sharp, is exactly adapted to it. Never before have his images come so naturally or played such an integral part in the whole. Examples can be chosen almost at random:

"In the main ward, beyond the open door, men could be seen walking about with their arms set in plaster, swathed in cocoons of bandages. Sometimes an arm, held by the splints in an unnatural position far from the body or at right angles to it, gave its owner the look of a strolling fiddler in the act of playing his violin. There was something particularly eerie in the scene; those monstrous, rigid arms paralyzed into fixed gestures, and the phantom violinists gliding like waxwork figures trundled to and fro in the green twilight, in a spectral silence murmurous with the low, incessant drone of flies."

The apparent lack of composition is at first disarming. In the first twenty pages one meets as many characters with no indication as to which ones will stand out a hundred pages further on. Unfortunately, they do not stay in one place either. But there is no central character, nor any focal point except the revolution itself. The composition is musical rather than literary. In this vast symphony there is a great number of themes, often interlocking, which recur insistently in the conversations between militants during the lulls in fighting. As the revolution organizes, the music swells and gains in cohesion and volume at the same time. In view of the fact that the mass movement is the subject of the novel, it is regrettable that the author has limited his attention so much to the leaders, the technicians and intellectuals. He would have achieved a greater universality if he had taken more figures directly from the anonymous crowd. His Garcia and Manuel and Magnin and Slade and Hernandez have all too much likeness with the intelligent observers whom we have already read on Spain. When he brings us close to the ordinary *milicianos,* the hard Asturian *dinamiteros,* and in the last pages the naïve Catalan peasants, he often writes his best pages.

But with all this André Malraux has not lost his sense of the individual and his tragedy amid the universal tragedy. The page in which Scali visits the aged father of Jaime Alvear, his friend who was blinded in a bombing expedition is one of the most moving in the novel:

"That's where Jaime always sits when he comes to visit me. You, too, are wearing glasses. When he takes his off I can't bear to look at his face." For the first time a note of grief throbbed in the old, toneless voice. . .

"Nothing's more horrible than the mutilation of a *body* that one loves."

"I'm his friend," Scali said, in a low voice, "and I'm used to wounded men."

"It so happens," Alvear said, "that exactly in front of his eyes, on those shelves over there, are all my books on painting, with thousands and thousands of the photographs over which he used to pore. . . . Still, do you know, when I turn on the gramophone—when there's music in the room—I can look at him, even if he isn't wearing his spectacles!"

The man who wrote that, moreover, is by no means an average writer.

On *Harvest* (*Regain*), by Jean Giono,
translated by Henri Fluchère and Geoffrey
Myers (New York: The Viking Press,
Inc., 1939). *The Nation,* June 3, 1939.

GIONO: "HARVEST"

Beside the overwhelming simplicity of Jean Giono's tales of peasant
life, all similar novels that come from France are frankly negligible. In
the high-perched village of Manosque in the French Basses-Alpes,
Giono writes of the life which he sees about him and which he himself
has led. He is one of those rare "naturals" like our own Steinbeck,
who effortlessly reproduce the direct accents of a primitive life. When
his novels run to any length, the reader, surfeited with simplicity, is
likely to lay them down unfinished. But when, as in the case of
Regain (*Harvest*), they do not exceed 200 pages, they are as refreshing
as a Cézanne still life after a gallery full of surrealism.

The natural decay and equally natural regeneration of Aubignane,
as witnessed by its one surviving inhabitant, the inarticulate Panturle,
form the story of *Harvest.* Panturle is a party to that transformation of
his village; in fact, he and Aubignane are one. It is only after he finds
a woman, mysteriously guided toward him by the aged crone Mamèche,
who has set out to find him a mate, that he and the earth and his goat
Caroline awaken and become productive again. If the blood of the fox
he flays, Arsule's breasts, old Gaubert's anvil, the goat's dry teats, and
Panturle's fall into the river are so many symbols, they all symbolize
substantially the same thing: the need for fecundation and its fulfillment.

Giono's realism is unforced, even in a passage like the following:

"Mamèche also hunted in her own way. She went in for small game:

257

sparrows tamed by the cold and all fluffed up like balls of wool. She did what people in those parts call 'embalming grain.' She boiled some old oats with some rue leaves and thorn-apple and then strewed the mixture in front of her door. The sparrows ate it and died on the spot. Before cooking them she removed their gizzards, cut them open with old scissors, and emptied out the grain onto a paper to use it again."

There is here no attempt to shock the reader, but rather simply a desire to record the old woman's life in some detail, as she ekes out existence on the barren heights where Panturle brings her his goat to milk and an occasional rabbit he has caught. Besides such details there are luminous bits of *nature morte:*

"On the kitchen table were three fine onions completely peeled, which showed up in violet and white tints against the plate. There was a jug of water, a jug of clear water, and the pale, light sun was playing in it. The tiles had been washed. Near the sink, in a big crack which had split the stones and through which the earth could be seen, a green shoot of grass had grown, holding up its head full of seeds."

With *Colline,* published here some years ago as *Hill of Destiny,* in an excellent translation by Jacques LeClerq, *Regain* is Jean Giono's best work. Its rich imagery is feelingly translated, and the book is very attractively presented with the aid of wood blocks taken from a French edition and skillfully fitted into a smaller page size.

On *Death on the Installment Plan* (*Mort à crédit*), by Louis-Ferdinand Céline, translated by John Marks (Boston: Little, Brown and Company, 1938). *The Nation,* August 27, 1938.

CÉLINE: "DEATH ON THE INSTALLMENT PLAN"

M*ort à crédit* is a long, dull book lacking the tragic quality that distinguished *Voyage au bout de la nuit*. Despite the title, which is an original way of saying the autobiography of an underdog, death no longer is one of the central characters, and the absence of the war cramps the author's style considerably. But the same unremitting violence, the same prolonged paroxysm, marks everything he writes. There is no relief for the reader, whom Céline attempts to crush just as the hero's father constantly attempts to crush his son by jumping up and down, foaming at the mouth, letting off steam through his distended nostrils, breaking up the furniture, and finally puking all over the chaos he has made. In fact there probably never was a book which contained, in the literal sense, so much vomit. The family's lark to England, Ferdinand's second arrival in England, the big fight in the Passage des Bérésinas, and Ferdinand's return from the country are scenes that testify to the documentation Céline has amassed on this subject during his service as interne and doctor. The hero brings up as easily and as frequently as the romantic hero wept, and all the big scenes end in retching.

Ferdinand, the protagonist, is of the abulic type that Dostoevsky probably created in literature and Duhamel introduced into French with his Salavin. On the surface inoffensive enough, he is only potentially harmful. His attempt to find a place for himself in life might be heart-rending if we could feel any sympathy for him. Ferdinand goes through some of the normal adolescent experiences—the breaking away from home, the revolt against conventions, the sex initiation, the adaptation to life—and completely misses others, such as the experience of friendship and love and the discovery of the beautiful. The life of Parisian small shopkeepers always on the edge of destitution and the atmosphere of one of those glass-covered passages on the right bank (now probably best visible in the Passage Choiseul) are recorded fairly faithfully. But there are no nuances in the picture. The author waves his arms too much. As he says of Ferdinand's father:

"He wound himself up again. He surpassed himself! He was swollen fit to burst. He tore open the front of his shirt. He bared his chest. . . . He's going to explode again. His fury revives. He's swelling up, his head and his eyes are enlarged. They're whirling in their sockets."

When he was awarded his M.D. in 1924, Céline had already shown an aptitude for violence. For his thesis on the life and works of Semmelweis, who committed suicide in Budapest in 1865 after making the mistake of discovering antisepsis fifty years too early, gave plenty of opportunity for outbursts against the stupidity of medical academies and of the public. Since then he has never turned off the valve. His later *Bagatelles pour un massacre* provoked a scandal by its resemblance to an anti-Semitic pamphlet, in which André Gide was the only one to see a vast ironic hoax.

Céline has been most frequently compared to Rabelais and James Joyce. To be sure, he has in common with them lengthiness, a love of scatology, and a dissatisfaction with the current vocabulary, but he lacks their learning and careful composition. When Rabelais and Joyce enrich the language, for instance, they make subtle graftings and invent onomatopoetic images, whereas Céline simply scrambles common words as a strong man bends iron. He dominates language as he does the rest of his material, crushing it with a heavy hand. His special sense of the comic manifests itself most often in elephantine exaggeration, not unlike

Rabelais at his worst—when he is carried away with the gigantic aspect of his heroes:

"Ever since the war I've had it, that whirring sound in my head. . . . It's amusing what noises it'll try: fifteen thousand different dins, a colossal hullabaloo. . . . I contain all the noises of nature, a symphonic Niagara of trumpets. I parade the big drum and an avalanche of violins. I tinkle my triangle for weeks on end. I can give anyone points on the clarinet. I've my own complete exclusive aviary of three thousand, five hundred and twenty-seven songbirds whose trillings cannot be stopped. The *vox humana* of the universe—that's me. All on my own, too, a one-man band, I'm the brass, the breath, and the inspiration. . . . I'm forever composing the opera of the Flood and the Hurricane. Then, when the curtain falls, the midnight express thunders into the station. The glass dome on high cracks across and explodes. Twenty-four valves shriek with escaping steam. The couplings clatter and jolt all the way down the train. In wide-open carriages three hundred well-oiled musicians rend the night."

If the Joyce-Rabelais comparison is misleading, there is ground for a better one, which unfortunately has less meaning here than it would have in France, where no one has apparently thought of it. In the eighteen-sixties Isidore Ducasse, self-styled Comte de Lautréamont—recently resurrected by the surrealists, whom he foreshadowed—wrote with the same unrelieved intensity, the same Gargantuan exaggeration, and the same hallucinatory manner. He suffered from a form of insanity for which pathologists have a name (his case has been studied on the basis of his writings). Certain pages from *Death on the Installment Plan,* chiefly the stampede in the Bois, the vision of the gigantic lady customer in the Passage, the pitched battle in the Tuileries, and the mass attack of the inventors on Courtial's office, sound as if they had come directly from *Les Chants de Maldoror* save that they lack Lautréamont's brilliant flashes and startling images. Céline, moreover, shows a poverty of imagination in these mad chapters, placed about every hundred pages throughout his work, since they all describe fantastic human stampedes.

In reality Céline belongs to the strictly contemporary school of hard-boiled writers, of which we know more here than they do in France. In saying that his work will survive, Leon Trotsky revealed his short-sightedness as a literary critic. In a very short time *Death on the Installment Plan* and all the novels of that school will possess merely an archeological interest.

On *Les Grands Cimetières sous la lune* (*A Diary of My Times*), by Georges Bernanos (Paris: Plon, 1938). *Partisan Review*, Winter 1938.

BERNANOS: CEMETERIES IN MOONLIGHT

It has been said that the only people who have any conviction today are the Fascists, the Communists, and the Catholics. Georges Bernanos is a Catholic who lacks the conviction. Probably he is no longer a Catholic in the eyes of the Church, which brooks neither insubordination nor criticism on the part of its faithful. M. Bernanos is gradually breaking away from his articles of faith. The *Action Française*'s approval of the rape of Ethiopia alienated him from the official French royalist party, to which he had belonged since its foundation. Now the clergy's support of Franco has done somewhat the same to his relations with his church. Like Joan of Arc—whom he optimistically invokes on the last page of this book—he has his own chapel. Architecturally, you might call it a free-standing chapel.

The chief interest of *Les Grands Cimetières sous la lune,* "Vast Cemeteries in the Moonlight" (to translate the title literally), is just that it shows the capitulation to evidence of a mind that had housed too many convictions. No matter how much we may admire the man's courage, this is bound to be a pitiful spectacle. M. Bernanos remains confused. It is much easier to determine what he is against than what he is for. His indignation showers itself upon the imbeciles (whom he used to call the "right-thinking people"), the dictators, the Spanish clergy, polemicists, the idea of progress, the philosophy of the lesser of two evils, Machiavelli and Mammon. He champions the poor and downtrodden and the fundamental dignity of man. Refusing to enroll himself, he points out that parties are a prerogative of the *bourgeoisie;* the masses—despite the plural in English—remain indivisible by any barrier between right and left. And he deplores the evolution that has made of those masses a proletariat—that is, "a vast reservoir of stultified workers plus a tiny nursery garden of future *bourgeois.*"

If he had not been living in Palma de Mallorca at the time the Spanish War broke out, Georges Bernanos might never have completely waked up. With an eighteen-year-old son in Franco's Falange and a pass in his pocket that identified him as a sympathizer of the Rebels, he witnessed the mass executions of suspects along the cemetery wall with a priest always in attendance to administer the extreme absolution. Along with his Spanish neighbors he got his summons to receive the sacraments and sign the register in church that would put him on the white list. He is thus able to judge the "Holy War" for what it is:

"I can easily understand how Fear and the desire for Revenge (but isn't Revenge simply the final manifestation of Fear) inspired the Spanish counterrevolution. But that such a state of mind should nourish the movement as long as it has remains a problem. Let me state, then, in no uncertain terms, that the Terror would long ago have worn itself out if the more or less open, or even conscious, complicity of the priests and the faithful had not finally succeeded in giving it a religious character."

It is impossible to question the impartiality of M. Bernanos' appraisal of the situation in Spain. But he returned to France not merely to tell what he knew of the trans-Pyrenean conflict. He has written his moving book as a warning to his countrymen. With subdued indignation, he shows the men of the right in France what they are heading toward and desperately calls on the French clergy not to emulate their Spanish colleagues. He raises his voice against that of Claudel, against Charles Maurras and André Tardieu and Pierre Flandin, against the whole ecclesiastical hierarchy. To him France is the last stronghold of Christendom and he fears mightily for its future. The men of today, he insists, "have hard hearts and soft guts. As after the Deluge, tomorrow the world may belong to spineless monsters."

Much too long and discursive, the book's great quality is its evident sincerity and its fairly calm accent of a man talking to us in the midst of a crumbling world. The frequence of incisive remarks makes up for the lack of any plan, surprising in the work of so accomplished a novelist. Some of the best passages are those self-justifying speeches that M. Bernanos ironically puts into the mouths of the Spanish bishops or the French royalists. The bishops recognize that "Society gets along well enough with her poor as long as she can absorb the dissatisfied in poorhouses or prisons. When the proportion of dissatisfied increases dangerously, she calls in her police and opens wide her cemeteries." But the Church being a society herself, she must deal with human societies as they are: "Do you want us to be forever on the side of the dissatisfied? Our temporal credit would soon be exhausted! Indeed, we never fail to respect poverty and to teach that it deserves to be honored. But there is not only poverty in the world; there are the poor. The only poor we can vouch for are the voluntarily poor, our own monks and nuns." The papal message to the rebellious Basques for use in the event of a Loyalist victory and the Saint-Theresa-of-Lisieux sermon by the agnostic constitute models of the type.

Macmillan has already announced a translation under the title of *A Diary of My Times* and promised that "to that great crowd of intelligent men and women who want to find some middle ground between Fascism and Communism, it gives a clear and eloquent response." This the book emphatically does not do. It offers no more than the testimony of a man of good will. Georges Bernanos has had the courage to do his awaking in public and he makes no attempt to hide the fact that he is still rubbing his eyes.

On *Earthly Paradise,* by Colette, an auto-
biography drawn from her lifetime writings
by Robert Phelps, translated by Herma
Briffault, Derek Coltman, and others
(New York: Farrar, Straus and Giroux,
Inc., 1966), and *The Delights of Growing
Old* (*La Douceur de vieillir*), by Maurice
Goudeket, translated by Patrick O'Brian
(New York: Farrar, Straus and Giroux,
Inc., 1966). *The Reporter,* May 29, 1966.

COLETTE: "EARTHLY PARADISE"

One of the easiest writers in the world to read, Colette is one of the hardest to write about. Perhaps this is because her means are so deceptively, so maddeningly simple. She herself, after using the word "masterpiece" to describe a friend's triumphant beef casserole—at once gratifying to the eye, the nostrils, and the palate—asked the cook what she put into it and received the reply: "Beef." That is the kind of masterpiece Colette turned out in abundance from 1900, when *Claudine à l'école* was published, until her death in 1954.

This is why, despite the fifteen volumes of her collected works, the bibliography of books and articles devoted to her is so much smaller than the list attached to any of the four other great names of the fabulous French generation to which she belonged: Claudel, Gide, Valéry, and Proust.

We know that she invariably wrote on blue paper and in ink, but that knowledge tells us less about her work than we know about Mme Yvon's casserole, for Colette, after all, saw and savored that dish and immortalized for us its tawny hue, its heady aroma, and its satisfying taste. "Regarde!" she insistently tells us, for during her eighty-one years she never ceased vibrating the multiple antennae of her senses.

An inborn sentience and highly developed awareness characterized every instant of her full life, from her birth in the village of Saint-Sauveur-en-Puisaye in 1873 to her death and state funeral in the glorious Palais-Royal of Paris in 1954.

Throughout this thick volume made up of excerpts from her many writings—a true *florilegium* appropriately decorated on the title page with an overflowing tub of varied flowers—we watch entranced as Colette watches the nature around her. But she herself has none of the intellectual's ingrown tendency, which tormented Paul Valéry, to see herself seeing herself. Indeed, it is almost never herself that she sees. When she does slip insensibly into viewing herself, she sees herself as a dog (p. 238) or as a cat (p. 199); when at the age of forty she gives birth to a daughter, for instance, she is "struck by the recollection that intelligent cats are usually bad mothers, sinning by inadvertence or by excess of zeal, constantly moving their kittens from place to place, holding them by the nape of the neck, pinched between their teeth, hesitating where to deposit them. What a comfortable nest that sagging seat of an armchair! However, less so than under the down quilt, perhaps? But surely the acme of comfort would be the second drawer of the commode?" The identification is complete, to the point that one forgets Colette the famous writer and her darling offspring to pace the house nervously with the cat dangling her kitten in her teeth.

From page to page here, we share her sensitive exultation in the changing seasons, her throbbing evocations of childhood, whether her own or someone else's, her affectionate reverence for Sido, her stalwart mother, her almost animal relationship to her father and the rest of the litter. The same gift for earthy identification provides unforgettable pages about quadrupeds, birds, butterflies observed as only the bright-eyed little girl of Saint-Sauveur could observe them in her mother's garden. What could be better pedagogy than her paragraph about a willful child's touching a butterfly, which ends: "A trace of lifeless ash on the tip of my finger, the wing dishonored, the tiny creature weakened."

Doubtless the same gift for putting herself in the place of others explains her acute observations of effeminate men and masculine women, her telling notations, when she was acting on tour in the provinces, about her fellow actors seen at close range in their shabby parts and paltry squabbles, her stunningly true re-creation of the gigolo *Chéri* kept by doting older women. Without that combined observation and identification she could never have written her indispensable sketches, which have long served as an adjunct to literary history, of such friends as Proust, Marcel Schwob, Sarah Bernhardt, Jean Cocteau, and Claude Debussy.

"I did not want to write," she once wrote. "Yet my life has been spent in writing. Born into a family without wealth, I had learned no profession or craft. I knew how to climb, how to whistle and run—gifts useful to a squirrel or bird or doe. The day when necessity placed a pen in my hand and I was given a little money in exchange for the pages I had written, I realized that every day of my life I would have to write, slowly, submissively, patiently, would have to match the sound to the word, would have to rise early by preference and go to bed late by necessity." But she possessed the instinct of a writer as surely as Cézanne or Van Gogh had those of the painter. "Just separate brush-strokes and splashes of color," she later advised the actress Marguerite Moreno, who was trying to write without that instinct. Her own sure sense of the splash of color, of the *mot juste* derived directly from her unerring *vision juste*. How else could she have ticked off so succinctly "the dark wrinkled faces of the pansies" or "the low wall embroidered with snails" or the "hairy gooseberries"? When she saw Marcel Proust again in his last days, she spoke of "the sooty telltale traces that an absent-minded malady had smeared haphazardly across his face." Like Proust himself, than whom Colette is no less great in her special way, she early recognized that style is not a matter of technique but of vision.

" 'The cat has caught a green lizard! She's caught a green lizard in the vines. Everyone come and look!' Can one say that she had caught it? The cat was lying on the ground. Suddenly, she turned into a dragon, into a flame, into a flying fish, and under her belly, between her silver paws, I saw a green lizard appear as though she had just that

269

moment invented it." If any other writer but Colette can match those lines for dazzling speed and absolute veracity, he belongs indeed among the greatest.

Poor Maurice Goudeket, who will go down in history as "the Man who Married Colette." At the moment he is suffering for it, as his little book about the joy of aging inevitably gets reviewed in conjunction with the so satisfying *Earthly Paradise* or synthetic autobiography of Colette. But in my generation we all married Colette. That is, if we had any sense.

By now, however, enough time has passed so that I can forgive Goudeket for being the only one among us to have really married Colette, to have shared in intimacy that wonderful, special spirit. His own book reveals in fact, as did his earlier *Close to Colette,* that he actually deserved to marry her and comfort her last years, for he possesses much of the same spirit as she. His childhood vision of the "cocotte" across the way (which can only remind us of the young Marcel spying on the Duchesse de Guermantes from some hidden vantage point) is as vivid as Colette's might have been: "The feathers of her boa tremble in the spring breeze. She has an immense hat on her head and a light-colored parasol in her hand; I am already conscious of the dancing gait of her walk. She gets in, the carriage sets off, and I gaze after her as long as I can, listening to the clip-clop of the horse's hoofs dying away in the distance."

I can even forgive Goudeket for having married someone else after Colette's death. After all, he had a vocation for marriage and he couldn't spend all his time guarding the documents left behind by Colette. I can go so far through sheer magnanimity as to forgive his translator, because of the excellence of his work, for not knowing how to spell his name. Did not Proust write: "The mere fact that someone has the same name as you without belonging to your family is a sufficient reason for scorning him"?

WAR AND OCCUPATION

Saturday Review, September 2, 1939.

FRENCH BOOKS, SUMMER 1939

The summer is not a dead period for French publishers. Not even this summer of 1939 when Parisians are constantly reminded of the international tension by the sand bags piled at their apartment doors and the underground shelter in the nearby park, when gas masks and a supply of canned foods seem more urgent necessities than books. The recent literary output by no means offers an escape from the grave preoccupations of the moment. The French are not even taking light reading with them to the mountains or the seaside this August.

Pamphlets and diaries—that is, the literature of the rostrum and of the private confessional—are sharing all the honors at the moment. Writing from Brazil, where he says he has gone to sleep off his shame, Georges Bernanos has issued two appendices to his virulent diatribe on the nationalist movement in Spain which appeared in America as *A Diary of My Times*. In *Scandale de la vérité* and *Nous autres Français* he continues to attack the Spanish Catholic hierarchy and the French nationalists and to warn his countrymen against following the example of Spain. The recent reception into the French Academy of his former spiritual guide, Charles Maurras, has made Bernanos feel even more deeply ashamed of his epoch which confuses "a petty bourgeois humanism" with the virile intellectual and moral movement of the Ancien Régime. In the period before 1889 he discerns a Catholic conscience, a monarchical heart and brain, and a republican temperament. In the royalist party's imitation of those virtues Bernanos sees only a preparation for dictatorship.

The title of Jean Giraudoux's new book, *Pleins Pouvoirs,* sounds like a dictatorial program. It marks the first venture into the political arena of a writer long distinguished for his effervescent novels and brilliant plays. At the outset Giraudoux explains that the writer no longer has the leisure to choose his subjects: "his subjects choose him; or rather his subject, for there is only one." To him the sole subject of interest today is how to keep France and the French alive at this moment of international misunderstanding and threatening war. In five chapters he succinctly outlines a program, based on statistics and expert research, for the repopulation of France by raising the birth rate and controlling naturalization, for an intelligent urbanism, for the encouragement of sports, and for a vast plan of construction that would utilize France's natural resources and accomplished engineers. By a happy coincidence, the very week this book appeared, the government, which must have been reading the proofs, voted new laws to encourage large families and promoted Giraudoux from the post he has long occupied at the Quai d'Orsay to the newly created position of High Commissioner of Propaganda (the French say "Information").

Even among the poets who write in verse—still numerous in France despite the large dose of poetry that goes into other literary forms—there is a marked tendency toward a poetry of social significance, often reflecting the author's anguish in the face of political events. Within the last three months, such admirable single poems as Jean Cocteau's *Incendie* (written during the Czechoslovakian crisis), Pierre-Jean Jouve's *Ode au Peuple* with its scathing scorn for the dictators, and Max-Pol Fouchet's *Prise de Barcelone* and Jules Supervielle's *Des Deux Côtés des Pyrénées,* both full of the Spanish tragedy and the shame of those who formed its helpless audience, have infused a new force into contemporary French poetry.

Just now the French seek relief from the problems of the day less in fiction than in the revelations of the intimate journal, passing from the public anguish to the private. If the second volume of Julien Green's diary has received very high praise and at the same time been called "as insipid as the first volume," this is because it reveals nothing but the personal. The loving description of what Green calls his photisms depicts the near-pathological state from which his novels spring. But the *Journal intime, 1928–1936,* of the self-made novelist Eugène Dabit and especially the 1,332 pages of André Gide's diary, stretching from 1889 through 1938, are limited neither to their authors nor to literary considerations. Dabit, who rose from a job as a subway guard to the deserved success of *Petit-Louis* and *L'Hôtel du Nord,* died in Sebastopol in 1936 while traveling with Gide and other Communist sympathizers. A great sincerity, a vast pity for mankind, and a fervent desire for social amelioration animate both the master and his young disciple. In his diary, now first published in a single volume and in a fuller form than ever before, Gide has put much of the best of himself.

The only novel to cause any stir this summer is *Les Lépreuses,* in which Henry de Montherlant concludes his series entitled *Les Jeunes Filles,* two volumes of which have appeared in America as *Pity for Women.* Costals, the too sensitive seducer, narrowly escapes marriage in Paris and leprosy in Africa. The reader cannot help thinking that either of these misfortunes would have served him right. Were it not for Montherlant's well-advertised ungracious attitude toward women, the novel might have passed unnoticed.

FRENCH LITERATURE AND THE WAR

Despite official assurances to the contrary, the war threatened last fall to leave no place in French life for literature. The young writers were called to the Maginot Line (the poet Patrice de La Tour du Pin was wounded and imprisoned in one of the first skirmishes) and the older writers, having seen active service twenty-five years ago, offered their pens to their country. All fall and winter the Commissariat of Information, organized in August with Jean Giraudoux as its director and lately transformed into a ministry, buzzed with the activity of Academicians, retired ambassadors, and literary prize winners. Placed in charge of all radio broadcasting, Georges Duhamel—who has seized every occasion in the past to express his mistrust of the radio—called in all the high dignitaries of the Republic of Letters and arranged several series of inspirational talks on such subjects as the literary heroes of the last war, the ideas and ideals of France, and France and England.

Several months ago, however, Duhamel gave up those functions as uncongenial. The French have used the radio well since last September, but no broadcasts have been better or more pertinent than those of Giraudoux himself, who has regularly explained to the French their duties and their privileges. With the greatest directness and frankness the subtle ironist of so many sparkling novels and comedies has dealt with the question of censorship, the conduct of the war in Poland, German propaganda, the recall of German nationals from the Baltic

277

states, and many other subjects. One of the best of his speeches, all of which would bear publication in book form, was delivered to the school children on October 7. After pointing out that their schools had opened in spite of the mobilization of thirty-eight thousand teachers, he vividly described the fifteen million German children studying falsified maps and expurgated history books in schools from which any mention of many of the greatest Germans is banished. Giraudoux ended his broadcast thus: "Young guardians of true history, of true geography, of a moral system which has no place for hatred, whose classroom regalia includes neither daggers nor powder, it is to you that France, bitterly engaged in fighting a war, delegates this autumn the mission of preserving two of its most precious possessions: gaiety and study."

French propaganda of a literary type got under way very early in the war. At least two Academicians early produced brochures of a timely nature. With his usual clarity André Maurois summed up in October *Les Origines de la Guerre de 1939* as a preliminary indictment of Hitler while waiting for the French Foreign Office's *Livre jaune*. In *Pourquoi te bats-tu?*, Louis Gillet, as a veteran of 1914, addresses the soldier of 1939 and clarifies the painful necessity for France's entry into war. September and October saw the birth of two magazines, *Notre Combat* and *Les Annales de la Guerre,* both aiming to give a faithful account of the war with all the diplomatic, military, and economic documents and statistics that present readers and future historians will need to get "an impartial view of events." At least half of each publication, however, is made up of radio broadcasts and articles signed by famous names.

Meanwhile, following the tradition of the other war, several newspapers and gazettes have already reached Paris from the front. *Franchise militaire, Le Vitaliste, L'Isard de Metz,* etc., reflect the inactivity of the Maginot Line, which a group of prominent writers in the capital have attempted to make more endurable by organizing a service for obtaining books and magazines for the soldiers. By November the intellectual exchange between the front and rear was very active. Some of the braver lending libraries were risking packages of books at the front, whence they returned looking as if they had been read by the whole regiment. The most popular reading among the soldiers is the French classics, with Montaigne well in the lead. One young lieutenant writes back that of the twenty officers in his group nine have brought along books and six of those have Montaigne. The ideal seems to be the one-volume, India-paper editions in the series known as the Pléiade which includes Shakespeare, Balzac, Corneille, Racine, Montaigne, etc.

Visible signs of a desire that literature should "carry on" normally are not lacking. Two such signs were the election to the French Academy early in January of the distinguished scholar Paul Hazard, beloved of so many Americans who have studied under him in Paris or at Harvard or Columbia, and the regular awards in December of the annual literary prizes to the best novels of the year. The coveted Goncourt and Femina prizes, each amounting to five thousand francs and to infinitely more in publicity, have given birth in recent years to two other prizes, the Renaudot and the Interallié, which are awarded by the journalists assigned to cover, respectively, the Goncourt and the Femina awards and which carry nothing but a great publicity value. This year all the prizes went to relatively young and deserving novelists; but a sharp cleavage is noticeable between the novels crowned by the Goncourt jury and its Renaudot shadow, which both present full-length portraits of social classes, and the novels preferred by the ladies of the Femina jury and the journalists of the Interallié, which are both works of action and intrigue.

The Goncourt winner, *Les Enfants gâtés* by Philippe Hériat, soberly recounts Agnès Boussardel's return to the bosom of her wealthy family after two years of student life, anonymity, and love in California. To French readers the novel owes its charm in great part to its picturesque (and to us rather false) descriptions of life in America; to American readers the cruel picture of a French banking clan seen through the eyes of its only rebel offshoot has far more value. Nothing but money counts in the life of the Boussardels, who are ready to sacrifice a daughter, a nephew, and their honor to satisfy their rapacious cupidity. The portrait is almost a caricature, but the great weakness of the novel lies in its construction, as is so often the case with novels in the first person.

The class depicted in *Les Javanais* by Jean Malaquais stands socially at the opposite pole. "Javanese" is the nickname for the migratory mineworkers from all parts of the world—outlaws, political exiles, criminals—who live in an amorphous group dominated by acts of violence. As an objective study in social pathology, this novel is brutal and often very moving, but the reader does not feel for these characters that deep sympathy that some of Steinbeck's specimens of humanity call forth. Though the social document here inevitably recalls Steinbeck, it is even more likely that the scenes of sexual violence owe something to the French translations of Faulkner.

Paul Vialar's *La Rose de la mer,* the Femina prize winner, and *Les Figurants de la mort* by Roger de Lafforest, which was awarded the Prix Interallié, belong to the classification of novels of adventure. Both are exciting tales and the latter, with its Pirandellian handling of action which is at once real and fictitious, offers something like a satire of the best tradition of this kind of novel.

But the outstanding recent literary events in Paris have certainly been the appearance of new installments of the three long cyclic novels being written by Georges Duhamel, Jules Romains, and Roger Martin du Gard. When such heavy bombers as these appear in the sky, the public immediately forgets the antics of the light scouting planes.

The eighth volume of Duhamel's *Pasquier Chronicles,* entitled *Le Combat contre les ombres,* brings the action down to August 2, 1914. On the eve of the last World War the Pasquier family is distinguishing itself in several ways: Laurent as a brilliant young biologist, Joseph as a financier, and Cécile as a musician. All seem unaware of the approaching catastrophe. Laurent's struggle against the stupidity, cowardice, and ill will of his fellow men starts with his discharging an incompetent but politically influential assistant and ends with his own resignation and an intolerant press campaign against him. In a series of brief scenes, Georges Duhamel, himself a doctor, editor, and Academician, builds up a pitiless picture of the medical and journalistic worlds he knows so well.

French Literature and the War

After the brilliant success of *Verdun,* the seventeenth and eighteenth volumes of *Men of Good Will* could not fail to disappoint Jules Romains's readers. In these two volumes Romains fairly faithfully reflects what we have until recently called postwar youth and the two popular postwar attitudes, but with too neat an opposition. If he maintains his intentions of a year ago, he still has nine or ten volumes in his inkwell, but from present indications he seems no nearer the end than he was when his cycle began that October day in 1908.

Martin du Gard, on the other hand, has finally terminated *Les Thibault* with a book of 350 pages simply entitled *Epilogue.* The preceding section took place in the summer of 1914 and ended with Jacques's appropriately futile death. The *Epilogue* completely winds up the story in what is artistically the most satisfactory manner. Antoine's return from the front, fatally gassed, permits the author to take up the tangled threads of the various Thibault and Fontanin lives and to show the transformations the years have brought. All the characters have changed greatly since those calm prewar days when we first met them, yet no one has failed to develop in harmony with his inner nature. Rarely has the impression of life, in all its flux, been so effectively created in a novel. At the end of the whole work, placed just after the Armistice, a new life has begun which combines the Thibault and Fontanin blood: Jacques's illegitimate and posthumous child whose mother is Jenny de Fontanin. When the last half of the whole work appears in English next fall, American readers will have the rare experience of reading an authentic masterpiece.

This new world war must have seriously upset the long-range plans of the French novelists engaged in writing cyclic novels. *La Chronique des Pasquier* has just reached the outbreak of the last war; Dr. Laurent Pasquier is setting out for the 1914 front with the conviction that he will fight to end all wars, and if he opens a newspaper in the train he will discover that he is headed for the Maginot Line. The *Men of Good Will* have weathered Verdun without loss of life or limb and are just beginning to enjoy the postwar years which turned out to be but a momentary armistice. Romains and Duhamel have let events get ahead of them—as who has not. Roger Martin du Gard has found the best solution to the problem, but the closing of his cycle was not forced upon him; for years he has been planning to end *The Thibaults* in much this way. The war of 1914 to 1918 has killed, maimed, or otherwise profoundly marked all his protagonists; having lived, they can now enter history as their flesh-and-blood brothers have done. Antoine's slow death from his wounds is subtly symbolic of a whole generation. Let us hope that the symbol will not soon be applicable to another generation.

College English, March 1940.

AMERICAN BOOKS AND FRENCH READERS

At the moment the French are not giving much thought to literature. One day last August they suddenly limited their reading to a diet of four or five newspapers a day and two or three fresh mobilization notices posted on the nearest public building. But right up to the staggering announcement of the Russo-German pact the terraces of the Left Bank had buzzed with talk of new books while—in the usual Parisian balance of body and mind—those of the Right Bank had hummed with analyses of the *couturiers'* showings and last-minute fashion tips. On both sides of the Seine the name of our country was constantly invoked. Though this may not be new among the stylists who have long designed models for the American market, the Parisian literary world's interest in the United States marks rather a revolution in taste.

The American in Paris last summer could not fail to notice how difficult it was becoming to discuss contemporary French literature with enlightened Frenchmen, since all the young and enthusiastic intellectuals would much prefer to talk of American literature. In this category must be included even André Gide, although he is nearing his seventieth birthday. A mention of Malraux or Romains would get no further than to call forth a remark about Steinbeck or Faulkner. Only after the American visitor had given his opinion of MacLeish's nomination as Librarian of Congress would his French friends consent to speak of Supervielle's latest poems. In certain groups knowledge of our literary output is so much more intimate and up to date than knowledge of French literature is in corresponding American groups that one comes to wonder if the French public reads chiefly in English. The popularity of the Parisian lending libraries for books in English—notably Sylvia Beach's and that of the Librairie Gallimard—would indicate that this is almost true, at least for an intelligent minority.

Within that minority must be counted the editors of certain magazines and reviews particularly susceptible to transatlantic influences and a lively group of young university critics. In recent years the monthly *Nouvelle Revue Française* has published stories, poems, and articles by a great many of the leading American writers of today. An editorial note in a recent number states that "there is perhaps no country in the world whose new poetry is more alive, more diverse, and at the same time more misunderstood than the United States." *Europe,* the liberal monthly of such men as Romain Rolland, Jean-Richard Bloch, and Louis Aragon, has welcomed many of our writers; its issue of August fifteenth contains a communication by Dashiell Hammett on tempo in the contemporary novel. Since its foundation in 1935, the very enterprising and well-edited quarterly *Mesures,* whose editors are creative writers possessed of an extraordinary flair, has published poems by Eliot, Frost, MacLeish, and Edgar Lee Masters, and at least one story by Saroyan. MacLeish and Eliot suffer no great sea change in translation, but *Spoon River Anthology,* though feelingly translated by Jean Prévost, who can quote Frost and Masters by the hour, is about as natural in French as Walt Whitman's *Feuilles d'herbe.*

The 380-page summer 1939 issue of *Mesures* is devoted entirely to the glory of American letters. Beginning with Cotton Mather and Franklin, it comes down through Irving, Poe, Whitman, and Emily Dickinson to Robinson Jeffers, Allen Tate, Dos Passos, Marianne Moore, and William Carlos Williams. Among our contemporary writers *Mesures* shows a marked preference for the poets, doubtless because they are necessarily less known in France. Each passage, whether in prose or verse, is given both in French and in the original, and the translations, by several hands, are generally excellent. To each writer the editors have devoted a brief and well-informed note, such as the following, literally translated:

"Hart Crane was born in 1899 in a small Ohio town. His schooling was brief. For a time he was an advertising copywriter. He made a trip to Europe and lived for a while in Mexico. He committed suicide in 1932 by jumping from the deck of the liner on which he was returning from Vera Cruz. His first volume, *White Buildings,* appeared in 1926. In *The Bridge* (1930) he sees in Brooklyn Bridge the myth of American civilization. A disciple of Whitman, close to Rimbaud, influenced by Eliot and Stevens, Crane revealed himself to be the most ambitious, and often the most obscure, of modern American poets." It is interesting to note that among these representative American writers figure two Negro poets: James Weldon Johnson and Langston Hughes.

The May 1939 issue of *Cahiers de Paris,* the review of the rather self-conscious Populist movement, which claims to write of and for the people and has so far achieved only half of its aim, was entirely filled with a discussion of the contemporary novel in the United States. Because of the awkwardness of giving extracts from the novelists, most of them available in complete translation anyway, the magazine is made up of a series of critical studies, many of them by university professors like Maurice Le Breton, Léon Lemonnier, Jean Simon, etc. Individual essays on Dreiser, "Sinclair Lewis and the Portrayal of Social Classes," Sherwood Anderson, Waldo Frank, John Dos Passos, Pearl Buck, and Josephine Johnson follow more general studies of currents. Lemonnier, in his introductory note, does not hesitate to qualify American literature as "at present one of the great literatures of the world." The profound knowledge and critical acumen of the contributors to this symposium would surprise many an English department in our universities.

Many of the same critics can be found in the very live, though scholarly, publication *Etudes Anglaises,* which succeeded in 1937 the former *Revue Anglo-américaine.* Its pages contain articles on such subjects as "Social Evolution in the Southern States According to the Novels of T. S. Stribling," "William Faulkner's Technique and Psychology," besides regular reviews of American writers from Edith Wharton to Sally Benson and from Van Wyck Brooks to Alexander Woollcott. Under the direction of members of this group of *américanisants,* the number of doctoral dissertations on American subjects is constantly increasing. At the Sorbonne alone, theses are now being written on many aspects of the American novel, on J. Fenimore Cooper, Willa Cather, Mark Twain; there is even one announced on Charles Eliot Norton.

In spite of the mixed impressions American tourists leave in their wake, America is decidedly the vogue in France. Within the last three months no fewer than six books have appeared which all treat what one publisher calls "the most urgent question of the day: how to understand America and the Americans." All but two of these volumes have something to say of the literary scene in the United States. In *Les Américains des colons aux penseurs* Edmond Privat sketches our history in a series of brisk chapters whose brevity, however, does not permit him to discuss American literature. Believe it or not, the thinkers who figure in his title are our political leaders. André Demaison's *Terre d'Amérique* limits itself to the impressions of a traveler who does not seem to have read on the train. *L'Amérique, miroir grossissant de l'Europe* by the brilliant young Léo Ferrero, who died a few years ago in a motor accident in New Mexico, presents a not especially flattering picture of the United States, where he found no real spiritual life. To this Italian exile, who with his distinguished father had elected France as his second fatherland and wrote directly in French, all the American intellectuals seemed exiled in their own country. Though more intelligent and more maturely expressed, Ferrero's reaction to American civilization recalls Duhamel's *Scènes de la vie future,* which was translated here as *America the Menace.* André Maurois, on the other hand, likes the United States and feels at home in them. His recent travel diary, entitled *Etats-Unis 39,* is full of sprightly comment on Roosevelt, *New Yorker* humor, Lewis and Conger's "sleep-shop," Mother's Day, and "Information Please."

For instance, Maurois characterizes the American brand of socialism as an aesthetic communism: 80 per cent William Morris, 10 per cent Rivera, 5 per cent Malraux, 4 per cent Freud, and 1 per cent Lenin.

On our recent literature Maurois has many interesting remarks. Above all, he finds it "rich and very much alive. No great classic art, often a lack of composition, a language of the people which is sometimes aggressively brutal. But a great deal of force; novel subjects, images and vocabulary; a strong and naïve poetry." Though this sounds like the classic noncommittal market report, these remarks do reveal rather typical French reactions. *The Late George Apley* strikes him as one of the most civilized American novels; *The Grapes of Wrath* makes him shudder and reflect on the inequalities of our capitalistic system. He sees America passing through a Romantic crisis. After the more realistic generation of Dreiser and Lewis comes a group of writers (Faulkner, Steinbeck, Caldwell) who provide a thrill through the horrible, the violent, and the brutal. The only poet of whom Maurois speaks is Edna St. Vincent Millay, whose *Conversation at Midnight* he considers very beautiful and he translates a page for his readers.

The young novelist and essayist Jean Prévost, who was the first holder of the Jesse Isidore Strauss Fellowship for study in the United States, has recorded his American impressions in *Usonie: Esquisse de la civilisation américaine*. Rather dryly, he has written a series of essays on various cultural aspects of life in the United States. His choice of subjects—Robert Andrews Millikan's physics, Thomas Hunt Morgan's biology, Clark Wissler's anthropology, Robert Lynd's sociology, Frank Lloyd Wright's architecture, and Walt Disney's cartoons—suggests that he spent much of his time on university campuses. The two essays on literary subjects are devoted to Eugene O'Neill and Robert Frost, both of whom appear to Prévost as figures of world importance. There is, unfortunately, nothing particularly French in Prévost's very able academic dissertations.

Though Bernard Faÿ, who now occupies a chair of American civilization at the august Collège de France, knows the United States as intimately as anyone, he still maintains a certain perspective in viewing us. Nor would anyone mistake his impressions for those of a German or an Englishman. His monumental *Civilisation américaine,* which appeared in July, has much to say of our literature, which "for the past forty years has been one of the most interesting in the universe as well as one of the most disappointing." Despite our many original and powerful writers, according to Professor Faÿ we have no general concept of an indigenous literary tradition. Of the novelists who write in what he calls the British tradition, he would save only Edith Wharton, though her novels "might have been written by a grandniece of Henry James who had married the cousin of one of Proust's servants and lived in Neuilly." But the most annoying group of writers to Faÿ is that which seeks to emulate the Italian Renaissance (Thornton Wilder, James Branch Cabell, etc.) and indulges in overwriting. What he calls the radical writers form the most vigorous group, in revolt against both the other tendencies. Though he recognizes the eminence of Sinclair Lewis among the "radicals," Bernard Faÿ is perhaps the only Frenchman writing on American literature who does not grant him supreme importance as a representative of the United States. He prefers John Dos Passos and Eugene O'Neill, and in the most vital American tradition he places Hemingway, Faulkner, and Sherwood Anderson. Among the poets Faÿ has always shown a tendency to glorify Gertrude Stein as the fountainhead of modern writing, but he also finds elements of greatness in E. E. Cummings, Marianne Moore, and T. S. Eliot. Like Léo Ferrero, Bernard Faÿ is sensitive to the strange position of the artist in America, where even the best writers are not so much isolated as "known, respected and neglected."

Maurois, Prévost, Ferrero, and Faÿ count among that ever growing number of Europeans who read our literature in the original. But the Frenchman who stays at home and does not read English has enough translations to keep him busy for months, if not years. It is not surprising if our Nobel prize winners, Sinclair Lewis, Eugene O'Neill, and Pearl Buck, are translated in their entirety. The most recent Lewis in France is *The Prodigal Parents,* which followed very closely on what is entitled there *Impossible ici;* the latest Pearl Buck novel to appear is *The Proud Heart.* Without benefit of the Swedish Academy, Louis Bromfield can boast at least seven volumes in French, and Hemingway three or four. Erskine Caldwell (*Le Petit Arpent du Bon Dieu, La Route au tabac, Nous les vivants*), William Faulkner (from *Tandis que j'agonise* to *Sanctuaire* and *Lumière d'août,* with prefaces by Malraux, Larbaud, and the translator Maurice E. Coindreau of Princeton), and John Steinbeck (*Des souris et des hommes,* also translated by Coindreau) enjoy the greatest popularity at the moment among enlightened readers, although *Gone with the Wind*—in which French critics unanimously recognize what they appropriately call *du souffle*—has broken all the records for sales. John Dos Passos—known to the French by *Manhattan Transfer, One Man's Initiation,* and *In All Countries*—reflects metropolitan life in America better than any other writer in their opinion. The Studs Lonigan series of James T. Farrell has begun to appear in translation, and many French readers wonder why they have not heard from James M. Cain since *Le Facteur sonne toujours deux foix* appeared. Dashiell Hammett has his faithful readers in France, and so has Ludwig Lewisohn. William Seabrook is known by two translations, while Josephine Johnson, Joseph Hergesheimer, and DuBose Heyward have each been translated at least once. The publishing house of the *Nouvelle Revue Française,* which with the house of Stock most vigorously promotes American writers, has issued several novels of Herman Melville in the last three years; the most recent volume, *Pierre; or, The Ambiguities,* has been receiving favorable reviews. Despite the esteem in which they are held in France as pioneer American realists, relatively little of Sherwood Anderson and Theodore Dreiser has appeared in translation; their reputation, like that of our poets, has in great part been established by those who have read them in the original.

Of course the American novel is better known in France than other literary forms. Our poets are for the most part accessible only fragmentarily in the quarterly and monthly reviews. While the quarterly *Commerce,* edited by Valéry, Fargue, and Larbaud, existed, it published numerous poems of Eliot and MacLeish besides some by English poets as diverse as Edith Sitwell, Robert Herrick, and George Meredith (*Modern Love*). *Mesures* has carried on the tradition of *Commerce,* but by almost omitting the English poets it has given double the space to the Americans. French knowledge of our theater should be more widespread than it is in view of the number of adaptations presented on Paris stages, but invariably the French can recall the name of only one American dramatist, Eugene O'Neill, whom Henri Peyre in a recent book calls "the only dramatic genius of our epoch." Maurois speaks of the great vitality of the New York theater, and so does Faÿ; but they have both had the advantage of visiting our country frequently.

Knowledge of America and her literature is visibly increasing in France. Of course the same people who think Detroit because of its French name must be in Canada continue to spell Sherwood with a *v*, as it would be pronounced in French. But the group of Frenchmen who do not have to hesitate over the number of *l*'s in the names O'Neill and Eliot is growing every year, and one almost never sees the *th* transposed in Whitman any more, as it always used to be, or the puristic dieresis over the last letter in Poe. A few years ago American books were generally announced as *traduit de l'américain*. This was rather a part of the blurb to catch the public's interest than an indication of the publisher's awareness of the difference between the American and English languages. The fact that today American books are *traduit de l'anglais* means simply that it has become unnecessary to make a distinction since all the new translations come from America.

On *Paris France,* by Gertrude Stein (New York: Charles Scribner's Sons, 1940). *The Nation,* July 27, 1940.

THE EXPATRIATE'S PARIS

Paris France might be called *The Autobiography of Paris, France,* since, like the other autobiographies by Gertrude Stein, it tells less about its subject than about its author. That smart-Aleck remark may not be altogether fair, for as we read about Miss Stein—her dogs, her friends, the village of Bilignin, and the town of Belley near her country home—we also learn much about the French and even something about Paris. In an appallingly and delightfully confused manner which simulates a one-sided conversation, Gertrude Stein does discuss fashions, cooking, Latinity, the French family, the peasant, and such very French concepts as civilization and equality. As if talking on the lawn at Bilignin, she illustrates her points with amusing or pathetic anecdotes—sometimes lost on the reader because he does not belong to her coterie—and peppers her speech with quaint expressions translated literally from the French. The book is full of charm, a very personal charm, and humor. Its 120 pages overflow with sententious remarks, such as, "The reason why all of us naturally began to live in France is because France has scientific methods, machines, and electricity, but does not really believe that these things have anything to do with the real business of living. Life is tradition and human nature"; or, "All Frenchmen know that you have to become civilized between eighteen and twenty-three and that civilization comes upon you by contact with an older woman, by revolution, by army discipline, by any escape or by any subjection, and then you are civilized and life goes on normally in a Latin way, life is then peaceful and exciting, life is then civilized, logical and fashionable in short life is life." The trouble with the postwar generation, she says, is that war prevents the process of civilization and that the young men "missed their time for becoming civilized." But this had already been said by any number of those very young men and before them by another lost generation, that of Alfred de Musset.

To Gertrude Stein, as to many of us, Paris has meant civilization. Firmly rooted in tradition, the French have been able to accept and try everything without losing their balance. Their keen sense of reality is so great that they can tolerate any degree of unreality. Yet with these qualities that she recognizes in them, and their logic and supreme degree of civilization, Miss Stein does not grant them any role, except that of "inevitable background," in the creation of twentieth-century art. In other words, the French looked on as picturesque and indulgent bystanders while the Picassos, the Steins, the Sir Francis Roses, the Bromfields, and the Hemingways made modern art. This is a parochial point of view, the point of view of the transients in the Sixth Arrondissement. Yes, it is the point of view of the tourist. On considering all that Gertrude Stein's art owes to her immediate French predecessors, one cannot but find this attitude particularly ungracious.

With all its charm and flavor and superficiality, *Paris France* is a pathetic little book. It is pathetic because, obviously designed as propaganda of the nicer sort, it fails to achieve its end. The larger public having been frightened away by the author's reputation and style, it will be read and enjoyed only by the initiates, the small minority who know both Miss Stein and France. And in view of Gertrude Stein's patronizing attitude toward her subject, this will be no loss. Written before the French capitulation, *Paris France* reflects the anguish that all civilized people felt during the spring. Like all of us, Miss Stein was worried about the possible loss of one of the most precious things in the world—an irreplaceable culture. It is unfortunate that to her that culture was important chiefly as the ideal atmosphere for the creation of expatriate art.

On the Editions de Minuit. *The New York Times Book Review,* March 4, 1945.

WRITERS AT MIDNIGHT

In November 1940, when more than half of France was a prison guarded by the ubiquitous green uniforms of the Wehrmacht, the leftist philosopher and essayist Jean Guéhenno, former editor of Romain Rolland's review *Europe,* wrote:

"It is time to paint the walls of one's prison. I do not know what I shall paint on the walls of mine, but I am sure that all my old dreams, all the images of my faith will be there. This is not the time to change them but rather to remain dangerously faithful. In my heaven the genius of liberty will continue to fly. Since the prison term will probably be long I shall work slowly. The time has now come to write simply for the pleasure of writing. We are now reduced to silence and solitude, but perhaps also to gravity. Whether or not our cell is full of light depends after all only on us. . . . No man with a heart can feel free when two million of his compatriots are hostages in the conqueror's prisons, when forty million men around him preserve only through silence and subterfuge the little dignity that remains to them."

A year later, when resistance to the conqueror had been better organized, when most self-respecting French citizens had learned to live periodically behind the mask of a false identity substantiated by an impressive series of forged papers and ration books, a little group of intellectuals met in the country and laid plans to adorn their prison. By that time every resistance movement had its newspaper, usually multigraphed or hand set on poor paper and passed from hand to hand by stealth. But Vercors and Mme Desvignes dreamed of a clandestine publishing house to issue works of genuine literary quality.

Neither one had any literary reputation and their business experience when pooled was very meager. Under his real name of Jean Bruller, Vercors was widely known before the war as an illustrator. His "Twenty-One Delightful Ways of Committing Suicide" and his frequent albums of black-and-white drawings entitled "Jean Bruller's Quarterly Statements" showed such an insight into man's foibles and such a sardonic humor that Roger Martin du Gard once said Bruller would eventually feel forced to write. And now, suffering under the Nazi oppression, he wrote in his middle thirties a little masterpiece of reticence of which André Gide might be proud.

In a pure, direct style *Le Silence de la mer* recounts the arrival in a French household of a German officer who, despite his extraordinarily sympathetic approach, cannot break the barrier of silence surrounding his hosts. When the German discovers that in dreaming of a Franco-German spiritual union he is in conflict with the entire Nazi ideology, he warns the French couple of their country's pivotal position in the "great battle of the temporal against the spiritual." Finally, in a gesture of suicide he requests his own transfer to the Russian front. *The Silence of the Sea* teaches by implication that there can be no collaboration in this war to the finish between a slave-creating tyrant and free men of all nations.

In December 1941, Mme Desvignes, who as Yvonne Paraf had been a secretary and translator before the war, found a small job printer named Aulard in the Rue Tournefort, one of those picturesque and smelly Latin Quarter streets so dear to Eliot Paul. Vercors—who now prefers to be known by his pen name—received 5,000 francs as a contribution from a professional man in Paris. And since Aulard was willing to risk his life by printing clandestinely without the official censor's imprimatur, the Editions de Minuit, as the new publishing house was to be called, came into being one dark night when his hand-set sheets were carried across the city to Mme Desvignes's small flat on the Rue Vineuse.

To understand the risks run by every member of the enterprise, one must attempt to re-create the atmosphere of the Occupation. Over a Paris bled to death "spread the spider-web of Nazi flags." Nothing but German automobiles on the streets. Every bistro had its enemy informants drawn from the scum of Europe's prisons; every subway car was full of the green uniforms with their highly polished holsters and short daggers; the entrance of every official building had its pair of heel-clicking black boots.

When Mme Desvignes and Vercors received me last November, the atmosphere was already very different: I had to climb the five flights to the famous apartment because the shortage of electricity had immobilized the elevator, but I drove past a Trocadéro free of swastikas and in my own Citroën car. No one had the power to ask what was in my brief case, marked with the gold U.S.A., or in my pockets.

In that apartment the two young people themselves cut and bound the sheets and arranged the distribution of the edition of the Vercors book, limited to 350 copies, ready in February 1942. Every copy, printed in a 4½ by 6½-inch format on fine white paper which Vercors himself bought in small quantities on the black market, bore a colophon reading: "This volume, published at the expense of a few patriotic lovers of literature, has been printed in Paris under the oppression." The putative subscription list was made up with great care and the copies addressed to Paris were delivered by hand, while those for the provinces were mailed singly, each in a different Vichy-controlled post office.

Jacques Mathieu, a member of the French Consultative Assembly, tells how, when he was heading an intelligence chain in France, he lent one of his minor couriers to deliver the books. After the latter had left in his room the suitcases containing one complete edition of the new publishing house he was picked up by the Gestapo for another reason. Mathieu miraculously found the address, though under a false name, and sent someone to recover the volumes at the risk of meeting the German police. Later two elegant young women regularly delivered the finished volumes. Each one was able to stuff thirty copies in the saddlebags that smart Parisiennes attach to the back fender of their cycles, and together they delivered sixty copies a day.

Soon subscriptions began to pour in through devious channels, together with requests for the precious little books. The 350 copies of *The Silence of the Sea* having proved lamentably insufficient, a second printing of 450 was begun at once. All later volumes were issued at 1,000 or 1,100 copies, but these figures give no adequate idea of the circulation, since many of the titles were smuggled into the so-called unoccupied zone where they were mimeographed or reset in type and widely circulated. In London as early as the summer of 1943 we had an English reprint of *Le Silence de la mer*, which also soon appeared in New York with an inexplicable plural in the title.

Altogether, in their effort to maintain "the pride of Letters," the new venture published twenty-five titles. Only two bore their author's names: *À travers le désastre*, by the philosopher Jacques Maritain, then a refugee in New York, and a French translation of Steinbeck's *The Moon Is Down*. Since Vercors had taken his name from a plateau in the Alps, famous for its maquis, most of the writers followed him by assuming geographical pseudonyms. The young essayist J. Debu-Bridal wrote, under the name of Argonne, a brief cultural history of England from Alcuin to Huxley; Edith Thomas (Auxois) gave a collection of stirring short stories. Jean Guéhenno, known for his studies of Michelet and Voltaire, issued his spiritual diary under the name Cévennes. Georges Adam (Hainaut) told a racy story of escape from a prison camp, and the well-known young novelist Claude Aveline (Minervois) told a pathetic tale of women in prison and under Nazi torture. The novelist and academician François Mauriac, as Forez, wrote *Le Cahier noir*. But, like Vercors's second volume, *La Marche à l'étoile*, it is out of print and I have not seen a copy.

The Editions de Minuit contributed greatly to the poetic renaissance that marked the Occupation and permitted many poets to see their verses "finally freed from the sobs that accompanied their birth." There is *The Musée Grévin*, by Aragon, the former surrealist, novelist, and editor of the Communist daily *Humanité*. In couplets reminiscent of the music hall satirists he consigns Pétain, Laval, Mussolini, and their henchmen to a waxworks museum. Aragon's wife, Elsa Triolet, of whom he had written in *Les Yeux d'Elsa,* contributed a collection of poems I have not seen, entitled *Les Amants d'Avignon. L'Honneur des poètes* includes twenty-one young poets, all writing with deep conviction of prisons, executions, and tortures, of swastikas, maquis, and penal trains.

But the finest poems are contained in *Trente-trois Sonnets écrits au secret,* by Jean Cassou, the poet, novelist, and authority on Spanish literature. "He had only the night for ink and his memory to serve as paper," says his commentator Aragon. A beautiful poem is translated from a sonnet by Hugo von Hofmannsthal which he found in a fragment of the filthy *Pariser Zeitung,* the only reading matter that ever reached his prison cell. The same objectivity toward the best in German art is reflected in another volume, *Les Exilés,* a collection of poems with French translation on facing pages of such as Heine, Schnitzler, Zweig, Werfel, Toller, and Kästner, who had been excluded from a large anthology issued by the German Institute of Paris in 1943.

Other volumes in the series have the value of political pamphlets. One such, called *Deux Voix françaises,* groups significant quotations from Charles Péguy, the poet and philosophic essayist who fell at the front in 1914, together with pages by Gabriel Péri, the Communist Deputy from Seine-et-Oise who was shot as a hostage in December 1941. Three other pamphlets collect the facts concerning three historical events: *L'Armistice,* by Roger Giron; *Toulon,* by Yves Farge, a Resistance leader of Lyon; and *Les Martyres,* by Aragon.

Two volumes titled *Chroniques clandestins* contain stories, essays, and poems by famous writers such as André Gide, Julien Benda, André Chamson, Charles Morgan, Jean Paulhan.

Indeed, Jean Paulhan, editor of the ever exciting *Nouvelle Revue Française* from 1925 until Otto Abetz replaced him with a fascist in 1940, occupied a central position in underground literary activity. Together with two young writers named Claude Morgan and Jacques Decour, the latter of whom was shot by the Germans, he founded *Lettres Françaises,* a clandestine literary periodical. Aged by his detention at the hands of the Gestapo, by the constant risk of further arrest, and by the torture and execution of many companions, he nevertheless basked in the friendship of young poets as he discussed hopes for the revival of his prewar periodicals.

The energetic Vercors and Mme Desvignes also played an important role in the publication of *Lettres Françaises*. Today, the leading weekly journal of the arts, it appears openly every Friday. Likewise, the Editions de Minuit now has a registered address and already announces the reissue of all its publications in a format almost identical with that of the little collector's items which appeared "sous l'oppression." For many years these brave writers and publishers will look back proudly on the dangerous days when they worked, as they now say "in clandestinity," and meanwhile the Editions de Minuit may grow, in the liberty for which they fought, to be one of the leading French publishing houses.

The New York Times Book Review, August 19, 1945.

A LETTER FROM PARIS, 1945

The French have always gloried in their past. Just now, for the sober intellectual in his study as for the swaggering FFI parading his unconventional uniform on the boulevards, the glorious past is the very recent period of Resistance. It is not strange that the nearly five years of struggle against the occupying forces have left a profound mark on French life and thought. Like demobilized soldiers with a reserve stock of unemployed heroism, the whole nation feels a letdown. Delighted as that liberty-loving people are by their new freedom, they cannot but feel a touch of nostalgia for the heroic period when they matched their wits with their cruel conquerors.

Much of the literary production in the spring of 1945 was originally written to escape the Nazi censor. It was correctly predicted in these pages in April that the Editions de Minuit would continue as a vigorous publishing house after the liberation of France. In fact, their 1945 books easily lead in interest other recent publications.

Les Oligarques by Junius describes the role of the Oligarchic Party in Athens between 415 and 404 B.C. Written by a specialist in ancient history who is still coquettishly hiding behind a pseudonym, it traces the machinations of the Athenian Fascists from the earliest weakening of the Republic by the mutilation of the statues through the Revolution of the 400, to the fall of the thirty tyrants. The last lines of this fascinating "Essay in Biased History" clarify the author's intentions:

"In this whole disconcerting story the evil-doing of the 'good men' is surpassed only by the clemency of the 'bad men.' I am writing these lines somewhere in France—in what was France—on Saturday, 17 October 1942: the 'good men' are still doing as much evil; it remains to be seen whether the 'bad men' will be as magnanimous."

But the striking thing about Junius' history is the discretion of his allusions to events of his own time. The alert reader is constantly aware of the parallel between the Cagoule and Vichy on the one hand and the men who wanted so badly to keep Athens for the "good" Athenians that they called in Sparta's arms. Yet only rarely does the author indulge in so direct a thrust as when, speaking of the council of ten ancients, he refers to the poet Sophocles, over eighty years old, and adds: "the revered name of a famous old man looks well on the letterhead of certain wrecking companies."

In issuing *Au rendez-vous allemand* by Paul Eluard, the same young publishing house has collected the finest, most stirring topical poetry to come from France—that is, to be written anywhere in our time. In anger, in pity, in deep disgust, Eluard, the surrealist who has best overcome and absorbed the lessons of that sterile movement, sings the horrors and heroisms of occupied France. The most memorable poems in the volume are those originally published secretly in 1942 under the title *Poésie et Vérité*, such as the "Hymn to Liberty" with its forceful repetitions, or "Curfew," or this quatrain entitled "Patience":

> Toi ma patiente ma patience ma parente
> Gorge haut suspendue orgue de la nuit lente
> Révérence cachant tous les ciels dans sa grâce
> Prépare à la vengeance un lit d'où je naîtrai.

Eluard's poems have easily recognizable subjects. There is one vitriolic statement, for instance, on the French intellectuals who served the enemy. There is a song for Gabriel Péri, the Communist martyr. There is another on the hostage's last night alive. There is even an outburst on the futility of shaving the heads of "horizontal collaborators."

"The forgotten giants were seen to rise up everywhere. In railroad stations where foreign sentries stood guard, young men passed with haversacks and hobnailed boots. Others, emaciated, with their little suitcases stuffed full. On street corners, in outlying deserted sections, men and women met and whispered, but not of love. At night the lights dimly lighted certain spots on the street which looked like dead bodies. Isolated houses were tenanted again. My country swelled with its myriad secrets."

Thus Aragon in *La Diane française* (Editions Pierre Seghers) sees the reawakening of France. Many of the poems collected here are already known to America in *Les Yeux d'Elsa* and *Le Crève-cœur*, but others have been published before only in underground periodicals. Somewhat less subtly than Eluard, Aragon treats the same subjects: among the most striking poems are "The Conscript of a Hundred Villages" and "The Abandoned Woman," in which a wife urges her husband to take to the Maquis rather than answer the German call-up of labor. In the last poem the poet glorifies the Communist party with the refrain, "My party has given me back the colors of France."

Picasso, too, is now a member of the C.P., but he can hardly yet have been touched by the special grace reserved for Communist poets, if one can judge by his first literary venture, *Le Désir attrapé par la queue* (Gallimard). This supremely silly playlet in six acts, written in four days of January 1941 (for it is scrupulously dated at both the beginning and the end), makes one doubt the serious intentions of Picasso, even as a painter. Some of the characters of the play are the Big Toe, the Onion, the Pie, Silence, Fat Anguish, Thin Anguish, and the Curtains. Even with the properly pious attitude, it is impossible to find any political implications or even any sense in this work.

La Fuite de M. Monde by Georges Simenon (Editions de la Jeune Parque) illustrates its author's belief that the panoramic novel is dead and must be replaced by the story of a crisis constructed like a tragedy. M. Monde's flight takes him, on a whim, away from family and business responsibilities into a dim world of night clubs, dubious hotels, gambling, and dope. Intending to act only as an observer and to enjoy his new carefree self, he finds himself repeatedly assuming new responsibilities and trying to save other people. But in the process he has learned something fundamental about himself. The famous creator of

A Letter from Paris

Inspector Maigret has here abandoned the detective novel for a more subtle form of fiction and in this latest creation he has delicately portrayed one man's psychology entirely by the method of implication. There is nothing topical in this novel, unless it be a lesson it contains for soldiers returning to civilian life. But this you have to read into the book yourself.

On *The Republic of Silence,* compiled and
edited by A. J. Liebling, translated by
Ramon Guthrie (New York: Harcourt,
Brace and Company, 1947), and *Three
Short Novels* ("La Marche à l'étoile," "La
Nuit et le brouillard," and "L'Imprimerie
de Verdun"), by Vercors, translated by
Eric Sutton and Haakon M. Chevalier
(Boston: Little, Brown and Company,
1947). *The Nation,* April 26, 1947.

VERCORS

Moved by a strong sentimental attachment for France and an intense dislike for the old French textbooks drawn from Alphonse Daudet's stories, A. J. Liebling came back from the war to make a living
text based on recent French history. He had the help of Eugene J.
Sheffer of Columbia, and the lively book they produced, full of extracts from French underground publications, has already had a de-
servedly successful career in high schools and colleges. Now the book
appears in a trade edition as *The Republic of Silence* with the French
passages by Vercors, Vladimir Pozner, Jacques Decour, Joseph Kessel,
and so on, translated by a college professor as no college student could
possibly do. What this will do for the class edition can only be
guessed.

The best writings to have come out of France's dark night are already widely known, but we are grateful to Mr. Liebling for preserving
often unsigned bits from the Resistance press that record the heroic
day-to-day struggle of the unions, the peasants, and the professions
against the heartless, stupid invader. The whole story is here, from the
fall of France to the Liberation, with its hostages, executions, reprisals, tortures, and mass atrocities. Intended as an appendix to history

rather than a literary anthology, this book constitutes excellent report-ing. In Africa, in London, in Normandy, A. J. Liebling had his eyes open to a mimeographed or badly printed clandestine newsheet as well as for the telling incident and picturesque detail. The latter he has in-corporated into his own running commentary, written in the style now so familiar in the pages of *The New Yorker,* bristling with irreverence and irrelevance, always colorful and memorable.

The book ought to shake our complacency. When it comes to liter-ature, however, only a few of the names cited by Mr. Liebling deserve to survive. High among them stands that of Vercors, the name of the high plateau above Grenoble which the artist Jean Bruller prophetically borrowed long before it became synonymous with one of the bravest Maquis and one of the most desperate battles of the war. By now every-one knows the story of how Vercors, who had not before written for publication, was moved by indignation to compose a subtle master-piece entitled *The Silence of the Sea* and then to found a clandestine publishing house to print it in late 1942. It was this little tale, variously attributed under its pseudonym to all the great writers of France, that launched the clandestine literature that was to flow from several secret presses—but chiefly from Vercors's Editions de Minuit—until we en-tered Paris. But many Americans do not know that Vercors has pre-served his new identity and gone on writing.

Probably no other French writer was more deeply marked than Ver-cors by the Occupation years which revealed him to himself. All his writings to date are concerned with the psychology of the underground worker and the political prisoner. Like most of the existentialists, he is tormented by problems of liberty, responsibility, and commitment. But there the resemblance ends, for Vercors has a more vivid sense of charac-ter and dramatization than they.

The heartbreaking tales contained in his *Three Short Novels*—at least one of which originally appeared in clandestinity as he and his friends would say—are typical. The first one, "Guiding Star," is the now famous "Marche à l'étoile," in which the star, symbolic of faith and hope, that draws a Moravian Jew across Europe to the land of freedom, is eventually sewed on Thomas' sleeve in yellow before his arrest as a hostage. It is characteristic of Vercors that the murder of that man's soul strikes us as more horrible than his actual execution. Similarly in the second tale, "Night and Fog"—which has recently been printed in France with the addition of a few sentences to attenuate the final horror and a new title that would translate as "The Weapons of Night"—the real horror lies less in any single act than in the systematic slaughter of a man's soul in a concentration camp. For cumulative effect it might have been preferable to publish this tale last, after "The Verdun Press," whose impact is somewhat less intense. But in each of these three gems of narration the simple, direct language coupled with the subtle technique and the sustained suspense reminds one of Maupassant at his best.

THE NEW WRITERS

Introduction to *The New French Writers,*
a brochure published by Alfred A. Knopf,
Inc., in 1947.

THE NEW FRENCH WRITERS

When France emerged from the First World War, she revealed a
brilliant galaxy of writers who were to dominate, in great part, the
literature of Europe during the next two decades. Chief among them
were two prose writers and two poets who had all begun writing long
before: Proust, Gide, Claudel, and Valéry. It was not entirely a coincidence that all four were over forty-five years old and had waited a long
time for recognition at home. Gide's revolutionary *Nourritures terrestres,*
read by but a few when it appeared in 1897, now became a handbook
for restless youths who also prepared themselves for *The Counterfeiters*
(to appear in 1926) by admiring his diverse and disturbing prewar
fiction: *The Immoralist, Strait Is the Gate,* and *Lafcadio's Adventures.*
Proust, an insufferable snob in the nineties, had succumbed in 1905 to
asthma and a literary vocation. Appearing momentarily in 1913 with his
first two volumes, he had again disappeared during the war, and this
enforced delay had permitted him to rework his *Remembrance of
Things Past* and double its size.

In 1890 Paul Claudel had begun composing his highly original poetic
dramas, one of which had finally reached the stage in 1912. By the
twenties when his distinguished diplomatic career led him to the Am-
bassadorship first in Tokyo and then in Washington, he was revered
as the great Catholic poet of modern France and the purest descendant
of Rimbaud. Paul Valéry had begun writing at the same time as a subtle,
hermetic lyricist of the school of Mallarmé. But after a scattering of

poems and a provocative essay on the pure intellect appropriately entitled *Monsieur Teste,* he had deliberately abandoned all literature for a period of twenty years. During the war he had suddenly resumed a career that was soon to lead to the French Academy. The hiatus of the war and the changed postwar attitude, which made so much of the past seem shopworn, brought these writers to public attention, just as it favored the reputation of such as Freud, Bergson, and Einstein.

After them came younger men, today equally famous, so numerous and of such varied genius that even university professors like myself already look back on the twenties and thirties as a great epoch of French literature. Long cyclic novels, ranging in length from ten to twenty-seven volumes each, rolled off the assembly lines of Roger Martin du Gard, Jules Romains, and Georges Duhamel, winning for their authors seats in the French Academy and Nobel Prizes; throughout the world people learned about French life from such varied panoramas as *The World of the Thibaults, Men of Good Will,* and *The Pasquier Chronicles.* Romains's novel is at once the most ambitious and the most typical. With the throbbing, multiform life of Paris as its center of interest and all Europe as its stage, it combines thrilling intrigue and vivid characters while incidentally tracing a picture of twenty-five years of French existence. In *The Bells of Basel* and *Residential Quarter* Louis Aragon opened the floodgates of another fictional river that was to flow most tranquilly and reflect most faithfully in the post-1944 supplement entitled *Aurélien.* But in the interval Aragon had become the great civic poet of France in travail and had thus forced us to change our attitude toward him.

Meanwhile three Jeans created each a special poetry of his own in prose: Jean Giraudoux enchanting, in both fiction and drama, with a faery realm peopled by his charming Suzannes and Isabelles and Amphitryons and Electras who speak the language of preciosity; Jean Giono bathing the life of ideal southern peasants in lush symbolism and imagery; and Jean Cocteau reflecting a sophisticated domain of hallucination and play.

At the same time André Malraux produced those harrowing novels of human brotherhood in revolution and social strife, *Man's Fate* and *Man's Hope,* whereas Antoine de Saint-Exupéry found a similar brotherhood and heroism among those who won their wings in *Night Flight* and *Wind, Sand and Stars*. Their contemporary, Henry de Monther-lant, after exhausting a personal heroism not so remote from theirs, took refuge in a haughty irony when he wrote *Pity for Women* and *Costals and the Hippogriff*, those emotionally exasperating and intellectually satisfying novels. While François Mauriac was probing the consciences of provincial bourgeois such as *A Woman of the Pharisees* and the hero of *The Vipers' Tangle*, Julien Green—an American born in France—was surrounding with a familiar Balzacian atmosphere the psychological abnormalities of the dream-laden protagonists of *The Closed Garden*, *Leviathan*, and *Then Shall the Dust Return*.

Now the second and more terrible World War, which was almost fatal to Europe, is finished. And France is the first country to come out of the concentration camp with a manuscript. In fact she is the only European country to offer us a new and vigorous literature.

Of the movement known as existentialism, Jean-Paul Sartre is the only member to have written prior to the war, when several original studies in psychology, a novel, a collection of short stories, and a series of perspicacious critical essays brought his keen analytical mind and his scornful cynicism to the attention of alert readers. With experience as a professor of philosophy, Sartre naturally organized his ideas into a system and became the leader of this new school founded on German phenomenology and Cartesian rationalism. During the war years he rapidly rose to eminence, as a philosopher can only in France, on the basis of a 720-page philosophical treatise and two plays, *The Flies* and *No Exit*. In 1945 his fictional trilogy, *Roads to Freedom*, began with *The Age of Reason* and *The Reprieve*. Within the last year two further plays, *The Unburied Dead* and *The Respectful Whore*, have caused sensations in Paris just as in New York *No Exit* was winning the annual Critics' Award for the best foreign play and *The Flies* was going into production.

In the shadow of Sartre, Simone de Beauvoir has written two novels, a play, and several philosophical essays inspired by existentialism. *The Visitor*, a novel, will be her first work to appear in English.

Albert Camus is that rare phenomenon: a Frenchman who knows Sartre intimately, has read Kierkegaard and the German philosophers, and yet is not an existentialist. In fact, all of his literary work to date rests on his anti-existentialist philosophical essay, *The Myth of Sisyphus,* which analyzes a contemporary intellectual problem not far from the one that tormented Dostoevsky and Franz Kafka. Camus's first novel, *The Stranger,* also bears comparison with the best of Kafka as literature.

Two plays, *Caligula* and *The Misunderstanding,* both published in 1944, again illustrate the conflict of free will and fate somewhat as Sartre was doing in *The Flies.* Just now there is appearing in Paris the second novel by Camus, *The Plague.* Most vividly it recounts the story of an imaginary plague isolating the Algerian city of Oran; but this serves as a discreet parable for the enemy occupation of France. This second novel proves what the first strongly suggested: that in Albert Camus France has again produced a major writer who at the beginning of his career set himself among the moralists who discourse for our edification upon our most fundamental problems.

With other young writers of today, such as the exuberant and be-witching southerner Henri Bosco, and the darkly poetic, even surrealistic, Julien Gracq, French fiction continues to reveal the variety that has made it one of the richest and most vivid in modern times.

It would be a great mistake for readers to shy away from Sartre, Simone de Beauvoir, Camus, and other new French writers because of all the talk of philosophy and moral issues that surrounds their names. Despite their popular reputation, the French have always been serious beneath their amiable exterior. If we were consistently to flee thought in fiction, we should have to avoid likewise Voltaire, Balzac, Zola, Anatole France—in short the whole great tradition of modern France that has had such a wide universal appeal.

Similarly, Paul Valéry and André Gide, giants of yesterday and of today, have always treated their readers as mature minds. It is particularly appropriate that—beside the young leaders of a new postwar renascence —we are reading Valéry's *Monsieur Teste,* begun in 1896, and Gide's *Journals,* of which the redaction, begun in 1889, is still going on. These two works are two of the masterpieces of our era. Of all the great predecessors, Valéry and Gide are the ones who have accumulated the least mold, and with them the present renews the vital continuity, despite wars and worse, of modern French thought.

On *The Reprieve* *(Le Sursis)*, by Jean-
Paul Sartre, translated by Eric Sutton
(New York: Alfred A. Knopf, Inc., 1947),
and *Troubled Sleep* *(La Mort dans l'âme)*,
by Jean-Paul Sartre, translated by Gerard
Hopkins (New York: Alfred A. Knopf,
Inc., 1951). *The New York Times Book
Review,* November 23, 1947 and January
21, 1951.

SARTRE: "ROADS TO FREEDOM"

In 1910, at a moment of earlier prewar tension in Europe, Charles
Péguy made his Joan of Arc say:

"An accomplice, an accomplice, it's like an author. We are ac-
complices in this, we are the authors of this. . . . He who commits
a crime has at least the courage to commit it. And when you allow
the crime to be committed, you have the same crime, and cowardice to
boot. . . . There is everywhere infinite cowardice."

Were he not so independent, Jean-Paul Sartre might well have used
this passage as an epigraph (quoting it more fully than I have done)
to his newly translated novel, *The Reprieve* *(Le Sursis,* the second
volume of *Les Chemins de la liberté*), the subject of which is the
week of European anguish leading up to the Munich agreement. From
Friday, September 23, through Friday, September 30, 1938, Sartre sweeps
his sensitive camera from one corner to another of France with an occasional parenthetical dash to Godesberg, to London, to Marrakech, or
to a small Sudetenland town.

The few familiar characters from his earlier *L'Age de raison* *(The
Age of Reason*) interest us particularly as they prepare for war. On
the 23rd, Mathieu is vacationing at Juan-les-Pins with his brother and
sister-in-law; the student Boris is living off his mistress Lola at Biarritz;
Boris' sister Ivich is fretting under a moderate parental discipline at

Laon in the north; the homosexual Daniel has married Mathieu's former mistress Marcelle, etc.

But their condition is generalized by the introduction of new characters: a Czech and his wife huddling in their house while Nazi hoodlums stone their windows; Chamberlain waiting for a message from Hitler; a young Communist workman in Paris preparing to leave his Zézette; Charles the paralytic being moved from the sanatorium of Berck; an illiterate shepherd ignorant of world events; an adolescent disciple of Rimbaud screaming against war in a drunken fit; a Jewish refugee from Poland, etc. By opening his lens wider and providing his camera with a more mobile mount, Sartre presents a rapid, densely packed world "loaded [Péguy wrote back in 1910] with peacetime responsibilities in the sense in which a donkey is loaded, loaded for war in the sense in which a gun is loaded."

Sartre, a bona fide philosopher, has been credited with making metaphysics the very substance of his novels. This is true if one adds that he has progressed in the art of fiction. His first novel, *La Nausée* (*Nausea*), tends to alternate action with reflection on action, somewhat as Gide, Huxley, and so many others had done before. *The Age of Reason* (published here in July 1947) effects a closer integration of philosophical thought with the narration, but remains unilinear and slow-moving.

Now *The Reprieve*—by means of a vivid, concrete dialogue, halting and broken as in real life, a natural use of the stream of consciousness, and a complete mastery of the cinema technique of simultaneity—suddenly achieves what Malraux accomplishes in his best novels. Yet Sartre's debt to Malraux and even more to John Dos Passos (whose *Manhattan Transfer* was a revelation to him) is unimportant, since he has made the device his own. *The Reprieve* is a brilliant kaleidoscope, realizing with ease (but with more demands upon the reader) what Jules Romains so strived for in his *Men of Good Will*.

The first five pages involve five separate scenes in five distinct places. Boris orders a glass of rum in a Biarritz café and by the time it is served the reader realizes (though he is still in the same sentence) that the waitress is setting down a cognac before Philippe in Paris. The best use of this technique is in the penultimate chapter with its parallel between the rape of Czechoslovakia and the rape of Ivich by another student in Paris. By the end of the novel the characters and the reader have lived intensely through a ridiculous epic of initial frustration, followed by decision and heroism and crushing anticlimax, expressed in the final bitter words.

Fortunately the future holds a meager element of hope, even so, for the last section of the novel that began with *The Age of Reason* is to be entitled *The Last Chance*. Doubtless it will continue to illustrate, as *The Reprieve* does more effectively than its predecessor, the urgent problems of freedom and commitment, of moral obligation and common responsibility.

Outside of Sartre's work it would be difficult to find more unpleasant scenes than in his latest novel, *La Mort dans l'âme* (*Troubled Sleep*), though within his work it would be impossible to find so good a novel. For, after portraying both the decay of prewar Europe and the ineffectual burst of energy and wrath that so soon subsided, Sartre gives us in the third volume of his cyclic novel the crushing defeat of France by concentrating on the period from June 15, 1940, to a few days or weeks after the armistice.

The skillful novelist, who is also a dramatist and a philosopher of no mean importance, again uses the same techniques of simultaneity and of stream of consciousness, broken by vivid dialogue. Yet there is less artifice here than in the earlier volumes; the method is now completely integrated. This is true of Part I at least, in which the defeat is viewed in turn by Lopez in a sweltering New York, by Daniel in a deserted Paris, where he admires the handsome Teutons as they ride into the city; by Boris in bed with Lola in Marseille, by various civilians on the roads of central France during the exodus, and finally by Mathieu among the demoralized soldiers of a headquarters unit in eastern France.

It was a brilliant idea to begin with an exiled Spaniard in New York and thus view the plight of France from a doubly remote perspective. It was equally clever to intensify the picture of the soldiers' moral collapse at the risk of nauseating the reader, since this serves as the ideal background for Mathieu's heroic and apparently futile sacrifice at the end of Part I. Yes, flabby and irresolute Mathieu Delarue (does his name suggest the man in the street?), who has been evading responsibility throughout two volumes, eventually commits himself during the last fifteen minutes of his life.

Part II deals with Brunet and Schneider in a prison camp and on their way to Germany, surrounded by some twenty thousand other French prisoners. Brunet is the noble Communist, far more likeable than the prototype Malraux offered in *Man's Hope*. He has matured since we last saw him, but he remains not very bright.

Schneider, the keen lawyer's clerk from Bordeaux who so easily dominates Brunet by the methods Brunet would like to use on him, is a second Mathieu, though more willing to engage in what limited action a prison camp offers. So far I like him better than Mathieu, but that may be simply because I have not known him so long.

The translation by Gerard Hopkins is smoother and more effortless than that of the two earlier volumes by Eric Sutton and does not make Sartre talk with the accent of Kensington. Yet why must even the best translator assume that in the French Army the term "major" refers to a specific rank?

Certain pages, such as Mathieu's shooting his first German from the church tower, the dizzying close of Part I, and the Alsatians' paying for their liberation by heiling Hitler, are masterful whether in French or in English.

On *The Words* (*Les Mots*), by Jean-Paul
Sartre, translated by Bernard Frechtman
(New York: George Braziller, Inc., 1964).
The Reporter, November 5, 1964.

SARTRE RESARTUS

In the beginning was the Word, many a writer could say as he looks
back to his initiation through the magic of the written word. This is
particularly true in France, where formal education, with its emphasis
on the specifically literary, tends to form writers. Everything in French
teaching, indeed, pushes the child to express himself pertinently and
elegantly, to know and admire his literary patrimony, and even to dream
of enriching that patrimony.

But the case of Jean-Paul Sartre is exceptional even in France. He
was a child prodigy. Teaching himself to read at an extraordinarily
early age, whetting his childish imagination simultaneously on the "classics" of his grandfather's library and thrillers from the corner kiosk,
then urged by example and mimetism to writing thrillers himself, he
precociously rushed the evolution, so that it was virtually completed
even before his real schooling began at the age of ten. Meanwhile, living
in the usual child's dream world, he acted out the breathtaking adventures of the swashbuckling heroes he met in books and films (there
is a marvelous evocation here of the pre-1915 movies) and even wrote
new scenarios for his solitary theater. But, worried by the compulsive
outpourings of such an overexcited imagination, his domineering and
doting grandfather, a smug Alsatian teacher of French to German pupils, dictated his future career by suggesting a safer combination of
two professions:

"Teaching gave a man leisure. Scholarly interests went hand in hand with those of men of letters. I would move back and forth from one priestly function to the other. I would live in close contact with the great writers. At one and the same time, I would reveal their works to my pupils and draw upon them for inspiration. I would beguile my provincial solitude by composing poems, by translating Horace into blank verse. I would write short literary articles for the local papers, a brilliant essay on the teaching of Greek for the *Pedagogic Review,* another on the psychology of adolescents. Upon my death, unpublished works would be found among my papers, a meditation on the sea, a one-act comedy, a few sensitive and scholarly pages on the monuments of Aurillac, enough to fill a thin volume that would be edited by former pupils."

This is precisely what Jean-Paul Sartre did in life, although his brilliant record at the Ecole Normale Supérieure provided a less provincial exile than Aurillac and his own writings have had far greater importance and enjoyed a much wider public than those foreseen here. Yet, as many passages in his memoirs show, he is the first to be aware of the ironic parallel.

Written as Sartre is on the point of turning sixty, *The Words* covers only the first eleven or twelve years of his life. Fortunately, there are hints in this very lively and too brief volume that there will be more memoirs to come. In view of his general revulsion against the past, clearly stated here, and his "loathing" of his "rejected, lost, forgotten childhood," such a record was decidedly unexpected. Viewing himself and his family with an acute lucidity bathed in an irony that is at times mildly indulgent and at times almost savage, he portrays the boy growing up between a young widowed mother, adoring and adored, and a somewhat tyrannical, opinionated grandfather, the uncle of Albert Schweitzer. It tells quite flatly of the mingling of Protestant and Catholic faiths which led to no faith, joyfully of the absence of a father, most unemotionally of his own ugliness, and pathetically of his rejection by other children.

Most of all, however, as the title suggests, *The Words* concerns "little Poulou's" initiation to literature. Its two equal parts, the first devoted to "Reading" and the second to "Writing," trace his whole precocious evolution in a world of indulgent adults. Without question, Jean-Paul Sartre is one of the few great writers of our time—a distinguished philosopher and founder of the French school of existentialism, a novelist of note with *Nausea* and the three volumes of *The Roads to Freedom*, the successful author of such plays as *No Exit, The Flies,* and *Altona,* and the timely, pungent essayist of so many volumes entitled *Situations*. Since 1945 he has occupied a unique place in universal modern letters.

Yet until now there was something lacking. Each of the great writers of the past has had something lovable about him, at once broadly human and peculiar to him. His readers could somehow identify with him while still admiring him. Until now, Jean-Paul Sartre has not inspired such an attitude in most readers. *The Words* introduces us into a new intimacy with the father of our new existentialism and the author of the rather cold dialectical works bearing his name. All at once, we see Sartre as a man.

On *The Miraculous Barber (Travelingue)*, by Marcel Aymé, translated by Eric Sutton (New York: Harper and Brothers, 1951). *The New York Times Book Review*, April 22, 1951.

AYMÉ: "THE MIRACULOUS BARBER"

Back in the mid-thirties France was in a parlous state. Rightists and Leftists clashed on the boulevards of Paris in civil strife; the franc was devalued; sit-down strikes spread throughout industry like a raging forest fire, and the Popular Front government strove to bring order out of chaos. Against this lurid background Marcel Aymé, the liveliest writer in France today, tells the complex story of two families or clans that touch at certain tangential points.

In *The Miraculous Barber* there are first the wealthy Lasquins with their factory, their indifference to the world, their prim and athletic son-in-law, their philosophic parasite, and their cousin who is a popular novelist. Then there is the utterly amoral clan of the Ancelots, living in the dream world of the movies with which they drug themselves daily, thriving on sensational and dynamic crises in their home life. Whenever the two clans meet, sparks are sure to fly.

Unrecountable incidents tightly pack the novel: a sudden death, several conjugal infidelities, two seduction scenes, a factory strike, an abortion, a pure love affair, a pederast's liaison, and finally a murder. Yet the novelist is less interested in such elements of plot than he is in satirizing his creatures with his moving camera. In any scene his lens is constantly traveling with fleet and irresistible humor from face to face; hence the original title of *Travelingue*, for Aymé has his own way of spelling words borrowed from our vocabulary such as "pineupe-gueurle" and "coquetèle."

Not the least of the author's inventions in this delightful satire of the Third Republic is Moutot, the placid barber who governs France from his little shop near the Gare de l'Est, keeping Cabinet members waiting in his back room while he shaves his customers. Appropriately, the fiction ends, after he has solved innumerable crises both national and personal, with his lively monologue which fills eleven pages with a single paragraph. The translation, usually faithful to the special flavor of Aymé's prose, often sounds a bit British to American ears.

No brief comment, however, can do justice to the alertness of Aymé's humor and the sharpness of his satire, for *The Miraculous Barber*—like *Uranus* (*The Barkeep of Blémont*), which appeared here in 1950—places its author in the heart of a very Gallic tradition. In France Marcel Aymé is just beginning to come into his own as a leading novelist, short-story writer, and dramatist, and in America there is already forming a group of discerning enthusiasts who prescribe him as a cure for all ills.

On *The Company of Men* (*Le Grand Vestiaire*), by Romain Gary, translated by Joseph Barnes (New York: Simon and Schuster, Inc., 1950). *The New York Times Book Review*, April 16, 1950.

GARY: "THE COMPANY OF MEN"

Romain Gary's first novel, *Education européenne,* won the coveted Prix des Critiques in 1945 and was translated into fourteen languages (not including the English); overnight he became one of the considerable young writers of the Paris school. His second novel, *Le Grand Vestiaire* (*The Company of Men*), opens with a hero of the French Maquis refusing to give up his machine gun after the liberation and ends with a boy of fifteen executing a pitiful, degenerate old man. This is strong stuff, which nonetheless presents a faithful picture of a low point in French social history directly after the recent war. Both the author and the translator lived in Paris during that moral anarchy, and this is doubtless why their collaboration produces so convincing and moving an image.

It is characteristic that a grafting police official who figures in the novel enjoys talking of the decay of France and that his sentiments are echoed in turn by a Gestapo informer who has sold his French comrades to the enemy, by the chief of a ring of automobile thieves, and by a run-down actor who lives as a drug addict in a negligée on the top floor of a brothel.

The principal characters, however, are a group of teenagers who move easily in this atmosphere of viciousness without knowing any other life. From dabblers in the black market, they become petty thieves and (thanks to the American movies) eventually big-time gangsters. Finally, the boy narrator awakens to the fact that he lives in a world of empty, cast-off garments posing as men (whence the original title which translates literally as "The Big Cloakroom"), and by assassinating one such spineless fake he asserts his right to enter "the company of men."

"It takes a lot of other people's love to make a traitor, many an outstretched hand to make a treachery," notes the articulate boy shortly before using his Colt automatic.

Despite the sordid substance of this novel, it is a powerful work of bitter satire and first-rate humor. Gary is a social critic who knows how to write. The French blame the blackness of his vision on the fact that he was born in the land of Dostoevsky. However this may be, his novel, as a picture of life in newly liberated Europe, should take its rightful place beside the Italian film *Shoeshine*.

On *The Castle of Argol* (*Au Château d'Argol*), by Julien Gracq, translated by Louise Varese (New York: New Directions, 1951). *The New York Times,* January 20, 1952.

GRACQ: "THE CASTLE OF ARGOL"

At the moment Julien Gracq is the most talked of writer in Paris. An obscure professor of geography and history named Louis Poirier with three novels, a play, and two essays to his credit under a pseudonym, he has achieved this position simply by being the first to reject the coveted Goncourt Prize. To be sure, the 5,000-franc award now provides merely a good dinner with a group of friends, but it still represents great publicity value and the sudden multiplication of sales by ten. On principle, Gracq refuses to be, as he says, a "pin-up writer," thus multiplying his own sales probably by twenty. Yet there is some misunderstanding: his writing is not intended for that many readers.

At the moment that his third novel is causing such a stir, we can read in a literate and feeling translation his first one, *The Castle of Argol.* (The second, *A Dark Stranger,* has been available in English since mid-1950.) By his own confession and by his book on André Breton, we know that Gracq belongs to surrealism—which he defines here in the foreword, appropriately placed at the end of the American edition, as "the only literary school . . . to revive the lost delights of the always childlike paradise of explorers." Gracq is an explorer in the childlike realms of dream. Consequently he is not easy reading: whoever continues beyond the first chapter feels like an initiate of mysteries reserved for the elect. For Gracq habitually applies the art of the lapidary to an already sumptuously complex adventure. His dazzling style is made up of long, involved sentences, multiple epithets, archaisms, incantatory repetitions, and frequent use of italics for emphasis.

Julien Gracq

The haunting and suspense-laden spiritual adventure in which the three exceptional characters of this novel are engaged is inspired by *Parsifal;* in fact, Gracq himself sees his narrative as a "demoniac version" of the Grail legend. But an even more direct antecedent than the mighty Wagner can be found in the early symbolist dramatist and novelist, Villiers de l'Isle-Adam. The nature of the protagonists (all strangely beautiful, both physically and spiritually, educated on Hegel and "qualified to penetrate life's subtlest arcana, to embrace its most exhilarating realities"), the romantic properties of desolate landscape, enchanted castle, secret passage, abandoned graveyard by the sea, and riderless horses combine with the persistent note of anxiety and the obsession of death to mark Gracq as a close descendant of Villiers, who stamped his mark also upon Maeterlinck.

Gracq's extraordinarily conscious art has already been likened more to the painter's than to that of the writer. And, indeed, Heide and Albert walking down the geometrically traced avenue of trees that closes behind them give one the illusion of an animated Dali.

On *The Voyeur* (*Le Voyeur*), by Alain
Robbe-Grillet, translated by Richard
Howard (New York: Grove Press, 1958).
The New York Times Book Review, Oc-
tober 12, 1958.

ROBBE-GRILLET: "THE VOYEUR"

Within a short time the name of Alain Robbe-Grillet may become a
commonplace among Americans interested in the *avant-garde,* as it already has in his native France. For the first three novels of this young
writer, who would surely be classed as an angry young man if he
lived in England, aim to upset our whole concept of fictional technique.

As he explained in a revolutionary article in the *Nouvelle Revue
Française* of July 1956, he refuses to accept psychological analyses and
auctorial interpretations, depth psychology, and all "visceral or incantatory adjectives." After all, man is surrounded by objects which,
despite any attempts to animate them, simply go on existing. "On the
other hand," he states, "the scientifically optical, descriptive adjective—
which is satisfied to measure, to situate, to limit, to define—probably
points out the arduous way to a new fictional art."

Consequently he gives us in his novels objects in their simple crudity
as the eye sees them, lighted as they are at 9 A.M. or 5 P.M., and without
any symbolic overtones. If the eye of a man who has just committed a
particularly horrible crime calmly notes a flattened frog in the roadway
and his brain wonders at length whether the stiff leatherish object was
a frog or a toad, this may reveal something of his psychology, but the
implications and conclusions are ours and not the author's.

In fact, the very meaning of the word "voyeur" helps us to understand
Robbe-Grillet, because all his heroes are men "affected with undue

visual curiosity." They seem to have set themselves up with T-square and rule and drawing-board to observe through a cold, camera-like eye which registers without ever commenting. Furthermore, everything they see, whether it is taking place at the moment or has transpired elsewhere and in the remote past, is happening now.

With such an original technique—which may well owe more to the films than its creator is aware—he can weave a spider web whose meshes of apparent anti-logic eventually catch us in a demonstration as convincing as if we ourselves had produced every thread. Thus at the end of *The Voyeur,* no reader can doubt that a monstrous crime—the rape and murder of a little girl—has been committed between the sale of a watch and the fixing of a bicycle chain, three acts of equal importance to the protagonist. Yet, until that point, the suspense, built up by skillful near-repetition, keeps us on tenterhooks.

That is, it does if we can get beyond the first infuriating pages (a distinguished and conservative Parisian critic confesses that he was put off from reviewing the first two novels of Robbe-Grillet by the quality of the opening sections). But once we have become accustomed to this young writer's particular kind of objectivity, we recognize his achievement as formidable and recommend it to all our friends.

On *A Change of Heart* (*La Modification*),
by Michel Butor, translated by Jean Steu-
art (New York: Simon and Schuster, Inc.,
1959). *The New York Times*, March 29,
1959.

BUTOR: "A CHANGE OF HEART"

As the shrill whistle pierces the early-morning gloom of the Gare de Lyon and the cry "En voiture!" interrupts the last embraces on the platform, you settle into your corner seat facing the engine and next to the corridor. You have twenty hours between Paris and Rome for reviewing your past and deciding your future.

As Michel Butor has written his absorbing novel *La Modification* entirely in the second person and consistently called his hero "you," the reviewer is obliged to involve you in his review and to force upon you the same identification the novelist uses so skillfully, which, merely intriguing at first, becomes increasingly justifiable while you progress toward your destination.

Ever since that first honeymoon trip with Henriette so many years ago, Rome has signified a kind of terminus in your dreams. Your frequent visits there as manager of the Parisian branch of an Italian typewriter firm had only intensified the contrast between the two cities. And taking Henriette there years after your marriage had failed miserably to introduce her to the Rome you loved and explain to her why you felt a different person, so much more genuine, in Rome.

Then you had met Cécile, who worked in the Palazzo Farnese, who showed you "how to explore Rome and that side of yourself that Rome fostered." After she had become your mistress, you made the mistake of accompanying her to Paris for her vacation and even of introducing her to Henriette and the children. And now you are on your way to Rome

329

once again, to tell her you have found her a job in Paris and will soon break with Henriette.

As a result of your protracted and fascinating monologue while the train glides through the rich French countryside, crosses the Alps, and stops in historic Italian cities, you undergo a change of heart. For after all it dawns on you, fifty pages after becoming apparent to me (your reader), that Rome is your real love and that transplanting Cécile to Paris will not help matters at all.

A Change of Heart—which received uniformly enthusiastic reviews in Paris a year ago—is the third novel by the thirty-two-year-old Michel Butor. Although it tells a traditional story, it distinguishes itself by its original technique. Even in this regard there are elements we should recognize, such as Valery Larbaud's subtle stream of consciousness flowing through an Italian railway compartment, Gide's forcing the reader to cooperate by reconstructing the truth, Proust's identification of the beloved with a landscape which one can possess only through possessing her.

There is also something Proustian in the final resolve, less motivated than in Proust, to make a novel out of these ruminations over earlier trips, with all the violence they do to chronology, whose differences and similarities eventually fuse in a strangely insistent unity. But Butor has combined these elements with a new twist, and he has added the device of calling his protagonist "you."

Like Alain Robbe-Grillet, Michel Butor is presently a white hope of young French literature, and in this, his first novel to be translated, he offers a haunting account of an average man's search for identity in an atmosphere charged with poetic overtones.

On *Zazie* (*Zazie dans le Métro*), by Raymond Queneau, translated by Barbara Wright (New York: Harper and Brothers, 1960). *The New York Times Book Review*, October 16, 1960.

QUENEAU: "ZAZIE"

It was not a purely disinterested sense of justice that made Zazie tell the court, during the trial of her mother for cleaving her father's head, that the ax had been lent by the blond butcher who spent so many evenings in their home. Nor is it sheer love of learning that urges her to pester her perfumed Uncle Gabriel by asking him repeatedly if he really is, as he has been called, a "hormosessual." No, there is a streak of mischief in the brat.

She has much in common with Eloise and Dennis the Menace, but, when her mother plumps this far from innocent provincial on her Parisian uncle, the world she discovers holds even more interest for us than the child does. Surrounded by cops in disguise, by "aunties," and by "sex-fiends" (her name for any male who tries to restrain her antisocial impulses), Zazie gets involved in a series of ribald adventures in the Flea Market, in an unorthodox nightclub, on the Eiffel Tower, without ever riding in the Métro which really symbolizes Paris in her eyes. For all who enjoy the novels of Marcel Aymé and for all lovers of Rabelais and Swift, *Zazie* is inevitable and required reading.

The imbroglios into which Raymond Queneau projects his heroine and the band of adults at her heels (even now being filmed in Paris with just the right urchin as the brat in "blewgenes") remind one of those early Chaplin films, for this author is one of France's most consummate humorists and ironists. Born in Le Havre in 1903, he lived through the experience of surrealism to emerge as the principal editor of the Gallimard publishing house, the compiler of the Pléiade Encyclopedia, and a member of the Goncourt Academy.

On the way, he wrote more than a score of books in prose and in verse, translated Sinclair Lewis, Marianne Moore, Wallace Stevens, and Amos Tutuola, wrote scenarios for films and songs for Juliette Greco, while acquiring a reputation as the leading *fumiste* or intellectual joker of his generation. Early in his career he absorbed the influence of James Joyce and of Henry Miller and crystallized his theory about the hiatus between our Sunday language and our everyday language, or written and spoken style. His deep interest in the mechanics of language led him to create a third French, corresponding to the speech of the common man, original in vocabulary, syntax, and orthography.

His best novels have all been written in this new demotic style, which frequently calls for reading aloud in order to be understood. His *Exercices de style* in 1947 hilariously recounted the same banal tale in ninety-nine different forms through metathesis, aposcope, paragoge, polyptoton, syncope, apostrophe, aphaeresis, anaphora, epenthesis, etc.

Such an almost pathological love of language (which in this novel has a young man proposing to his beloved say: "Zit yes? Rizit no?") makes Queneau, like Joyce, seem untranslatable. But Barbara Wright has achieved the impossible, although she has used some expressions that ought not to be in her vocabulary.

On *Tropisms* *(Tropismes)*, by Nathalie
Sarraute, translated by Maria Jolas (New
York: George Braziller, Inc., 1967). *The
New York Times Book Review,* May 21,
1967.

SARRAUTE: "TROPISMS"

"Tropisms! No sooner was the word invented than people could see
nothing else; a whole category of psychologists would admit of nothing
but tropisms. *Tropisms!* What a new light those two syllables suddenly
cast! Obviously the organism obeyed the same impulses as the heliotrope
when the involuntary plant turns its flower toward the sun. At last
the cosmos was endowed with a reassuring benignity. In the most
surprising movements of the living creature could be uniformly recognized an utter obedience to the agent." So wrote André Gide in 1914,
when the word was new and fresh, to mock a biologist absorbed in
his experiments on rats.

Nathalie Sarraute, one of Gide's numerous descendants, has carried
over the odd word, now fully acclimated in the scientific vocabulary,
to mean "those subtle, barely perceptible, fleeting, contradictory,
evanescent movements, faint tremblings, ghosts of timid appeals and
recoilings, pale shadows that flit by, whose unceasing play constitutes
the invisible woof of all human relationships and the very substance
of our lives," as she states in her seminal essay on Dostoevsky and
Kafka.

In the current series of sensitive vignettes (which is not so current
as all that, for the original French edition was Mme Sarraute's first
book, published nine years before "Portrait of a Man Unknown"
caused Sartre to hail her as a great innovator), we have minutely
observed persons and things with the human psychology implied so

333

insistently and vividly that the page or two of the vignette long reverberates in the reader's mind. A less explicit Andrew Wyeth, Mme Sarraute suggests so much more than can actually be found in the painting. An empty chair, a half-open door, a back turned, is enough to call up in us subtle sensations analogous to those suggested in her images. We cannot, for instance, watch her good little children walking gently in a circle and holding one another's "sad, moist little hands" without simultaneously sensing "the invisible adult looking after them."

Because Mme Nathalie Sarraute is inevitably concerned here with the little futilities, the quotidianities, the ephemerides of life, she may seem caustic to some. But is this comment not true?—"And they talked and talked, repeating the same things, going over them then going over them again, from one side then from the other, kneading and kneading them, continually rolling between their fingers this unsatisfactory, mean substance that they had extracted from their lives (what they called 'life,' their domain), kneading it, pulling it, rolling it until it ceased to form anything between their fingers but a little pile, a little grey pellet" (p. 33). To be sure, her frequent centering on characters tending toward asthenia or a vague debility and her repeated implied contrast between childhood's freshness and the dull, weary present of maturity suggests the same.

Her material, however (and *Tropisms,* says the author, "contains *in nuce* all the raw material that I have continued to develop in my later works"), "is the immediate data of consciousness," as W. M. Frohock points out in his recent *Style and Temper.* "A study of Mme Sarraute's imagery, for example, shows that it operates on the level of the first recognition of phenomena, rather than on the level of evaluation, and thus identifies a kind of psychic activity very rare in earlier fiction."

This is why she is, with but four or five novels to her credit, all attentively recreated in English by Maria Jolas, universally recognized as one of the few inventors of the "new novel" ("held between quotes

as though between tongs," as she wrote of the word "psychological").
And now, with her first two plays staged this winter in Paris by
Jean-Louis Barrault and already translated for Off-Broadway, her skillful
manipulation of dialogue and unspoken sub-dialogue may well place
her among the leaders of the "new theater" (same tongs, please).

POETRY

The University Review (Kansas City), December 1939.

FROM DADA TO SURREALISM

That a nation of rationalists like the French, to whom clarity has always been the touchstone of beauty, should deliberately set out to annex the irrational shows to what an extent the First World War upset their scale of values. The war was not alone responsible, for as early as the nineties Henri Bergson had opposed intuition to reason and in many minds had taken the place of Descartes as *the* French philosopher. But by destroying all values the war cleared the way for all experiments and eccentricities. In an atmosphere of intense revolt, the young—known as the lost generation in distinction to their immediate elders the mutilated generation—took over literature and the arts as their playground.

The result was a characteristically youthful anarchy in all the arts as an escape from the horror of 1914–1918. The revolt against the reason, invoking Bergson as its tutelary genius and favored by the example of such older writers as Marcel Proust, André Gide, Paul Claudel, and Paul Valéry—who began to achieve wide recognition only after the armistice—reached its paroxysm in the movements known as dadaism and surrealism. But outside those relatively limited groups, literature in general showed a preference for the nonrational aspects of man. The twenties marked the literary discovery of the subconscious and the application of such techniques as the stream of consciousness and automatic writing as aids to translating its flux into words.

The natural postwar demand for facile pleasures reflected itself in the universal popularity of the novel, that most facile kind of reading matter. The public had no time for meditation and little patience for the subtleties of dialectics; the poetry of the symbolists and neo-symbolists needed to be adapted to the tempo of the epoch. Now, the most successful type of novel immediately after the war was the novel of psychological analysis. But this seems to be a contradiction: how did a public which called for easy reading and fought shy of intellectual effort enthusiastically accept the *finesse* of the analytical novel? The answer lies in the fact that this kind of novel paradoxically offers at once a lesson applicable to the reader and at the same time the additional, and by no means negligible, attraction of taking the reader outside of himself. On the one hand, "the novel," as François Mauriac wrote in 1928, "loses all reason for existing if it does not add to our knowledge of the human heart." On the other hand, the young Jacques Rivière prophesied, as far back as 1913, the coming popularity of the novel of adventure, adding that there was room also for a type of psychological novel of adventure such as he found in the works of Dostoevsky. It would contain a picture of the spontaneous development of souls, the gradual formation and evolution and eventual transformation of emotions. The adventure within the human mind and heart would be no less thrilling, the incidents no less varied and unforeseen, the suspense no less poignant than in the old-fashioned melodrama.

Rivière was not wrong in his prediction, for as we watch Marcel Proust analyzing the most subtle reactions of an invalid, Georges Duhamel depicting in Salavin the spiritual dryness of a man without will, Jacques de Lacretelle, Jean Cocteau, and François Mauriac among others following the serpentine intellectual processes of dreamy adolescents, Georges Bernanos tracing the course of spiritual elevation in the disease-ravaged body of a village priest, André Gide pursuing the inner combat of a soul in crisis, or Henri-René Lenormand putting on the stage the gradual evolution of an incestuous passion—we are transported beyond ourselves as surely as if we were reading *Treasure Island* or Poe's *Tales*.

And yet the pretext for writing most of these novels is the writer's or the narrator's need to see clearly what has happened and is happening within him. Such a spiritual inquest must be conducted with absolute sincerity to have any value. Someone has said that it became as necessary, for instance, to know a character's sexual tastes as Balzac had earlier thought it was to know his financial standing. This pitiless need to dissect every slightest element of the emotional and intellectual life left nothing intact. Proust tells us of one of his characters:

"Then he tried to tell her that he had deceived her with another woman. He tried to do so, not out of revenge or the desire to make her suffer as he was suffering, but rather so that in return she would tell the truth too, especially so that he would not have to live any longer with a lie, and could expiate his sensual sins, since it sometimes seemed to him that (to create an object for his jealousy) it was his own lie and his own sensuality that he was projecting into Françoise."

Or there is that abnormally lucid child, Raymond Radiguet, who, while assuring himself in *Le Diable au corps* that only the presence of her parents keeps him from kissing the married woman he loves, at the same time congratulates himself that they are there since if he were alone with her he wouldn't really dare to kiss her and yet would have no excuse for not doing so.

Zola and the naturalists had demonstrated the failure to seize life by means of documentation. Consequently the new writers, brought up under the influence of Bergson, aimed to do so through the intuition. Literature therefore turns to the study of those elements and moments of life in which the instinctive and the irrational predominate: the child and the adolescent, hitherto largely neglected by writers, primitive races, inarticulate peasants, Parisian *apaches,* even animals, become subjects of predilection.

If the probing of abnormal states of consciousness and of unconsciousness provided an escape from material reality, how much more so did the exercise of the free imagination! There has probably never been a period in French literature which has produced so much pure fantasy as the postwar years. Whether through preposterous humor or through an equally incredible use of the supernatural, writers of all types turned their back on the problems of the day. Often they mingled humor and the supernatural, as our own Gertrude Stein was to do in her *Four*

Saints in Three Acts, in which two St. Theresas, dressed alike in a parody of a cardinal's costume, release pigeons from a large Easter egg while symbolizing the mystic's state by standing "half indoors, half out of doors."

The word fantasy is applied to a composition in which the author has permitted his fancy to run wild regardless of the consequences. The work may be visionary, even hallucinatory; often, on the other hand, it is a cold and deliberate attempt to mystify the public. But one should avoid thinking of a particular school of writers of fantasy, for nothing is more dangerous than to attempt to group certain writers under the catch-all heading of "les fantaisistes" as certain manuals do. In fact, perhaps the chief advantage a writer derived from indulging in this kind of mental acrobatics is that they helped him to escape classification. Moreover, where is the common denominator that will put André Gide and Max Jacob, Jules Romains and Jean Cocteau, in the same school? Gide's *Caves du Vatican,* that rollicking account of Amédée Fleurissoire's pilgrimage to Rome to free the Pope from captivity and his final unmotivated murder at the hand of a peculiarly picturesque adventurer, is a good example. From Gide's *sotie* to Jules Romains's comedies about the *débauche* and marriage of the geographer Le Trouhadec or Fernand Crommelynck's farce of the *Cocu magnifique* the distance is not so great as it might at first appear.

Meanwhile Jean Giraudoux's irrepressible fancy continued to create visions of a more articulate and more sharply pointed kind, such as the following from *Eglantine:*

"Unable to sleep, he spent the night trying out on this new nation, from New York to Los Angeles, the great scenes of injustice of the old world. The company on tour included all the great actors: one night, for example, it was Socrates' death in Chicago. It was terrifying. You can't imagine what became, on the shore of Lake Michigan, of the most beautiful lesson given to men before Christ. The Negroes added ten cents to their price for shining the shoes of all those who were going to the execution; the ten cowboys galloping in front of the Ford in which the Assistant Professor of Chemistry from the University of Michigan was bringing the hemlock donated by the President of the

University; the 22nd regiment of the National Guard interrupting its parade in the 22nd armory to form this sentence in which each letter was made up of an entire company: SOCRATES DIES. It was snowing. Electric signs announcing the stages of the operation—right toe dead, left leg paralyzed, right knee out of life—cut through the snow like hot irons. The imitation Greek façades of the public buildings, of the prison itself, emphasized the universal hypocrisy. The virgin phonograph records—those records without which Xenophon and Plato once had to be recorded—were handled impatiently, for Socrates was talking in too low a voice. Socrates was talking through his nose. And what can we say of Socrates' suit, that suit with vertical white and green stripes. . . Heart attacked, Assistant Professor Robinson says that Socrates' last minute has come. . ."

In poetry, which even in the most reasonable ages has always been the refuge of fantasy, the comic, both frank and sly, and the supernatural, especially the tongue-in-cheek supernatural, are inextricably intertwined. In the third quarter of the nineteenth century several adolescents had independently broken off relations with the so-called poetic subject, and in the works of Rimbaud, Lautréamont, Laforgue, and Corbière there is an almost constant overtone of sardonic humor. All four walked deliberately and delicately on the edge of the abyss of madness. In the immediately postwar years in which their state of mind was universal among the young, their poetic revolt was multiplied many times over and they, particularly Rimbaud and Lautréamont, were resuscitated as the leaders of the new movements in poetry.

The fantasy of their imitators and admirers ranged from the subtlest preciosity to scandalous coarseness. The most various devices were employed—anything in fact to make fun of conventional literary technique: far-fetched images, verbal surprises, plays on words, ridiculous alliterations, repetitions *ad nauseam,* daring typographic arrangements. Indeed, this humor is often bitter and the laughter it provokes is primarily a grimace. Guillaume Apollinaire had set the style of calligraphic poetry, writing his words in the form of a mandolin when describing a mandolin or disposing in the form of a fountain of lightly falling waters his modern version of the "Snows of Yesteryear." Jean Cocteau, his most ardent disciple, wrote verses which had to be read aloud to yield their meaning since the whole poem was one long rebus.

In all such conscious playing with words, there is necessarily an element of chance, just as in building anagrams or composing a poem with the aid of a rhyming dictionary. Often the thought of such a poem is dictated by the possible rhymes.

With such devices do the poets set inspiration in motion when it refuses to start under its own power. If they generally write with a mocking intent and use all their ingenuity to multiply their comic technical devices, they nevertheless agree with Rimbaud that one must "consider sacred the disorder of one's mind." The poet's happy find, the gift of inspiration or of his own subconscious, is akin to a miracle.

With this definition of inspiration as something within the poet, the dadaists were in agreement. The sole affirmation of that movement of total negation, in fact, was that of the supremacy of inspiration. Dada is the most violent form of the postwar revolt of youth. Less a literary movement than a satiric philosophical revolt against the insanity of modern existence, dada is so direct a product of the war that it couldn't even wait for the armistice to declare itself. Born in Zurich in 1916, this movement found its name when Tristan Tzara, the Roumanian Jewish leader of the group, opened his Larousse dictionary at random to the word "Dada," that primitive onomatopoeia, which in the language of French children means horse and figuratively means hobby. The most frequently repeated phrase of the dadaist writers is "Dada means nothing." They managed to say this in all the known languages of the world and to lead up to it in a thousand different manners. Dada negates everything, and first of all literature.

To those who asked why men who revolted against all forms of literature wrote at all rather than expressing their disapproval by complete silence, the dadaists answered that only by writing could they make known their revolt and win new adherents to their views. In addition to their frequent manifestoes (Tzara alone published as many as seven in one volume), they had their own periodicals: *Le Bulletin Dada,* the well-named *Cannibale, Littérature, Nord-Sud* (named after a sub-way line), and *Sic,* perhaps the best-named of all. In Zurich and Paris they organized meetings in which two spokesmen would lecture unintelligibly at once from the same stage while a phonograph barked incessantly or shouted a third speech. From the start the movement clearly manifested a love of scandal for its own sake. These young men simply refused to accept the universe.

With its utter negation of the inner world as well as the outer world, dada was an *impasse;* only two possible solutions offered themselves to its adherents, suicide or a miracle. Some of them did commit suicide as the supreme gesture of revolt; others waited for the miracle. In October 1924 one of their number, André Breton, issued his *Manifeste du Surréalisme* and two months later began publishing the periodical entitled *La Révolution Surréaliste.* While preserving some of the destructive philosophy of dada, the surrealists who grouped around Breton centered their attention on the miracle and presented a constructive program. Still refusing to accept the universe, they insisted on going beyond so-called reality to the super-reality of the imagination. Their whole effort consists in entering into relations with spiritual reality, which reveals the absolute that we cannot see as long as we accept the physical world. To discover that absolute, surrealism began by throwing away the usual instrument of knowledge, the reason. In this way does André Breton define *Surréalisme* in his first manifesto:

"Pure psychic automatism by means of which we propose to express, orally, in writing, or in any other manner, the real functioning of thought. Thought-dictation, free from any check exercised by the reason, outside of all aesthetic or moral preoccupations."

The movement has had two periods distinguished by the means which have been used to achieve the "pure psychic automatism." In the first period automatic writing seemed to offer the solution: a surrealist would sit in a dark room and write as fast as possible whatever came into his head; as he became more and more fatigued the intellectual effort would decrease until he was, or seemed to be, writing at the dictation of his subconscious. Bald accounts of dreams were also acceptable material since the dream comes from beyond the conscious mind. In the second period, fearing to exhaust the bottomless well of their own subliminal selves, the surrealists entered into relations with insane people and recorded their insanities.

In a book written just as they were entering the second period (and to which Breton and Paul Eluard gave the brilliant title of *L'Immaculée Conception*—conception free from the intervention of reason) there are several attempts to simulate various mental ills: mental debility, manic depression, general paralysis, delirium of interpretation, and dementia praecox. Under the influence of Freud, the surrealists had decided that creation was the function of the subconscious. Hence they recognized and practiced inspiration, not as an inexplicable visitation, but as a faculty which can be exercised.

Like all the other advance-guard movements in contemporary literature, surrealism has its reflection in the visual arts; it is in fact the paintings of the surrealists that have made the movement known abroad. As do the writers, the painters take infinite pains to transpose the subconscious onto canvas. Gertrude Stein says in her *Everybody's Autobiography*, "Since Picasso no painter uses a model at least no painter whose painting interests anybody and so they paint what is inside them as it is in them and the only thing that is outside them is the painting they have just been painting. . ." In their attempts to do so they do achieve a kind of super-reality by showing us the surprising things that habit hides from us. The amazing circumstances in which they place a house, an egg, a rubber glove, a plaster head, confer upon those objects a novelty which we were unable to see in them.

Though the surrealist movement still lives today, its prestige is declining. The economic depression has had a sobering effect in Europe as well as in America. As it approaches the forties, the lost generation of the twenties appears to be finding itself. In an era that looks anxiously for a social significance in literature, the periodical that began life as *La Révolution Surréaliste* has been renamed *Le Surréalisme au service de la Révolution*. In recent years several poets have actually published under the noncommittal title *Poèmes*. Novelists like Louis Aragon have yielded to the popular trend of sketching in many volumes the social history of the epoch. Jean Cocteau has become a successful dramatist whose images are now interpreted in terms of fascism and antifascism. Salvador Dali has painted his opinion of Hitler and made the fantasia of the unconscious pay on Fifth Avenue. Cloud-Cuckoo Land is being rapidly deserted. The Post-War is over, and the world will soon be producing a new war literature.

Kenyon Review, Autumn 1939.

FRENCH POETRY IN THE THIRTIES

In some regards the last decade has witnessed but few changes in the history of contemporary French poetry. The implements necessary to a study of the most recent poetic production all point to the truth of the adage that "Plus ça change, plus c'est la même chose." The three-volume anthology of Adolphe Van Bever and Paul Léautaud entitled *Poètes d'aujourd'hui* and the fresher, if less comprehensive, *Anthologie des poètes de la N.R.F.* (1936)—limited to the varied poets who have been published by the review or the publishing house of the *Nouvelle Revue Française*—and the indispensable critical work of Marcel Raymond, *De Baudelaire au Surréalisme* (1933) are as valuable today as when they first appeared. The two great tendencies stemming from Baudelaire—that of the artists and that of the seers (which Raymond was the first to distinguish) can be traced almost as clearly in the poetry of the thirties as in the immediate postwar poetry. Among the "artists," deriving from *Les Fleurs du mal* by way of Mallarmé, Paul Valéry still occupies the foremost position, though he has written considerably more prose than verse in the past ten years. His credo that "The subject of a poem is as foreign and as important to the poem as to a man, his name" simply restates in milder form his fidelity to the doctrine of pure poetry, about which the debate is, however, definitely closed. His "weakness for the formal" reveals itself again in the delicately chiseled lines of "Colloque," published in the June 1939 issue of the *Nouvelle Revue Française:*

349

Que me compares-tu
Quelque rose fanée?
L'amour n'a de vertu
Que fraîche et spontanée. . . .
Mon regard dans le tien
Ne trouve que son bien :
Je m'y vois toute nue!
Mes yeux effaceront
Tes larmes qui seront
D'un souvenir venues. . . .
Si ton désir naquit
Qu'il meure sur ma couche,
Et sur mes lèvres qui
T'emporteront la bouche. . . .

The whole poem, of which this is but half, might easily be incorporated into one of Valéry's earlier collections *Charmes* or even *Album de vers anciens*. But if Valéry would prefer, as he has said, to write in complete lucidity and full consciousness something weak rather than to produce a masterpiece while in a state of trance, the poets are legion who distinctly prefer the evocative sorcery achieved by recourse to the subconscious.

The tradition of the *voyants* or "seers" who plunge with another Baudelaire "into the depths of the unknown to find something *new*" and like Rimbaud systematically cultivate a confusion of all the senses reaches its highest point in Paul Claudel and its extreme in surrealism. And it is significant that whereas the French Academy consecrated the Mallarmé-Valéry formula by admitting the latter to a place among the immortals it rejected the Rimbaud-Claudel vein, with all that it implies in the direction of complete nonconformism, when the former ambassador's candidacy proved unsuccessful.

During the last ten years Paul Claudel, who strikes many critics as the one French writer of this century to give indubitable signs of genius, has produced two works of epic significance, *Le Livre de Christophe Colomb* (1933) and *Le Soulier de satin* (1931). In both, the seventy-year-old poet, who has spent the greater part of his life in diplomatic outposts on remote continents, turns to the Spanish Renaissance with its voyages of discovery, its deep mysticism, and its impressive equilibrium of the physical and the spiritual. When Columbus—whose first name recalls the Christ-bearer while his last name symbolizes the dove, that is, everything spiritual and everything winged—is asked what drives him westward, he replies:

> L'amour de la Terre de Dieu! le désir de
> la Terre de Dieu! le désir de la possession de
> la Terre de Dieu!

In his original and very free *verset,* which has influenced such diverse writers as Paul Fort, André Gide, and Henry de Montherlant, Claudel sings in a deep, throaty voice—the voice of a man descended from peasants and possessing a close affinity with the saints—at once the reality of the universe and the joy of renunciation. *Le Soulier de satin,* grandiose drama in five parts each as long as the ordinary play, may very well come to be considered its author's masterpiece. Revealing in its structure and its verse the deep influence that both Aeschylus and Shakespeare have exerted on him, this epic of worldly power and spiritual growth tells a story of universal application. Ever since his consummately poetic miracle play of *L'Annonce faite à Marie,* Claudel's admirers have hoped that he would give them a Joan of Arc similarly conceived. In Ida Rubinstein's performance in May and June 1939 of Claudel's dramatic oratorio *Jeanne d'Arc au bûcher* with Honegger's music, those admirers finally got Joan in all her peasant naïveté and sublime heroism.

If Valéry and Claudel best represent the opposing tendencies which find their common source in Baudelaire, it is also true, as it would seem from a comparison of their activity during the last decade, that the Rimbaldian current is more vigorous than the Mallarmian. Among the older poets who follow the more astringent, more intellectual example of Mallarmé, François-Paul Alibert, Roger Allard, and Vincent Muselli have published only rare poems in periodicals. The survivors of the Belgian contingent—Maeterlinck, Albert Mockel, and André Fontainas—have maintained an almost complete silence, although André Fontainas illustrated in a severe exhortation to a young poet (published

in *Le Pont Mirabeau* in November 1938) how valiantly he has kept
alive the manner of the master:

> Songe à tes odes. Scrute, au point où se dessine
> Presque informe le germe issu d'un sourd ferment,
> Le beau suc nourricier qui creuse la racine,
> Monte, et jaillit au faîte en feux de diamant.

Francis Jammes, whose last ten years yielded two volumes of rich poetry,
could still strike the note that Mallarmé loved in such a poem as
"Salon" with its voluntarily deceptive echoes:

> Un liseron bleu s'enlace,
> Coupe avide de rosée,
> Aux simples roses rosées
> Que répercute la glace
> De Venise, biseautée.
> Et la lèvre d'une tasse
> Verte qu'un liséré dore,
> Où le café fume encore,
> Attend la lèvre de Laure.

His symbolist contemporaries would doubtless have appreciated also
his pastoral tragedy "Diane," but Jammes, whose death last spring
came just as he was beginning to be more widely recognized, was more
at home in a simpler elegiac mood, as when he relates his hunting experiences in his native Béarn, or in a charmingly playful mood that was
entirely his own—

> Dans la transparence de l'eau
> Les poissons font dodo.

Emmanuel Lochac has cultivated the Mallarmian ideal of purity to the
point of whittling down a poem to a single line, many of which he has
published under the title of *Monostiches* (1936). The first of these
"vers solitaires," as one might maliciously call them, is a justification
of the method:

> Maint poëme est la cage où chante un vers captif.

Others leave one with the impression that one might have from the last line of a perfect sonnet—

> Il fallait me guider, Ariane, ou me suivre.

The other tradition is more robust in many of its realizations. Ten years younger than Claudel, Léon-Paul Fargue lived through the height of the symbolist movement without ever enrolling himself under the pastel-colored banners. Even then he was drawn, like Claudel, to the most introspective of his elders: Rimbaud, Corbière, Laforgue. In recent years, "tired of the sonnet for the poor, the alexandrine for weddings and banquets, the ballade for Ph.D.'s" this prestidigitator of neologisms and inventor of lush images has expressed himself in a prose that must be classified as poetry. *D'après Paris* (1932), with such creations as "chemindeferrique" and "faune sonipède" (for horse) and images like that of the bat signing his mail against the sky, is a model of Farguian evocation. In what seems at first a mere description of exterior objects there always erupt phantoms and larvae of the author's childhood. In *Le Piéton de Paris* (1939) he reveals that his message to a putative disciple would be: "Sensitive . . . strive to be sensitive, infinitely receptive. Forever in a state of osmosis. Get to the point where you no longer need to look to see."

Undergoing much the same influences as Fargue, and others as well, Jules Supervielle nevertheless brought into French poetry a certain freshness from South America where he was born, and a profound feeling of solidarity with everything in nature. A metaphysical anguish torments the poems of *Le Forçat innocent* (1931) and *Gravitations* (1932). In *Les Amis inconnus* (1934) the poet is haunted, like Whitman, by unknown faces in the street, by the half-effaced features of a lost friend. Like Whitman again, he is the poet of the interpenetration of all things in such a way that "from the most lost inland villages one hears coral being formed in the depths of the sea." At rare intervals he strikes a Baudelairean note, as in "Un Poète":

> Je ne vais pas toujours seul au fond de moi-même
> Et j'entraîne avec moi plus d'un être vivant.
> Ceux qui seront entrés dans mes froides cavernes

Sont-ils sûrs d'en sortir même pour un moment?
J'entasse dans ma nuit, comme un vaisseau qui sombre,
Pêle-mêle, les passagers et les marins,
Et j'éteins la lumière aux yeux, dans les cabines,
Je me fais des amis des grandes profondeurs.

The poetry of Pierre-Jean Jouve, who took part in the prewar unanimist experience with Jules Romains and Supervielle, today records
in moving language the transports of a religious mystic tormented by a
lucid awareness of his libido. In his preface to *Sueur de sang* (1935)
Jouve tells of his attempt to find a fundamental relation between the
super-ego and the non-ego or universal erotic basis of personality. No
less characteristic, however, is "Destruction," which might more appropriately have been published yesterday rather than in 1935:

Ces traits de fer et ces chevelures délabrées
Te conviennent, forme aujourd'hui de la ville.
Les visages déformés par l'angoisse et les regards
Troués au cœur! et toujours des mousses légères.
Ce sont les cavaliers avant-coureurs
Ils sont marqués du doigt de Dieu
Ils errent encore avec des journaux à la main
Quand les troupeaux de canons changent de pâturage.

No greater tributary helped in prewar years to swell the river Rimbaud than the rapid, though tortuous, stream which bears the name of
Guillaume Apollinaire. Although he died in 1918, his influence continues to be felt on such poets as Cocteau, Jacob, and all the *Surréalistes*
(it was he who coined the word). Greater in personal prestige than in
his published works, Apollinaire had time in his short life to annex
many new domains to literature and painting and to utter the definitive
prayer of all *avant-garde* writers to come:

Nous voulons vous donner de vastes et d'étranges domaines
Où le mystère en fleurs s'offre à qui veut le cueillir
Il y a là des feux nouveaux, des couleurs jamais vues
Mille phantasmes impondérables
Auxquels il faut donner de la réalité

Nous voulons explorer la bonté contrée énorme où tout se tait
Il y a aussi le temps qu'on peut chasser ou faire revenir
Pitié pour nous qui combattons toujours aux frontières
De l'illimité et de l'avenir
Pitié pour nos erreurs pitié pour nos péchés

In the chaotic Paris immediately after the war, Max Jacob and Jean Cocteau fought on the same frontiers between reality and the land of dreams. As a specialist in literary mystifications and hoaxes, each of these poets—instead of imagining "as his audience an ideal normal man who is an educated member of his own community and is basically at one with the poet in his attitude to life," as Louis MacNeice does—visualizes rather an abnormal reader who, says Cocteau, "has the same sense of mystery as the poet." Max Jacob has by no means abandoned poetry since his conversion to the Catholic Church and his retreat from Montmartre to the shadow of an eleventh-century basilica at Saint-Benoît-sur-Loire. In the past decade *Rivage* (1934) and *Saint Matorel* (1937) have contained poems in his new manner which, among others that unpleasantly recall the "religious art" of the Place Saint-Sulpice, might almost be translated from the Latin of Jacopone da Todi:

> Terre où pourrit le péché et l'erreur,
> terre où la vie dure quelques heures,
> te quitter est la seule envie
> que me laissent mes terreurs.

But as Morven le Gaélique, reincarnation of a Breton bard, Jacob has occasionally untethered his fancy in periodicals.

As for Jean Cocteau, who by common agreement succeeded in 1918 to Apollinaire's position as impresario of the modern spirit, he gives an account of himself in his long poem "L'Incendie" published last May in the *Nouvelle Revue Française*:

> Depuis quinze ans (oui juste) il n'avait plus écrit.
> Il attendait un ordre et qu'un destin l'y force.
> Et voilà que, pareil à l'arbre, sans un cri,
> Sans un geste, un sang bleu coule de son écorce.

355

The event that forced this "playboy" (as he has often been characterized) to leave Paris during the successful run of his melodrama *Les Parents terribles* and to write of his anguish in the poetry he had abandoned years before was the Czechoslovakian crisis of September 1938.

> Nous n'en pouvions plus d'attendre le pire;
> Il fallait, il fallait que nous nous en allions
> Loin du tambour voilé, loin des cirques d'Empire,
> Où Rome aussi livrait Israël aux lions.
>
> . . . .
>
> Et la fuite. Vers où? Vers un autre soi-même
> Vers un linge encor frais où l'on n'a pas rêvé,
> Où des cauchemars neufs construisent leur poème,
> D'où l'on se sauve, à peine était-on arrivé.

Developing his image of a conflagration in a fairly free form of verse which nevertheless preserves rhyme, using concrete metaphors in place of the puns he used to exaggerate, Cocteau makes us feel a very real emotion here. Only in the Epilogue does the tongue-in-cheek author of *Opéra* pop up, and there the manner is justified since Cocteau is referring to the Munich conference:

> Que faut-il pour qu'un coup de dés réussisse?
> Rien, sinon que la chance lasse,
> S'installe obscurément sur l'os de l'as
> Et mette en l'air les tétines du double six.

Stemming from dadaism and from Apollinaire and therefore directly in the tradition of the conquest of the irrational which goes back to *Les Illuminations* and *Une Saison en enfer,* surrealism began as a rather absurd rhetoric of revolt and transformed itself, through a conscious use of a kind of verbal delirium, into a search for the supernatural in the subconscious. "A monstrous aberration," says André Breton, "makes men think that language was born to facilitate their mutual relations." The very incoherence of most surrealist poems makes it impossible to follow their subtle alchemy intended to transmute the unreal into the real. The artificial simulation of mental ills (see *L'Immaculée Conception* of Breton and Eluard) has definitely petered out as literary material, and too often members of the group (for instance: Benjamin Péret in *Je ne mange pas de ce pain-là*) continue to wallow in the cheaply erotic and scatological manner of bad boys who will shock at any price. Paul Eluard, the only real poet to issue from the movement, has published several volumes since 1929 containing many poems of great purity achieved through the complexities of a very learned verbal manipulation:

> Une rafale une seule
> D'horizon à horizon
> Et ainsi sur toute la terre
> Pour balayer la poussière
> Les myriades de feuilles mortes
> Pour dépouiller tous les arbres
> Pour dévaster les cultures
> Pour abattre les oiseaux.

Aragon, Breton, and Philippe Soupault write almost exclusively in prose now. While the Communist party absorbs the spirit of revolt of former dadaists and surrealists, the surrealist revolution is agonizing. In March 1939 it received something like a *coup de grâce* when an impartial monthly *Yggdrasill* voiced a call for a general liquidation of surrealism.

Since the two main currents in contemporary French poetry flow from Rimbaud and Mallarmé, one might turn about the question that Edmond Jaloux addressed to Stuart Merrill in 1905 and ask: Who is not still a Symbolist today? It is true that, though the symbolist movement reached its apogee between 1885 and 1905, it has continued to influence even the younger poets whose work differs as much from that of Verlaine and Maeterlinck as T. S. Eliot's does from that of Yeats. Poets like Lochac and Perse, Jouve and Supervielle, are symbolists, if you will, in the broad sense in which Edmund Wilson discerned this same tradition in Joyce, Gertrude Stein, and Proust.

Although such poets are by no means out of touch with their

time—one has only to recall Cocteau's "Incendie" or Jouve's "Destruction" with their very contemporary anguish of the intellectual pursued by the threat of war—there are many other poets who would gladly echo Louis MacNeice's "plea for *impure* poetry, that is, for poetry conditioned by the poet's life and the world around him." More and more in the past ten years, in fact, French poetry has tended to discard its voluntary obscurity (deriving at one and the same time from a concentration of meaning and from an unwillingness to submit the spontaneous products of the mind to an artificial elaboration, as Romains points out) and to come into closer contact with life. Many of the younger poets illustrate this double movement toward "impurity" and greater communicability. Marthe Boidin, discovered by *Mesures* in 1936, writes this simple and beautiful "Prière du matin":

> Faites que par ce jour d'azur incandescent,
> Rien ne puisse arriver de ce que je pressens.
> Faites que ce seul jour soit encore une trêve,
> Que rien ne bouge ou crie avant qu'il ne s'achève.
> S'il faut que le silence enfin soit déchiré,
> Qu'au lourd soleil qui gagne un volet soit tiré,
> Que des chants éclatants dans la cour de derrière
> Annoncent un œuf blanc pondu dans la poussière.

In spite of her playful use of puns, Louise de Vilmorin occasionally strikes a sincere note in her *Fiançailles pour rire* (1939) that recalls, through the verse-forms of Verlaine, the so feminine Marceline Desbordes-Valmore:

> En plein cœur de ma vie
> L'inconnu se fait beau
> Qui venu me défie
> Et m'impose ses maux
>
> . . . . . .
>
> Car il a fait de moi
> En plein cœur de ma vie
> L'enfant qui autrefois
> Rêvait d'être ravie.

358

No poetess has yet come, however, to replace Anna de Noailles, who died in 1933, but Yvonne Ferrand-Weyher's *Fontaines de mémoire* (1935) and Elisabeth de Vautibault's fairy-like *Matines* (1935) possess decided qualities, and one can justly expect excellent poetry from Marthe Boidin's skillful handling of the alexandrine.

Raymond Queneau opens his *Chêne et chien* (1937) with this prosaic autobiography:

> Je naquis au Havre un vingt et un février
> en mil neuf cent et trois
> ma mère était mercière et mon père mercier
> ils trépignaient de joie. . . .

While bringing the same directness into his highly personal poems, Louis Brauquier continues the tradition of exoticism inaugurated by Valery Larbaud and enriched by Henry J.-M. Levet and St.-John Perse. From Australia he looks nostalgically across the world to his native Marseille:

> Je voudrais revenir dans un vieux port du monde,
> Comme ceux d'où partaient ces premiers découvreurs,
> Encor mal assurés que la terre fût ronde,
> Qui levaient l'ancre pleins d'audace et de terreurs.

Though he is constantly thrilled by the "Brise marine" that Mallarmé felt but never yielded to—

> Et la vie est courte et la mer est grande
> La route des eaux reste la plus longue
> Et trop de vaisseaux sont partis sans moi—

Brauquier, as a man who has rounded the cape many times, is also keenly aware of the joys of the return.

The contemplative, sometimes religiose art of the Catholic poet Patrice de la Tour du Pin often expresses itself with the greatest clarity, as in "Les Enfants de Septembre" or in this beginning of "Légende":

> Va dire à ma chère Ile, là-bas, tout là-bas,
> Près de cet obscur marais de Foulc, dans la lande,

Que je viendrai vers elle ce soir, qu'elle attende,
Qu'au lever de la lune elle entendra mon pas.

Tu la trouveras baignant ses pieds sous les rouches,
Les cheveux dénoués, les yeux clos à demi,
Et naïve, tenant une main sur la bouche
Pour ne pas réveiller les oiseaux endormis.

Even such poets as Henri Michaux and Jacques Audiberti, ordinarily difficult, have written simply of simple things. In "Sur le chemin de la Mort" Michaux abandons his usual analyses of nightmares which make one think of Racine's line: "C'était pendant l'horreur d'une profonde nuit"—

Sur le chemin de la Mort,
Ma mère rencontra une grande banquise;
Elle voulut parler,
Il était déjà tard,
Une grande banquise d'ouate.

Elle nous regarda mon frère et moi,
Et puis elle pleura.

Nous lui dîmes—mensonge vraiment absurde—que nous comprenions bien.
Elle eut alors ce si gracieux sourire de toute jeune fille,
Qui était vraiment elle,
Un si joli sourire presque espiègle;
Ensuite elle fut prise dans l'Opaque.

In "Demandez le programme" Audiberti cries out his joy upon starting for a vacation:

Que se repose le mystère!
Je ne veux plus toucher mon coeur.
J'ai hâte de gagner la terre,
d'y trinquer, charmante liqueur,

au sang des herbes anonymes,
au suc des pierres sans douleur,
loin des cités d'où nous bannîmes
la paix, le rire et la chaleur.

The two opening lines are significant: a vacation implies freedom from the poetic mystery and the poet's usual probing of his emotions.

Though there is still much good poetry being written in Paris which proves that, as Michael Roberts says, "It is possible . . . for a poem to be professedly realistic and yet to have the vigour and insistence of a dream or nightmare," nevertheless (to quote again from Patrice de la Tour du Pin) there are also indications that

> Il est fini, Seigneur, le siècle des isolements,
> Il menaçait de mourir dans la contemplation de soi-même,
> Peut-être encor plus loin; mais jamais plus
> Nous ne recommencerons ces découvertes stériles
> Et cet enfoncement dans l'inquiétude du corps.

The two most encouraging indications are *Encore un instant de bonheur* (1934) and *L'Homme blanc* (1937) which mark the return to poetry, after many years, of two very successful novelists: Henry de Montherlant and Jules Romains. Most beautiful among the former's poems are those of African inspiration in which he employs the long Claudelian *verset,* loosely rhymed or not at all, as in this one from "Thèmes pour une flûte arabe":

> Toute chose précisée, vigorée, dans l'humidité qui suit l'averse.
> Les jeunes filles avec un lustré, un soyeux, un brillant d'oiseau.
> Abenamar, en plein conseil des ministres, tourne la tête à droite et à gauche, comme la jument qui entend l'étalon.
> Il n'y tient plus. Il feint qu'un message lui arrive. Il sort, il va humer cette belle pleureuse, la terre après la pluie.
> Chaque feuille est une petite tasse pleine. Abenamar au passage, incline les branches pesantes et reçoit sur son front la bénédiction de l'eau.

Pierre Louÿs would doubtless not have rejected that poem from his *Chansons de Bilitis.* In other poems Montherlant very happily uses a combination of five- and seven-syllable lines that recalls Verlaine. Less revolutionary than Claudel and Montherlant in prosody, Romains employs a freely cadenced, generally assonanced verse of fourteen syllables (permitting three different rhythmic measures of traditional form: seven-seven, six-eight, eight-six) which alternates with poems in octosyllables or decasyllables. Such off-rhymes as Romains occasionally uses (azur—gourds; montagne—enseigne) suggest that French poets are rhyming much as English poets are. This is true. Where Spender uses such end-words as concrete, wire, pillars, secret; endures, anger, danger, future, Audiberti often rhymes thus in *Race des hommes* (1937): veuve—trouve; citron—brun; ombre—novembre; violons—lents. In René Chalupt's "Vie de château," published by *Le Pont Mirabeau* in 1938, we find: rouille—treilles; barbe—herbe; amazone—alezane; brume—brame. On the other hand, Audiberti occasionally employs hyper-rich rhymes of a precious variety, such as hors de—horde; durci—mais si; donzelle—dans elle.

But what is more important, though Romains can claim to be a specialist of versification, is the vast epic inspiration of *L'Homme blanc,* for it sings nothing less than

> . . . l'Homme blanc, l'Homme premier, la race belle;
> La chair non déguisée où le sang fait des pas visibles;
>
> . . . .
>
> La peau de l'Homme blanc, la coléreuse, la décente,
> L'amoureuse, l'impudique, la seule qui soit nue.

At the risk of being called prosaic, the author of *Men of Good Will* wishes poetry to cease withdrawing from life, to reach out and annex great masses of prose, since

> Les peuples ont cessé d'entendre le poète;
> D'autres jeux les ont pris; de plus mornes amours.
> Pense-t-il se venger en détournant la tête?
> Par son mépris muet leur donner des remords?
>
> Ou pour se consoler de l'extase commune,
> Fera-t-il du poème un rite ténébreux?
> Mots troubles, mots tordus, caressantes fumées,
> Saurez-vous bien cacher le monde à ses yeux bleus?
>
> . . . .
>
> Je préfère garder la même voix tranquille
> Que si toute la terre écoutait notre chant,
> Et qu'on vît jusqu'au ciel les gradins qui reculent
> Chargés de laboureurs, de femmes, de marchands.

The end of this epic (which, by the way, contains some beautiful lines on: "New York, bouquet de bourgeons/Et furie de floraison. . . .") sings of Jules Romains's favorite dream, the Universal Republic of free men, of which the great instrument, in the eyes of this former Normalien, is the schoolmaster—

> L'école est neuve au flanc de la montagne.
> Le vent est vif; il gèle dans l'azur.
> Les écoliers réchauffent leurs doigts gourds.
> Ne faiblis pas, homme qui les enseignes.
>
> Dis-leur que rien ne vaut contre l'amour;
> Qu'il n'est qu'un temps pour le flux des délires;
> Et qu'on vaincra les anges souterrains
> Par le compas, la balance et la lyre.

Thus Jules Romains comes to the same conclusion in favor of the epic that has apparently been Paul Claudel's since the beginning of his career. But whereas Romains, bred in the most anticlerical tradition, hopes to revive poetry through recourse to a broad human theme, Claudel, the religious mystic and the greater poet, is inspired rather by man's relations with the divine. Though France has as yet produced but little verse of "social significance" and even less topical poetry (the French fear to combine poetry and journalism), the move away from the hermetic and the gratuitous is very marked. Despite the great variety in inspiration and technique which French poetry of today tolerates, there is becoming manifest a greater unanimity of attitude; as the influence of both Rimbaud and Mallarmé decreases, the number of poets writing in a major key grows constantly.

On *The Imposter (Thomas l'imposteur)*, by Jean Cocteau, translated by Dorothy Williams (New York: The Noonday Press, 1957), and *The Holy Terrors (Les Enfants terribles)*, by Jean Cocteau, translated by Rosamond Lehmann (New York: New Directions, 1957). *The New York Times Book Review*, November 3, 1957.

JEAN COCTEAU: MYTH-MAKING

Jean Cocteau is a poet who on occasion expresses himself in plays, novels, ballets, drawings, or paintings. The novels form the smallest part of his output, for he wrote but three between the ages of thirty and forty and never returned to the form. All are highly poetic novels of adolescence, catching much of the elusive charm of that transition period. And now, many years after Cocteau's excursion into fiction, the best two of those novels are made available in very sensitive English translations by Dorothy Williams and Rosamond Lehmann.

The very starting point of *The Imposter* lies in the heart of Cocteau's poetic theory, for he has always been concerned with the relation between falsehood and reality. The poet, he tells us, cares nothing for admiration; he merely wants to be believed. Hence Cocteau gives a portrait here of a young myth-maker having a field day during the First World War. Thomas, the impostor, comes to believe his own inventions, like the child playing horse who literally becomes a horse. Thus his death on the battlefield just as he feigns death to avoid being shot provides a perfect ending to his life of prevarication as reality catches up with the make-believe.

Aside from this basic conception, however, which equates the poet with the child, the poetry of this novel becomes apparent only superficially in ingenious images and verbal artifices. The author remains so playful throughout that many readers back in 1923 were shocked by his personal view of the war. Yet one has only to read the memoirs of his friends and certain poems by Cocteau to see that the poet has faithfully depicted the war as he experienced it.

In *The Holy Terrors* (originally titled *Children of the Game* on its appearance in London) the artifice is less apparent and the atmosphere of make-believe more convincing. Starting with a brother and sister who resist the process of growing up as they live in a nonadult world of their own fabrication, Cocteau has told a moving and tragic story.

In the odd, unhealthy atmosphere of their common bedroom, which is a perfect projection of their personalities, they indulge in a calculated trance they call the Game. And such an escape from life—it must be remembered that Cocteau wrote this novel during a sort of waking sleep while trying to cure his addiction to opium in 1929—admirably foreshadows their simultaneous suicide.

The plot subtly traces the groping evolution of the love instinct in Paul, who first loves a boy, then a girl of the same facial type, before recognizing on the point of death that his real love is for his sister Elizabeth. It is with Elizabeth that he has shared the gypsy-like room that is their shell, the hallucinatory Game, the precious childhood treasure of sundry magical talismen and even his most intimate dreams. Yet the form of his death, and this fully identifies the novel as a poem, harks back to the initial scene in which the handsome bully Dargelos fells Paul with a snowball, for Dargelos prompts that death by sending Paul a ball of Oriental poison evocative of the snowball.

As surely as any of his lyrics, this novel derives from what Cocteau calls his "mythology of childhood" which made him use the snowball fight again in his first film, *Le Sang d'un poète* (*The Blood of a Poet*), the dream and sleepwalking in many of his best poems, and the death by poison in poems, novels, and plays.

The twenty drawings by the author used in this American edition (chosen from the sixty he brought out some years after the novel) reflect the same inspiration and strike precisely the same disturbing note as do his prose and verse. Cocteau also illustrated *The Impostor* most handsomely not long after its first publication, and this makes it particularly unfortunate that the present publisher has commissioned such an ugly and inappropriate drawing for his cover.

On *Dialogues* by Paul Valéry, with two prefaces by Wallace Stevens, translated by William McCausland Stewart (Volume IV of *The Collected Works of Paul Valéry*, edited by Jackson Mathews, Bollingen Series, XLV; New York: Pantheon Books, Inc., 1956). *The New York Times Book Review*, March 24, 1957.

PAUL VALÉRY: "DIALOGUES"

This is another book from the busy *bottega* of Jackson Mathews, which, specializing in introducing French poets to America, has recently produced for New Directions the most authoritative edition of Baudelaire and for Random House a dazzling translation of René Char entitled *Hypnos Waking*. Long before his own translation of Valéry's *Monsieur Teste* for Knopf ten years ago, Mr. Mathews was deeply concerned with the great French poet, and *Dialogues* is but the first volume to appear of *The Collected Works of Paul Valéry*, translated into English under his general editorship by many expert hands. If all are as felicitous as William McCausland Stewart, through whose version one never feels either the lack of the original or its obtrusive presence, America may yet discover the greatest poet of twentieth-century France.

When Paul Valéry died in 1945, Paris accorded him the most magnificent funeral since that of Victor Hugo—and rightly so, for he had become the spokesman for French art and intelligence. Like his contemporaries Claudel and Gide and Proust, he had begun to write in the early nineties with rather hermetic poems and elliptical essays exalting silence and experimental thought. In 1896 he took his own advice and for twenty years abandoned literature in favor of mathematical and philosophical speculation. His sudden emergence in 1917 with a long poem, *La Jeune Parque*, which might be called *The Waste Land* of

France, marked him as a major poet who harked back through Mallarmé and Baudelaire to the French classics. Other slim collections of polished verse and several profound prose works easily assured his election to the French Academy in 1925.

"How could I have been so slow to discover his work?" wrote Rilke in 1921 on reading one of the Valéry dialogues that he eventually put into German, and at about the same time Gide wrote to Valéry of the same dialogue: "*Eupalinos* forces me to wonder at times if I do not prefer your prose even to your verse." It is surely wise, therefore, for the present edition to begin with six sparkling dialogues combining depth of thought with remarkable subtlety of style.

The form was ideal for Valéry because it permitted the expression of contrary ideas without dogmatism. Of course, he took his model from Plato, in whom dialectic brilliance, myth, and poetic beauty are combined; but beyond the names of the speakers (Socrates, Phaedrus, etc.) he has made no attempt at local color nor aimed at a pastiche. The subjects derive directly from the modern poet's constant meditation and the myriad reflections he consigned to the notebooks that are now being published in Paris in thirty-two facsimile volumes of 1,000 pages each.

There is no need to be either dancer or balletomane to enjoy the delicate description and analysis of dancing in "Dance and the Soul," nor is this description by a Greek builder addressed solely to architects: "This delicate temple, none knows it, is the mathematical image of a girl of Corinth, whom I happily loved. It reproduces faithfully the proportions that were peculiarly hers. It lives for me! It gives me back what I have given it. . . ." The same might be said of the classification of buildings into those that are mute, those that speak, and those that sing, or of Socrates' witticism in Hades that "life cannot defend herself against those undying death scenes" such as he had experienced.

Everything in this handsome little book is quotable, simply because Valéry possessed the gift of making the abstract a thing of palpable pleasure, combining thought and sensation in a mental interplay as delightful to the mind as a ballet, a Greek temple, or a spreading tree.

On *The Art of Poetry,* by Paul Valéry, with an introduction by T. S. Eliot, translated by Denise Folliot (Volume VII of *The Collected Works of Paul Valéry,* edited by Jackson Mathews, Bollingen Series, XLV; New York: Pantheon Books, 1958). *The Reporter,* July 10, 1958.

PAUL VALÉRY: "THE ART OF POETRY"

In Paris last winter the bookshops were full of new Valeriana. The first volume of the definitive Pléiade edition of Valéry's works, meticulously edited by Jean Hytier, had just appeared, as had Octave Nadal's luxurious and scholarly presentation of *La Jeune Parque,* a fresh volume of the poet's ever-stimulating correspondence, and two new collections of his obiter dicta made by the indefatigable Henri Mondor. The huge photographic edition of Valéry's 30,000 pages of notebooks, now in course of publication, was not generally exhibited, doubtless because it is so expensive that only a library could afford to buy it.

And yet this year does not mark one of those anniversaries that the French so scrupulously observe, for Paul Valéry died just thirteen years ago and the centenary of his birth will not come until 1971. The number of new editions simply attests to the perennial interest in this great poet who has miraculously been spared the period of limbo usually reserved for recently dead idols. Long before his death, in fact, Valéry had become a touchstone for French intellectuals. "Have you read his poems in the latest *N.R.F.?*" "What do you think of *Amphion?*" "I rank the prose of *Monsieur Teste* even above the chiseled lines of *Le Cimetière marin*"—such remarks were commonplaces in the 1920's and 1930's, when the young could establish their poetic sensitivity or aptitude for rigorous thought by reference to a single writer.

As a member of that prodigious generation born at the time of the Franco-Prussian War (including Claudel and Gide and Proust), Valéry had appeared rather late on the literary horizon. Then after *La Jeune Parque* of 1917, fame had come rapidly with his election to the French Academy in 1925 and his unofficial position as spokesman for French intelligence. The fact that after a brilliant start as Mallarmé's closest disciple he had almost completely abandoned literature for a period of twenty years only added to his prestige. The man who had had the courage to remain silent so long must now, when he finally deigned to speak, have something to say. And he did, for his highly distilled poems, subtle dialogues, and aphoristic reflections all grew from the years of secluded philosophical and mathematical inquiry that prepared him to write with urbane profundity on any subject that engaged his attention.

In America, thanks to the Bollingen Foundation and more specifically to the editorship of Jackson Mathews, Valéry is beginning to become available in a form that he himself, for all his nicety of taste, would have approved. The care exercised in selecting, combining, and presenting the texts (with just sufficient annotation to satisfy the curious) is no less admirable than the simple classical format and typography that Pantheon has given these volumes.

Coming a year after the *Dialogues, The Art of Poetry* is the second to appear of the projected fifteen volumes. Its nearly threescore essays—comprising lectures, prefaces for others' books, articles, even a radio broadcast and an after-dinner speech—span the whole of Valéry's career, for the earliest was written in his eighteenth year and the latest shortly before his death at seventy-four.

Yet as T. S. Eliot points out in his sensitive introduction, the occasional character of the essays does not make them perfunctory, as it might have done with other writers. Each occasion or assignment merely served as a pretext for Valéry to return to the unchanging themes of his lifelong meditation as recorded in his more than two hundred notebooks. This is why, as Mr. Eliot states, "If the best of his poems are among the masterpieces, the best of his critical essays are among the most remarkable curiosities of French literature." It is a pity that in the present translation, by no means comparable to Walter McCausland Stewart's version of the *Dialogues,* he too often speaks with a marked French accent.

Many of the essays concern the making of poems, and particularly the making of Valéry's poems. Hence Eliot tends to see them as a sort of vindication of the brevity and paucity of those poems and to note a harmony between practice and theory. But we might well ask with Jean Hytier (in his exhaustive study of 1953 entitled *La Poétique de Valéry*) if the doctrine is not often built up and added unto the work as the result of an altogether independent meditation. To be sure, everything Valéry thought about the process of creation relates to his own finished poems, but he never misses a chance to tell us that he was even more interested in the creative activity than in the product of that activity. An implausible family tradition claims that the first word the infant Valéry pronounced, back in 1872, was "clef"; and nothing could be more appropriate for the man who never ceased seeking the key to knowledge, to poetic pleasure, to creation in general. In this very volume does he not tell us that "there is no theory that is not a fragment, carefully prepared, of some autobiography"?

Perhaps the focus of his poetic art can be found rather in the opposition he himself felt between creative intention and realization. At the age of twenty he wrote to his master Mallarmé, in a letter not included in this volume, "This is what I think and here is what I wrote; which represents the truth?" Again and again in these essays, this most conscious of modern poets returns to the intimately felt contradiction. And with his characteristic disdain, he disposes once and for all of the accusation of "obscurity" when he notes: "If my mind is richer, more rapid, freer, more disciplined than yours, neither you nor I can do anything about it."

The major points Paul Valéry makes in his *Art of Poetry* are few because he so frequently returns to the same ones. The first is the reduction of inspiration to its proper proportions; he revolts against what Eliot calls the "mediumistic" view of the poet by setting against it a salutary insistence on technique and hard work. Still, he never completely denies the element of dream, or inspiration, or intoxication; he simply wants to subject it to some more sustained organization "than is shown by a flame following a trail of powder," which is all he finds in most famous lyrics. "The gods in their graciousness," he says here, "give us an occasional first line *for nothing;* but it is for us to fashion the second, which must chime with the first and not be unworthy of its supernatural elder. All the resources of experience and of the mind are not too much to render it comparable to the line which was a gift." A second point is his equation, wonderfully illustrated by analogy with a very small child, that poetry is to prose as dancing is to walking—a free, nonutilitarian activity in which form is its own justification.

As a third point there might be adduced the many references to rhythm as the starting point for a poem and the consequent conclusion that form frequently determines the "content" of a work. And finally, forsaking the poet's relation to his work for his relation to his reader, there is Valéry's statement: "A poet's function—do not be startled by this remark—is not to experience the poetic state: that is a private affair. His function is to create it in others. The poet is recognized—or at least everyone recognizes his own poet—by the simple fact that he causes his reader to become 'inspired.' Positively speaking, inspiration is a graceful attribute with which the reader endows his poet: the reader sees in us the transcendent merits of virtues and graces that develop in him. He seeks and finds in us the wondrous cause of his own wonder." Or, as he stated in an aphorism not included here, "The man of genius is the one who infuses genius into me."

Well, this is something that Valéry himself undeniably does for his readers; we feel elevated by having absorbed his thoughts and made some of them our own. His prose, like his verse, is not for hasty reading; but, provided we read him attentively and thoughtfully, he becomes a part of our intellectual substance.

On *A Barbarian in Asia (Un Barbare en Asie)*, by Henri Michaux, translated by Sylvia Beach (New York: New Directions, 1949). *The New York Times Book Review*, June 5, 1949.

HENRI MICHAUX: "BARBARIAN IN ASIA"

U*n Barbare en Asie* is the first book to appear in English translation by the sensitive Franco-Belgian poet, Henri Michaux, creator of a certain M. Plume, discoverer of Great Garabagne and the Land of Magic. Most appropriately it reached us in a taut, faithful translation by Sylvia Beach, ever a defender of the new and original. Through her famous Shakespeare and Company in Paris she effectively introduced to France the best in English and American literature; now she is continuing her work of initiation in the opposite direction.

For years those who read French have delighted in the colorful, violent world of Michaux, cherishing the little volumes entitled *Qui je fus, Entre centre et absence, Exorcismes,* and the collection appropriately called *L'Espace du dedans.* Beside the poems in verse and in prose, his hieroglyphic drawings and hallucinatory paintings have reflected the same world. André Gide, René Bertelé, and more recently Richard Ellmann have written intelligently and enthusiastically of him.

Michaux is a barbarian in Asia as all Occidentals must be in the East. But in another sense the true poet is ever an alien in any but the special world of his own devising. "Poets travel," he says, "but the adventure of travel does not possess them." He should know, for he early embarked as a cabin boy bound for South America, explored Ecuador, and descended the Amazon in a canoe. Some fifteen years ago, he roamed throughout Asia gathering the reflections on India, China, Japan, and Malaya of which this book is made. In the interval and down to the present, he has not ceased to travel widely in the strange latitudes of his own mind, where he came upon Great Garabagne, Poddema, and other haunting countries which still remain half mysterious even to him.

Imagine Arthur Rimbaud carrying his peculiar poetic vision with him to Abyssinia and describing the country, natives, and customs for us. Or just fancy Lewis Carroll—with whom Henri Michaux also has something in common—reporting a trip to Africa. In either case the result would be somewhat like this original and stimulating refraction of the Orient through a very special personality.

This brief note is characteristic: "It is believed that the Chinese swarm because they have so many children. Not at all; they have a great many children because they like to swarm [. . .] and to occupy space. They like the general effect, not the individual; the panorama, not the single object."

On *Selected Writings: The Space Within*
(*L'Espace du dedans*), by Henri Michaux,
translated with an introduction by Richard
Ellmann (New York: New Directions,
1951). *Saturday Review,* December 29,
1951.

HENRI MICHAUX: "SPACE WITHIN"

Without New Directions such French writers as Mallarmé and Apollinaire and the more recent Eluard, Queneau, and Michaux would be unknown or inadequately known in America. That young publishing house consistently introduces to the American public the best in the *avant-garde* writing of Europe. Those who read French sometimes feel that the translations are not always worthy of the originals, but Henri Michaux, one of the three or four most considerable French poets of the present, has been fortunate in this regard. This is the second of his books to appear in America; the first was translated by Sylvia Beach and the second by Richard Ellmann, both scrupulous and intuitive translators.

The Space Within—a faithful rendering of *L'Espace du dedans,* the title Michaux gave this anthology—reflects the content of his original poetry, in which everything takes place in the mind. In another volume Henri Michaux characteristically wrote: "Man is inclined to walk on riverbanks, thinking of nothing. In the belief that he is contemplating the river or simply walking aimlessly, he contemplates his own river of blood, in which he is a delicate island, despite his organs, his hard bones, his even harder principles, which would like to delude him." For him the skeleton, the prison-frame of man's eager heart and hypersensitive nerves, symbolizes the emotional ossification which the poet must escape. In praise of childhood he once pointed out that a drawing by the eight-year-old Louis XIII was indistinguishable from one by the eight-year-old son of a New Caledonia cannibal, thus proving that the French boy of 1609 was as old as humanity, or two hundred and fifty thousand years old. But a few years later "he is merely thirty-one, he has become an individual, he is merely a king of France, an *impasse* from which he never escaped. What is worse than being finished?" For Michaux adult, finished, dead, are but different ways of saying the same thing; and he concludes: "The worst criticism against Aristotle is still this: that he was definitively Aristotle. Before dying one becomes all bone."

Opposed to the rigid there is the fluid which the poet finds and liberates in sickness, travel, and magic. Painfully sensitive to all that is unpleasant, he undergoes a series of ordeals and exercises his neurotic obsessions in his poetry; hence the pathological show of violence of many pages beside the Kafka-like timidity of his Mr. Plume. And yet Henri Michaux himself is such a deceptively gentle, gracious man, distinguished in every gesture and every articulation; perhaps this merely proves that his catharsis is effective.

Certain of these poems in prose or in irregular verse strongly suggest satire: "The Spermatozoon's Heaven," for instance, or the one about the brutalized child martyrs reared by the Hacs in order to be sure of having "great artists, poets, but unfortunately also assassins, and especially reformers." But the satire is merely incidental, a by-product of a particular anguish projected into words.

Someday Michaux will be known in America as the great painter he is. If he worked on canvas and in oils rather than in water colors and on paper, he would doubtless already have taken his rightful place beside such as Paul Klee and Miró. As a painter, he has hauntingly portrayed the same Parpue, the Darelette, "Hypedruches with black tails," and all that fantastic zoology that figures in his poems.

THEATER

On *L'Ecole des femmes,* by Molière, produced by Louis Jouvet. *New York Herald Tribune,* March 18, 1951.

JOUVET'S "SCHOOL FOR WIVES"

One evening in the spring of 1936 Molière began to live again as intensely as when he had charmed the court of Louis XIV. For when the curtain went up on *L'Ecole des femmes* at the Athénée in Paris, he seemed to be reincarnated in Louis Jouvet. Yet this play, in which Jouvet will open tonight at the Anta Playhouse, was the great French actor-director's first Molière production, his reputation having been built on his brilliant collaboration with such moderns as Jean Giraudoux, Jules Romains, Marcel Achard, and Jean Cocteau.

Since he has come here for less than a fortnight with but one offering, he could not have made a better choice from his large repertory. Nothing could be more French than this comedy on *cocuage* combining a healthy common sense with rollicking farce, and nothing is more French than Jouvet's way of playing it, measuring his broad and his subtle effects with perfect finesse. Essentially French too is the single set by Christian Bérard which, I, having remembered it vividly since 1936, was delighted to see again in all its fresh whiteness last month in Paris. Sober and yet fantastic with its arcades, tall house, and garden walls in the form of a prow, it employs machinery to open those walls and reveal the garden with its rose trees and espaliers. There the naïve Agnès can take the air presumably safe from contacts with the outside world. Overhead, four hanging candelabra remind us, if need be, that we are in the theater and add to the carnival aspect of the stage.

As Arnolphe, the cocksure guardian whose clever plans are designed to foil fate, and, later, as the rejected elder suitor, Jouvet makes effective use of grimaces, silent laughter, repeated tics, and muffled tears as Molière himself must have done, if he was the great actor he was reputed to be. Beside him the lovely Dominique Blanchar plays Agnès with such simplicity and directness, confessing the loss of her ribbon without any of the false implications that once shocked critics, as to make us even forget Madeleine Ozeray, who created the role in Jouvet's company.

In the past fourteen years Jouvet and his company, composed of some of the most consummate actors in Europe today, have made this comedy more widely known than the Comédie-Française has done in two hundred and seventy years. In addition to hundreds of performances in their elegant little theater near the Paris Opera, they have taken it on tour throughout Europe, North Africa, and Latin America and produced it at the International Festival of Edinburgh in 1947. Jouvet's highly original versions of Molière's *Don Juan* and *Tartuffe* have not yet been attempted abroad, for with him as with Molière the chief rule is to please and he insists on thoroughly "breaking in" a play, as he says, in Paris before taking it on the road.

In America Louis Jouvet is best known through his films as the ingenious charlatan of *Knock*, the priest in *La Kermesse héroique*, and the night-club proprietor in *Carnet de bal*. But some of his public the next few nights will remember him in the roles of Géronte and Sir Andrew Aguecheek on the stage of the old Garrick during the First World War, when he came here with the famous Vieux-Colombier. Indeed, it was as actor, stage-manager, and general assistant to that genius Jacques Copeau that he learned his art in all its aspects to become the greatest French *Theatermensch*. He himself recalls how much more enthusiastically American audiences took to the classics than to the modern dramatists Copeau presented. To be sure, French dramatists have vastly improved since then, thanks in great part to the work of such enlightened producers as Louis Jouvet. Yet it is doubtless due to that earlier experience of New York that he is giving us tonight one of Molière's masterpieces.

New York Herald Tribune, November 9,
1952.

THE RENAUD-BARRAULT COMPANY

When the French theatrical company of Madeleine Renaud and
Jean-Louis Barrault opens Wednesday night at the Ziegfeld Theater,
New York will have a chance to welcome the most successful independent repertory theater of Paris. And Paris is the city of exciting
repertory companies; for the brilliant history of the contemporary stage
in France is not entirely due to its revelation of such powerful new
dramatists as Claudel and Giraudoux, Romains and Sartre, Cocteau and
Anouilh. Without the *avant-garde* repertory theaters that have flourished
there since the end of the last century, many of those writers, indeed,
might not have had a hearing. In 1913 (to go back no further) dramatic
art in France was revolutionized by Jacques Copeau, that French
counterpart of Stanislavski, who brought his Vieux-Colombier group
to us during the First World War. Two of the members of his troupe,
Charles Dullin and Louis Jouvet, later branched out to form independent theaters of their own. Together with the Russian Georges
Pitoëff and the French Gaston Baty, they dominated the Parisian theater
of the twenties and thirties.

Eighteen months ago New York was fortunate enough to see
Jouvet's company in one of Molière's masterpieces, *L'Ecole des femmes,*
and after his successful engagement Jouvet planned to return with a
more extensive sampling of his repertory. But his untimely death in
the summer of 1951 left to others the mission of representing the French

381

theater abroad. Dullin and Pitoëff had died before him, and now Baty, the last of the famous "cartel," has also succumbed; not one of the three ever produced a play in New York, although the Theater Guild staged adaptations of some of their productions.

At present Jean-Louis Barrault is their undisputed heir. When, as an art student of twenty-one, he felt drawn to the stage, he naturally wrote to Charles Dullin and thus in 1931 entered Dullin's Atelier Theater as a student-actor. There he was drawn at first to study the art of pantomime with Etienne Decroux, another of Copeau's pupils. And when in 1935, to practice his newly acquired technique in that field, the young Barrault spent his patrimony staging an almost silent adaptation of Faulkner's *As I Lay Dying,* it was natural that Louis Jouvet should ask him to put on a special matinee so that the ever-busy director of the Athénée could see the revolutionary performance.

It was equally natural that in 1940 Jacques Copeau, come out of retirement to administer the Comédie-Française, should call the freshly demobilized Barrault to Paris to play the title role in *Le Cid.* During his six years of association with that great national theater, the young actor discovered the French classics and Shakespeare, distinguished himself internationally by being the first to stage Claudel's *Le Soulier de satin* (which had long been thought unplayable even in a five-hour performance such as Barrault gave), and met there the accomplished actress Madeleine Renaud who was to become his wife and co-star.

It was but natural, likewise, that when Madeleine Renaud and Jean-Louis Barrault left the Comédie-Française and set up their own troupe in 1946, they should gather around them a young, alert group of actors, some of whom had been trained by Copeau or Dullin. And, like their predecessors in the great modern tradition, they patiently elaborated a repertory of varied plays ranging from Shakespeare and Molière to Montherlant, Anouilh, and Camus.

The eight plays that the Renaud-Barrault company is bringing to New York represent a perfect cross section of the last several seasons at the Marigny, that most elegant of Paris theaters, free-standing in a grove of horse chestnut trees set in the ultra-chic quarter midway between the Presidential Palace and the shops of the leading dressmakers.

The first production, which will have five performances, includes a little gem of French taste and psychological subtlety, *Les Fausses Confidences* by Marivaux. Its freedom in stylization personifies the delicate art of the eighteenth-century Regency and provides an ideal vehicle for the charm of Madeleine Renaud, who seems here to have stepped out of a painting by Watteau. With it Barrault will give his own pantomime-ballet of *Baptiste*, already known to us through the film of *Les Enfants du Paradis*. Better than anything else, this sophisticated ballet, based on a work by Jacques Prévert with music by Kosma, summarizes Barrault's long cultivation of the technique of the mime that so happily distinguished the Italian comedians for whom Marivaux wrote.

The second week will open with four performances of a play equally new to Broadway, the Gide-Barrault adaptation of Kafka's novel *The Trial*. In October 1947 that daring dramatization of an indescribable nightmare of alienation was not only a *succès de scandale* but even a financial success at the Marigny. By staging the play in a manner reminiscent of the expressionist drama, the enterprising director has caught and communicated in tangible form the theory of the absurd that his friend Albert Camus (who recognizes Kafka as a brother) has made the cornerstone of his philosophy. The inclusion of this unusual production on the limited program should not only provide greater variety but also dispel any illusions as to the Parisian theater's chauvinism. Under present circumstances, the French Government seems consummately disinterested in contributing to the New York performance of a work adapted from the German of a Czech writer.

The third production, which will hold the bill at the Ziegfeld for three evenings and one matinee, combines two facets of Molière's comic genius in the admirable court comedy of *Amphitryon* and the popular farce, *Les Fourberies de Scapin*. Barrault as the perplexed Sosie and again as the amazingly resourceful Scapin will remind theatergoers of the finely nuanced performance Jouvet gave here as Arnolphe and make them wonder if Molière ever had better interpreters. Indeed, Louis Jouvet staged the farce for his colleague, and the late Christian Bérard, who also created the ingenious mobile set for Jouvet's *Ecole des femmes*, designed sets and costumes for both plays with breath-taking success.

The Renaud-Barrault Company

The week of the twenty-fourth will be divided between Georges Feydeau's light comedy, *Occupe-toi d'Amélie*—a mad and rapid imbroglio of carefree Paris life as seen by a caricaturist whom Barrault likens to Daumier—and a sombre recent play by Jean Anouilh entitled *La Répétition ou l'amour puni*. This curious tour de force by the author of *L'Invitation au château* (*Ring Round the Moon*) and *Eurydice* (*Legend of Lovers*) centers around a group of wealthy idlers gathered in a handsome eighteenth-century château to put on an amateur performance of one of Marivaux's plays. Their own complex and decadent loves become constantly confused with their stage parts as they rehearse in the costumes worn in the age of Louis XV. This subtle play within a play, as it shuttles between past and present, offers a dazzling vehicle for both leaders of the troupe, whereas in the Feydeau comedy Barrault himself plays but a minor role in the shadow of a deliciously effervescent Madeleine Renaud.

Doubtless aware of his boldness in presenting *Hamlet* in French to a New York audience, Jean-Louis Barrault has reserved for it the final place on his program, the first week in December. It is easy to see why he felt tempted by the challenge of giving us Shakespeare with a French accent. Although he may have been told how jealous we are of our Anglo-Saxon heritage, surely he also knows that *Hamlet* always interests us in any language or in any dress. Furthermore, his new interpretation with evocative incidental music by Honegger and scenery and costumes by the painter André Masson marked the initial success of the Marigny troupe back in 1946, and it has also proved successful when taken across the Channel. Nor must we forget either, Barrault's natural pride in having commissioned of André Gide this most lyrical and most moving French translation of Shakespeare's masterpiece.

The Reporter, November 13, 1958.

THE STYLE OF FRANCE'S T.N.P.

Trumpets sounded as the curtain rose on an almost bare stage that rapidly filled with colorful Florentine Renaissance costumes, and suddenly two pages dressed in red, yellow, and black rushed toward the audience furiously twirling enormous bright flags. For an instant, at the Théâtre National Populaire's first performance on Broadway last month, we saw again the Palio at Siena, the celebration of the Calcio in Florence. The Palazzo Strozzi and the Piazza della Signoria were conjured up before us with the first lines of Alfred de Musset's *Lorenzaccio,* so superbly directed by Gérard Philipe that one almost forgot it was not by Shakespeare. The bare stage, the absence of footlights and reliance for effects on the fusing of discreet spotlights from the balcony and sides of the proscenium, the bright and somewhat massive costumes, the reduction of the sets to a minimum of accessories outlined against dark curtains hung on frames of different sizes, and especially the flawless acting of the whole ensemble—these are all marks of the T.N.P.'s style.

Louis Jouvet once said to a young actor named Jean Vilar that Parisian producers were merely presenting the public with the familiar fare wrapped up in a new sauce. "In order to do something new, we shall have to have new theaters or else act in the street." Until he had his great chance at Avignon in 1947, when he staged Shakespeare in the Cour d'Honneur of the Palace of the Popes, Jean Vilar had experienced the long and difficult apprenticeship of all good actors. He was born in

1913, the son of a shopkeeper in a small Mediterranean city. His only early artistic training was daily violin lessons; at twelve he was already earning pocket money as a jazz violinist. After desultory literary studies in Paris and intensive work in the theatrical studio of Charles Dullin, where Jean-Louis Barrault was also a pupil, he did his military service and lived through what was then called "the phony war." Married at twenty-eight, he managed to get a wedding trip through war-torn France by joining the traveling theatrical company of André Clavé called La Roulotte. They gave performances all over the country in dance halls, parish halls, barns, inn courtyards, and cafés, generally receiving their payment in food that had escaped the black market.

Back in Paris, he staged Strindberg's *Dance of Death* in a private house in the Rue Vaneau. But a commercial theater, which had acquired the rights to the play, put a stop to his performances. He finally received wide critical acclaim in 1945 for the staging at the Vieux-Colombier (sacred to the memory of Jacques Copeau) of Eliot's *Murder in the Cathedral*.

At the age of thirty-four, Vilar began his experiments at Avignon in the first move toward a permanent theatrical decentralization in France. Rather suddenly, as a result of his extraordinary success with the festivals, he was named director of the T.N.P., founded in 1920 by the idealist Firmin Gémier. Its home was the Palais de Chaillot in Paris.

The first official theater constructed in Paris in some fifty years, it is huge and cold and acoustically bad. Furthermore, the audience has to reach it by walking through endless hallways and down flights of stairs. But it boasts twenty-seven hundred seats, a proscenium opening eighty feet wide, and a stage seventy feet deep. With a subsidy from the state, and required by law to give at popular prices two hundred performances or concerts each year (the number has since been greatly reduced), Vilar could finally realize his dream of a popular theater appealing to the masses. By the end of the third year of producing the classics of all literatures and such modern dramatists as Brecht, Claudel, Gide, Henri Pichette, and Pirandello, the T.N.P. had rung up the impressive total of about a million and a quarter tickets sold.

Even today the top price for an orchestra seat at the Palais de Chaillot is a little over a dollar. And for a somewhat larger inclusive price, one can attend a T.N.P. "weekend" consisting of two plays, a lecture or discussion with the actors, a concert, two picnicky meals, and a dance extending on toward Sunday dawn. Furthermore, tickets for all performances can be bought all over Paris in the hundreds of local book-shops that display the familiar stenciled letters "T.N.P." Doors are closed to latecomers, who are led into a large buffet like a railway wait-ing room, where they may listen over loudspeakers until the first inter-mission. Anyone who has sat thus through the first act of Claudel's *La Ville* (which lasts fifty minutes) is not likely to forget the lesson.

Soon after the initial staging of Bertold Brecht's *Mother Courage* in November 1951, Gérard Philipe, young and already famous, offered to work under Vilar's direction. But despite the fame of Philipe and of the tragedienne Maria Casarès, who joined the company a little later, the T.N.P. under Vilar has consistently avoided the dangers of the star system. In all T.N.P. productions the human element far outweighs all others, for Vilar insists upon "reducing the show to its simplest and most arduous expression—the scenic effects created by the actors themselves. Hence it is essential to keep the stage from becoming a meeting place of all the arts, major and minor (painting, architecture, electromania, music, stage machinery, etc.)."

Like Jean-Louis Barrault on his latest visit to New York, the T.N.P. brought us for its three-week stay at the Broadway Theatre a repre-sentative sampling of their wide repertory. Musset's *Lorenzaccio* and Hugo's *Marie Tudor* are typical Romantic dramas with just enough historical color and melodrama to catch the imagination of both the most naïve and the most jaded publics. And far from concessions to the student population of New York, the two seventeenth-century classics, *Le Cid* and Molière's *Don Juan,* are perennial favorites at the Palais de Chaillot.

In the minds of those who know their French classics, *Le Triomphe de l'amour,* the second offering of the season, represents the most hazardous of the T.N.P. undertakings, for both the Barrault company and the Comédie-Française have already shown themselves supreme in the re-creation of Marivaux's Dresden figurines and sophisticated dialogue. Furthermore, his traditional setting—the precious eighteenth-century *salon* and equally stylized garden—do not fit the austere aesthetic of Jean Vilar. But to everyone's surprise, he used here a rather traditional if somewhat summary set, composed of a small temple of love flanked by four tortured trees, two stone benches, and a formal balustrade. And those accustomed to applaud Maria Casarès when she plays the somber heroines of Albert Camus, the stepmother of Hippolytus, or the star-crossed queens of Victor Hugo, discovered that she could also play the graceful and elegant coquette practicing the intellectual anatomy of love in a charming comedy of errors. Perhaps, after all, there is but one way to interpret Marivaux, and the T.N.P. has clearly demonstrated that it knows the way.

Introduction to *The Condemned of Altona*
(*Les Séquestrés d'Altona*), by Jean-Paul
Sartre, translated by Justin O'Brien (to be
published by Samuel French, Inc.).

SARTRE: "THE FAMILY CELL"

The Condemned of Altona is not my title for the play by Jean-Paul
Sartre that I adapted. It has two strikes against it in my opinion. To
begin with, Altona sounds dangerously like a certain place in Penn-
sylvania which does not enjoy the best reputation in theater circles.
Furthermore, as a conscientious translator who strives to put himself
within the mind of his chosen victim, I wonder if Sartre really meant
Altona. Even though he has been in Hamburg whereas I never have,
he could have come away with confused memories. Germans, who ought
to know the geography of their own country, assure me that Altona
is an industrial section of the city of Hamburg near the waterfront
filled with cranes, wharves, and screaming sirens. But it is hardly the
setting for the spacious estate and thirty-two-room mansion of the
wealthy industrialist Gerlach. And if Altona lies in the heart of the
city, why does Johanna in the play wail about returning from there to
Hamburg? No, the name does not make sense. There must be a
spacious suburb out along the Elbe within easy drive by Mercedes or
Porsche. Sartre probably saw such a place but forgot its name. After all,
didn't someone say that even Homer nodded?

To be sure, "The Condemned" can be justified in a pinch, although
it is too close to the title of the only published English version of the
play. As that version is not mine, I could hardly approve it whole-
heartedly. What Sartre actually wrote was *Séquestrés d'Altona*. Obviously the accent falls on the idea of sequestration as it does in André

Gide's title of 1930, *La Séquestrée de Poitiers,* which records a true case of criminal sequestration and which may well have inspired Sartre's title of 1959. Years ago, I had to translate the Gide title—just the title, to be sure—and rendered it as *The Poitiers Incarceration Case.* There must have been people, real people squestered at some time or other in Chicago or Bronxville or even Duluth; but we Americans tend to think rather of the sequestration of property. Possibly the French treat their retarded children or batty relatives more harshly than we do.

After all, Sartre asked me to make the acting version of his play for its production in London several years ago, giving me, as the French picturesquely say, a white card. At that point, not having thought much about the title, I failed to ask if the title itself was included on that white card. This was foolish because Jean-Paul Sartre, who talks very readily, shows a marked hesitation to write letters. Consequently, when I did finally write him about my brilliant idea for a title in English, he simply didn't reply. His silence could have been interpreted as a refusal; it *was* so interpreted because I failed to wave my white card.

And then the fun began. In London my title got nowhere. Perhaps the late George Devine and Oscar Lewenstein remembered the passage at arms—or was it a legal suit in a U.S.A. court?—back in 1948 when someone dared to produce *Les Mains sales* ("Dirty Hands") in New York as *Red Gloves.* In vain I pointed out the possibility of valuable publicity resulting from such a suit against the Royal Court Theater. Either they were thinking of the probable judgment against them or else they didn't fully understand my arguments. I do speak their particular foreign language, but somewhat more haltingly than I speak French. In any case, the play was called merely *Altona* when it was billed in London, whence I returned crestfallen but convinced that the same thing could never happen in New York, which is too close to Altoona, Pa.

There I was wrong—or rather partly wrong—for *The Condemned of Altona* is at least better than just *Altona.* But I have noticed that over in the plush subterranean labyrinths of Lincoln Center the title is invariably abbreviated on the doors of rehearsal rooms, or at the top of notices to the cast, to that unpleasant place name.

The Family Cell

Does the translator or adaptor or whatever he may be called have a right to change the title of the original work? Most of those who have never translated anything because they know no language but their mother tongue are by nature purists who insist on a literal rendering. Recently one such reader took me to task for the well-known title of a work by André Gide, *If It Die,* pointing out that the French title reads *Si le grain ne meurt.* Shouldn't the negative have been retained in English? The late Dorothy Bussy having translated that book long before I became associated with André Gide, it seemed unfair for me to take the rap. However, my respect for Dorothy Bussy is such that I replied with full references to the French translation of the Bible and the King James version of the Vulgate. Mme Bussy, née Strachey, knew her Bible in both English and French as well as André Gide did. But the lady from Fort Lauderdale always feels justified in taking a busy journalist's time instead of puzzling out the question for herself or toddling down to the local library under a parasol.

What *was* your title for *The Condemned of Altona,* Mr. O'Brien? Oh, that! I am almost afraid to mention it now after such a build-up. Besides, I never pronounce it today without my trauma of several years ago rising to the surface, for I fear those huskies lurking just outside the circle formed by the spotlight. Aren't they wearing Nazi uniforms? Do they carry truncheons? What about those Mausers in their smart holsters? I am *not* guilty! It was all Herbert Blau's fault! Leave me alone, please mister!

If you insist on knowing, my title for the play was *The Family Cell.* Frantz lives in a cell upstairs, which his sister Leni goes up to occupy at the end of the play. The baronial mansion is a cell; Altona or whatever we shall call it is a cell; all Germany is a cell in this play; the rich and powerful Gerlachs are all immured with no real chance of getting back to Hamburg. In addition to being a prison cell, the family, as one right-thinking Roman Catholic novelist of the late nineteenth century said, is the social cell. And in this case, what with incest and all the rest, the social cell bears added overtones.

These, then, are some of the things the public might have read into the title of *The Family Cell* by Jean-Paul Sartre. Some of them—because as Lincoln is reputed to have said, you can't fool all of them all the time—would probably have seen other implications.

Where would this leave Sartre? He could have sued me, except that as a former professor he might have hesitated to attach my university salary even if he didn't like me. He might also have thought about the question over lunch and decided to rename his play in French as *La Cellule de famille*. After all, don't we call the family vault in the cemetery *Le Caveau de famille?* Forgive me, I am thinking again in his name. I swear I never asked so much.

INDEX

Index

Ponsard, François, 126
Pont Mirabeau, Le, 352, 362
Populism, 285
Portugal, 163, 205
Poucel, Victor, 69
Pound, Ezra, 187
Pourtalès, Guy de, 113
Pozner, Vladimir, 303
Prague (Czechoslovakia), 88
Prévert, Jacques, 383
Prévost, Jean, 123, 179, 284, 287, 288
Princeton University, 289
Pritchett, V. S., 86
Privat, Edmond, 286
Prix des Critiques, 323
Proust, Marcel, 1–46, 69, 73, 93, 103, 125, 126, 134, 149, 173, 175, 177, 179, 183, 185, 193, 194, 199, 215, 228, 239, 245, 251, 267, 269, 270, 309, 330, 339, 340, 341, 357, 367, 370
Puvis de Chavannes, Pierre, 50

Quai d'Orsay, 274
Queneau, Raymond, 180, 331–32, 359, 375
Quennell, Peter, 215, 219

Rabelais, François, 127, 183, 260–61, 331
Racine, Jean, 22, 60, 279, 360
Radiguet, Raymond, 179, 200, 341
Random House, Inc., 253, 367
Raphael, Pierre, 6
Raymond, Marcel, 349
Redon, Odilon, 50
Régnier, Henri de, 50
Rembrandt van Ryn, 37, 128
Renan, Ernest, 34
Renaud, Madeleine, 112, 381–84
Renaudot Prize, 279

Renoir, Auguste, 27
Reporter, The, 33, 115, 187, 215, 267, 317, 369, 385
Revista de Occidente, La, 174
Revolution, Russian, 153
Révolution Surréaliste, La, 345, 346
Revue Anglo-Américaine, La, 285
Revue Blanche, La, 122
Revue Critique des Idées et des Livres, La, 175
Revue des Deux Mondes, La, 182
Revue de France, La, 206
Revue de Littérature Comparée, La, 105
Revue de Paris, La, 206
Rhineland, 181
Ribbentrop, Joachim von, 235
Richardson, Samuel, 198
Rilke, Rainer Maria, 41, 52, 368
Rimbaud, Arthur, 40, 129, 183, 285, 309, 314, 343, 344, 350, 351, 353, 354, 357, 363, 374
Rivane, Georges, 7
Rivera, Diego, 286
Rivière, Jacques, 101, 125, 177, 178, 179, 181, 182, 183, 184, 340
Robbe-Grillet, Alain, 327–28, 330
Roberts, Michael, 361
Roberty, M., 78
Rodker, John, 209
Rollan, Henri, 118
Rolland, Romain, 41, 215, 246, 284, 293
Romains, Jules, 126, 177, 179, 215, 221–44, 246, 280–81, 283, 310, 314, 342, 354, 358, 361–63, 379, 381
Rome (Italy), 79, 206, 231, 329–30
Rondeaux, Madeleine, 76
Ronsard, Pierre de, 127
Roosevelt, F. D., 286
Rose, Sir Francis, 292
Rosenberg, Hans, 235
Rostand, Edmond, 125

IN THE COURSE of a long and distinguished teaching career at Columbia University, beginning in 1931, Justin O'Brien not only has written innumerable critical articles and an outstanding book on Gide, *Portrait of André Gide,* but also has been a translator of Gide, Camus, and Sartre. In the years 1945 to 1951, when he was engaged in translating the four volumes of Gide's *Journals,* author and translator were in almost constant communication. Other translations followed: Gide's *Journal of the Counterfeiters, Madeleine, So Be It,* and *Pretexts,* Camus's *The Myth of Sisyphus and Other Essays, The Fall, Exile and the Kingdom,* and *Resistance, Rebellion, and Death,* Sartre's *The Condemned of Altona,* and others.

Mr. O'Brien relates that it was Camus who inoculated him with a passion for the theater by inviting him to the daily rehearsals of *Caligula* in Paris in 1959, the last year of Camus's life. Hence it is appropriate that the first of Mr. O'Brien's adaptations for the theater was the Broadway production of this play in 1960. Since then Mr. O'Brien has adapted Camus's *The Possessed,* for the Mermaid Theater in London, Sartre's *The Condemned of Altona,* for the Royal Court Theater in London, and two plays by Henry de Montherlant, not yet produced.

Mr. O'Brien holds a Ph.B. from the University of Chicago and his M.A. and Ph.D. from Harvard University. During World War II the OSS sent him to London to help train secret agents and drop them into France. One such operation was called the Proust Plan because it started "à la recherche des hommes perdus."

Mr. O'Brien is the recipient of the Denyse Clairouin Prize for the best translation from the French (1947), the Prix du Rayonnement Français of the French Academy (1965), and an honorary Doctorate of Letters from Wesleyan University (1966), besides war decorations from three governments.